Rivers of Texas

NUMBER THIRTY-TWO:
The Louise Lindsey Merrick Natural Environment Series

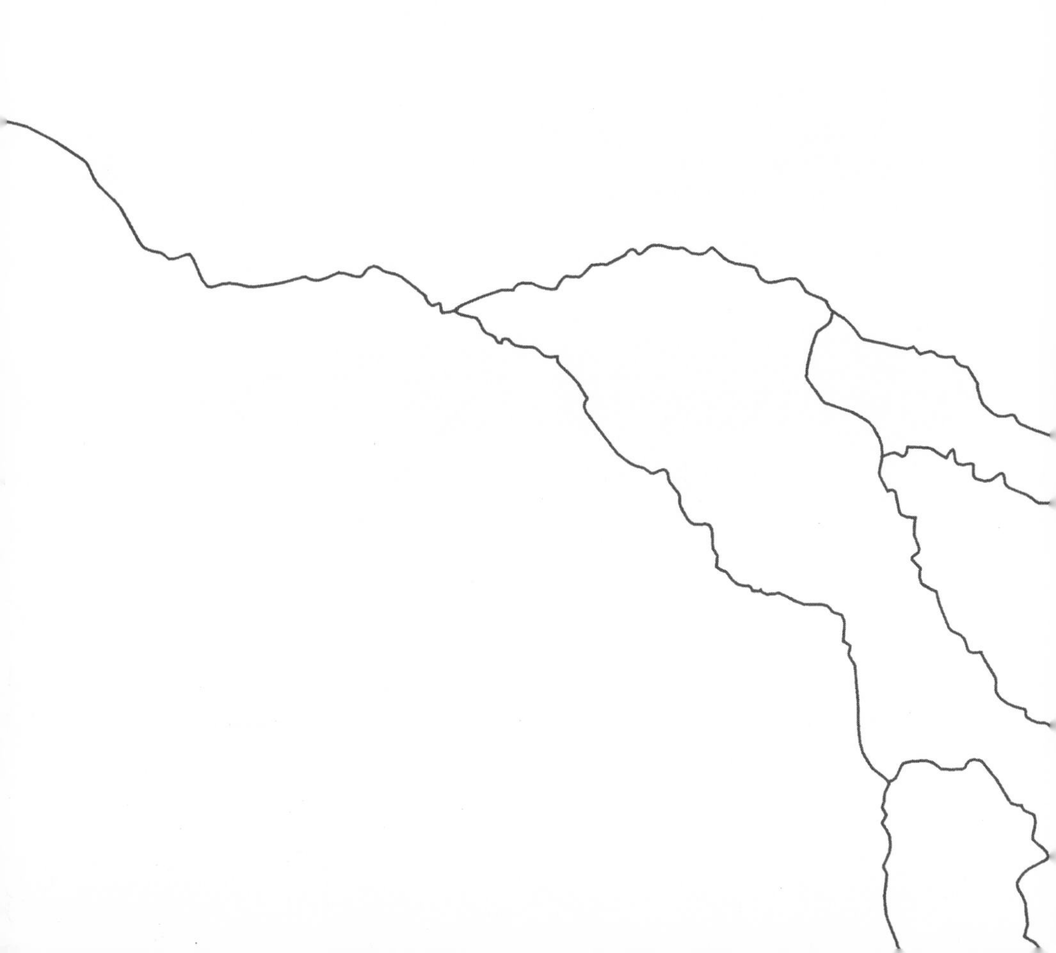

Rivers of

Texas

VERNE HUSER

TEXAS A&M UNIVERSITY PRESS
COLLEGE STATION

Second printing, 2004

Map by Heidi Huser Hackler

Dedicated to my granddaughters:
Rachel Marie Sonnenreich,
Noelle Claire Huser, and
Sarah-Jane Evans Huser

The paper used in this book meets
the minimum requirements
of the American National
Standard for Permanence
of Paper for Printed Library
Materials, z39.48-1984.
Binding materials have been
chosen for durability.

Library of Congress Cataloging-in-Publication Data

Huser, Verne.
Rivers of Texas/Verne Huser.
p. cm.—(Louise Lindsey Merrick
natural environment series ; n.32)
Includes bibliographical references (p.).
ISBN 0-89096-905-1 ; ISBN 1-58544-369-7 (pbk.)
1. Rivers—Texas. 2. Rivers—Texas—
History. 3. Texas—Description and travel.
4. Texas—History. 5. River life—Texas.
I. Title. II. Series.
F392.A17H87 2000
917.64'09693—dc21 99-26673
CIP

Contents

Illustrations

Acknowledgments

I have many people to thank for this book, not least of whom is my wife, Willa, who tolerated five years of my studying and writing, not to mention my disappearing on several trips to Texas to do field research. Thanks to paddling partners Dave Green and Henry Holman and river companions Hans Weichsel, Jr., David Reichert, and Gib Hafernick and other members of the Alamo City Rivermen. River consultants Mark H. Andrus, Joe Butler, Lorraine Bonney, Tom Goynes, Don Greene, Vic Hines, and the Texas Parks and Wildlife Department's Bob Spain, Jerry Sullivan, and Ernest G. Simmons (now retired) all offered valuable counsel.

I also thank my brother Paul and his wife Lindy of Schulenburg; my high school English teachers I. E. and Lila Clark, who live on the Navidad; Earle Oldham of Tomball on Spring Creek; Billy Gilbreath and his wife Annalon of Midland near the Pecos; Sammy Franklin, who grew up on the Atascosa; Charlena Vargas-Prada, who grew up on the Pecos; Elmer Kelton of San Angelo on the Concho; Dean Smith of Eliasville on the Clear Fork of the Brazos; Ken (now deceased) and Pat Lorfing of Orange on the Sabine; Cecile Kuhne of Dallas on the Forks of the Trinity; and Gilbert Gutierrez, who fished the Brazos and its reservoirs while in the army stationed at Fort Hood.

I want to thank a number of writers for creating fine books that I've enjoyed during my library research, books that have taught me much about Texas rivers: Joe C. Truett and Daniel W. Lay (*Land of Bears and Honey*), Thad Sitton (*Backwoodsmen*), John R. Erickson (*Through Time and the Valley*), Louis F. Aulbach and Jack Richardson (*The Lower Pecos River*), Lucia St. Clair Robson (*Ride the Wind*), Pat Dearen (*Crossing Rio Pecos*), Edward C. Fritz (*Realms of Beauty*–photographed by Jess Alford, whom I met quite by accident in New Mexico), and of course John Graves (*Goodbye to a River*).

Also, thanks are due to the Texas A&M University Press staff and Sally Antrobus for making this a better book.

For technical assistance and moral support I thank the library staff and computer experts at Albuquerque Academy, and I appreciate the encouragement and support of Tim McIntire, former headmaster at Kinkaid School in Houston and now head of school at Albuquerque Academy, where I serve as archivist.

Introduction

Reflections on the Texas Landscape

The rivers of Texas are as varied as the land that bears them, landscapes they have created and carved, drained and decorated, watered and weathered. From the Panhandle to Palacios, from Big Bend to Big Thicket, Texas rivers generally flow southeasterly to the Gulf, although they meander like so many sidewinders to every compass point in their convoluted courses across the Lone Star state.

Few people outside Texas appreciate the vastness and variety offered by streams of the Lone Star state: pineywoods bayous and moss-draped, cypress-lined streams of East Texas; spring-fed, limestone-bedded rivers of the Edwards Plateau; rain- and snow-fed perennial creeks and sandy arroyos of the Trans-Pecos mountains and the high plains; previously pirate-plied tidewater creeks, where some still believe they may find buried treasure; and the steep-walled canyons of the Rio Grande. The rivers vary from region to region, and the same river may display different characters in a trip of several hundred miles to the sea.

For this book I have grouped Texas rivers into four categories: border rivers, those of the heartland, some regional specialties, and those with a short course into the Gulf of Mexico. I have also included at the beginning of each river chapter a sidebar summarizing important information about that river. The sidebar includes the river's general location, the source of its name (if known), its major tributaries and recreational activities, its length, and the area of its watershed. It also includes public lands and special features. *Public lands* may be federal, state, or local and are listed from upstream to downstream. *Features* may not necessarily be protected, but they represent important association with the rivers.

The Rio Grande, which forms roughly a thousand miles of international border between the United States and Mexico, serves as the southern and western boundary of Texas. The state's oldest villages, Ysleta and Socorro near El Paso on the Rio Grande, were established by transplanted New Mexican Indians who fled with the Spanish during the 1680 Pueblo Revolt. The Rio

Grande serves as the state's historical contact with the Pueblo people of New Mexico, whose jewelry, pottery, basketry, and artwork Texans buy to decorate themselves and their homes, and with the Colorado and New Mexican high country where Texans like to ski.

Texas' northern and eastern boundaries, the Red and Sabine rivers—except where straight artificial boundary lines fix the limits of the state—are less distinct because miles of these stateline rivers have become reservoirs, widening those natural boundaries into unnatural impoundments. The Red forms the northern boundary, roughly half the Rio Grande's border distance, between Texas and Oklahoma (480 miles), and about forty miles of the Texas-Arkansas border. The Sabine, third longest Texas river and the one that discharges the most water into the Gulf, marks nearly two hundred miles of the Texas-Louisiana state line in a swampy morass of interconnected channels and the huge reservoir known as Toledo Bend.

The rivers of the heartland—those that flow almost entirely within the state and course her breast from their headwaters to the Gulf—flow crooked and winding through the very heart of Texas, geographically, historically, and demographically: the Colorado, Brazos, and Trinity. Stephen F. Austin's land grants, which first brought Anglo-American settlers to Texas from the United States, lay between the Brazos and the Colorado, and the Trinity had to be crossed to get there. The Trinity flows through the Dallas–Fort Worth area on its way to the Gulf, a third of the population of Texas living within its watershed. More than half of Texas' population lives in these three adjacent watersheds.

Four special rivers represent four greatly differing regions. The Neches, which drains the wettest parts of Texas, is the quintessential East Texas river, along with its tributaries the Angelina River, Attoyac Bayou, and Village Creek and Pine Island Bayou in the Big Thicket country. What more appropriate river than the Nueces—with its tributaries the Frio, Sabinal, and Atascosa—to represent South Texas? The Pecos not only typifies West Texas but lends its name to the region known as the Trans-Pecos (and, with apologies to the Devil's River, it *is* practically the only river in the region). Three Texas rivers begin in the Panhandle—the Brazos, the Colorado, and the Red—but only one flows completely across it, the Canadian, my choice for Panhandle river.

The Gulf Coast rivers course the coastal plain, some of them flowing from the limestone hills of the Edwards Plateau: the San Antonio with its tributary Medina; the Guadalupe with its tributary San Marcos and Blanco, and the Lavaca with its tributary Navidad. I also include the streams of the Houston area: the San Jacinto River, Buffalo Bayou, Spring Creek, Cedar Bayou, and Oyster Creek.

The Power of Floods

Stories of floods on Texas rivers are legion: the massive amounts of water they have to carry has given them wide floodplains. Thirty-eight inches of rain fell in a twenty-four-hour period at Thrall in the San Gabriel River (Brazos) watershed of Central Texas on September 9 and 10, 1921. Many Texas rivers may barely trickle a few inches deep, a few feet wide, during the dry season, but their riverbeds may be a mile wide, carved by runoff from the big sudden "cloudbursts." Floods on several Edwards Plateau rivers in 1997 and 1998 are well remembered.

I grew up near the headwaters of the Navidad River halfway between Houston and San Antonio, and I saw its destructive flooding during the middle

1. The San Gabriel River is a Brazos tributary, though it rises near Austin. It flows into Little River.

and late 1930s—though for much of each year it flows only a few inches deep, and in drought years, not at all. Brief heavy rains characterize much of Texas. Along the Gulf Coast during hurricane season, heavy rains may last for days, as those precipitated by Hurricane Charlie did in August, 1998. All the dams in the world won't cure those kinds of floods.

Bridges across some Texas rivers sometimes seem ridiculously long, but bridge builders have learned from hard lessons that they must anticipate floodwaters and must give the rivers room to do their job of draining the land. From semiarid West Texas and the Panhandle to well-watered East Texas, bridges may seem absurdly high above the water flowing beneath them; but come the flood, that vertical space pays big dividends. Check the high-water mark on bridges along the frequently dammed and well-controlled Colorado in slightly drier Central Texas.

Once, as I was hunting with my college buddy Jimmy Hand along an old abandoned oxbow of the Brazos during a rainy June, we kept hearing explosions. Investigating, we found the Brazos in full flood, the "explosions" caused by sections of riverbank suddenly collapsing into the swirling flood. For all the man-made "flood-control" structures along Texas rivers, we still experience destructive floods because we insist on building in the floodplain. Texas weather just won't listen to logic any more than Texans will listen to the reasons they should *not* build in the floodplain.

Floods on Texas rivers create a distinctive phenomenon: trenchlike troughs through which many Texas rivers flow. At high water, they roar through their whole floodplains, cutting banks, undercutting trees, and scouring deep, steep-sided channels, the type that Luna Leopold, in *A View of the River,* characterizes as Type A from David L. Rosgen's classification system. Once the floods subside, they leave rich silt beds on the upper benches of the river valley, steep muddy slopes along the main channels, and whole trees that form massive debris dams and clutter. I have observed such channels on several Texas rivers in modern times, in particular on the Brazos, San Antonio, Navidad, and on many small creeks.

Another phenomenon of many Texas rivers, the low-water crossing, often has dual purposes: to facilitate vehicular traffic without the necessity of building a real bridge, because most of the time you can simply drive through the shallow flow; and to create small dams that turn low-flow rivers into a series of long impoundments serving as stock tanks, fishing and swimming holes, and reflection pools. Some stretches of the Pedernales illustrate this practice, and flood gauges at each crossing remind one how the river can rise.

Even in the driest parts of the state, the rivers flood; and floods can be especially severe when rivers are bound by artificial barriers such as dikes and levees and when natural runoff increases due to human activity: from roofs and driveways, from parking lots and roads, from bare farm fields and overgrazed rangeland. We keep drowning rivers with dams, permanently inundating thousands of acres of rich river-bottom land. We try to keep the water within man-made boundaries that fail to anticipate floods. And we keep building within the floodplain. We must give rivers room to run and roam, or they will bite us in the end and find their own way to the Gulf.

If Texas rivers have not always been kind to Texans, neither have Texans been kind to their rivers. Historically most Texas rivers were better known for their floods than for their aesthetic values. Today many are better known for their pollution than for their recreational possibilities, better known for their impoundments than for their free-flowing segments (which have become rare on some rivers), better known for what's been lost than for what remains.

2. A typical low-water dam in the Texas Hill Country with cypress and pecan trees growing in the floodplain.

3. A Texas grasshopper pumps in a pasture near the Brazos River.

What Are Rivers For?

Do we really prefer reservoirs to free-flowing rivers, or have we been so grilled by chambers of commerce and river basin authorities, the Army Corps of Engineers, and the Bureau of Reclamation that we know nothing else? We have used our rivers as sewers and sumps; dammed them for flood control, recreation, and hydroelectric power; used their waters to dilute pollution, to ship products to world markets, to process manufactured goods, to irrigate crops, to create jobs, and to make some people rich and others poor. We have drained swamps, filled wetlands, and manipulated natural rivers until we hardly know one when we see one.

To understand the whole story, we need to reflect on rivers' complete courses through time and the landscape. Geologically speaking, the Staked Plain formed from deposition of materials eroded from the ancestral Rocky Mountains. The red soil, silt, and sand that colors all the Texas rivers that head on the Llano Estacado came from the Rockies. When bison roamed these headwaters, they ranged freely and migrated seasonally. The land had time to recover from their heavy grazing and pounding hoofs, and there were gophers and prairie dogs to churn the earth. The native people lived with the land as it was except that they used fire to call back the grass and the bison herds that depended on the grass. Like the bison, they drank from the surface streams and bubbling springs.

While rivers in many eastern states served as transportation routes for settlers and as a means of getting their products to market, many Texas rivers provided ready routes for the raiding Comanches, who harassed Texas pioneers with deadly intent. Texas rivers were often too shallow for reliable transportation due to low water levels. Some were blocked by sandbars at their mouths, like the Brazos—wherever flowing water slows, it drops its suspended load of silt, sand, and organic materials; or by logjams upstream, like the Great Raft on the Red River above Shreveport, a gigantic logjam almost a hundred miles long of durable red cedar and bald cypress. (Although a barrier to river transportation, this logjam acted as a natural bridge for overland travelers, enabling people to cross, to ride horses across, even to drive herds of cattle across.) The Colorado also had a considerable natural obstacle in the series of driftwood-and-debris rafts near its mouth.

Nevertheless, steamboats plied the lower reaches of several Texas rivers: the Brazos, the Colorado, the Sabine, the Red, and the Rio Grande. In Sam Houston's 1836 retreat eastward across Texas ahead of Mexican troops under Gen. Santa Anna, the Texas commander requisitioned the steamboat *Yellow Stone,* which had been built for use on the Upper Missouri, to ferry his soldiers and equipment across the Brazos, thereby getting the jump on Santa Anna. In fact, this delay led the Mexican dictator to split his forces in an attempt to catch the fleeing Texans. It was a mistake like Custer's at the Little Bighorn, and it cost Santa Anna dearly at San Jacinto.

Later that year the same steamboat carried the body of Stephen F. Austin, Father of Texas, down the Brazos to his burial place at Peach Point. Austin's cousin, in a steamboat named the *Ariel,* tried to develop river trade on the Rio Grande but failed. Many early steamboat explorations of Texas rivers ended like that of the *Ceres,* which made her way into Sabine Pass in 1838 but wrecked on a submerged log.

Ultimately few Texas rivers proved navigable on a regular basis for anything larger than keelboats and pirogues. As Elmer Kelton writes in *Water Trails West* (145): "Texas was never vitally dependent upon river transportation. . . . Commercial boat traffic was confined to the eastern part of the state and to fewer than a dozen rivers." In Texas, he notes, "the traffic crossed the rivers; it did not move upon them."

Rivers blocked overland routes, sometimes by brief but serious flooding, which necessitated the location of fords, the development of ferries, and eventually the building of bridges. Rivers were soon being used for irrigating crops along several dry-land rivers, following patterns that native tribes had used for hundreds of years. As early as 1729 the San Antonio River was diverted for irrigation. Steamboat traffic on the Rio Grande had become impractical early in the nineteenth century in part because irrigation along the river regularly lowered the water level.

Today rivers continue to serve Texas in multiple industrial ways. People in agribusiness—rice growers, cattlemen, wool and mohair producers, truck farmers, citrus growers, cotton farmers—provide jobs, but such industries manipulate rivers for private profit, often to public detriment and at taxpayer cost. Vast fishing fleets harbor in river mouths along the coast to harvest the estuarine and offshore bounty of the Gulf. Petrochemical companies have located polluting, often toxic facilities on tidewater streams for easy access to raw materials and Gulf shipping and in the process have fouled many waterways. The dredged ship channel in Galveston Bay makes Houston one of the nation's leading seaports.

Traditional kinds of river uses persist alongside more modern ones. Besides constituting state boundaries, rivers and creeks also serve as natural divisions between counties. On a good map, notice how many Texas counties are delineated by the rivers of the region, except in West and North Texas where most counties are laid out in a grid pattern. Look especially at the Trinity, Pecos, Neches, Brazos, and Colorado. Hunters, trappers, and fishermen use rivers recreationally as well as commercially, and wildlife watchers find rivers a means to an end: getting closer to birds, deer, alligators, raccoons, or whatever wildlife they can find. Water-skiers, jet-skiers, and windsurfers may be more accustomed to enjoying their sports on reservoirs, but broad, slow rivers offer them similar opportunities.

River Advocacy

When I was a youngster growing up between the branches of the Navidad, our interactions with rivers were more limited than today. They were considered too dangerous. My father hauled home washtubs full of sand from the Navidad beaches to fill my sandbox; later, I hauled sand home myself to fill a

4. Raccoon tracks mark the riverbank mud on every Texas river I visited in my five-year research for this book.

5. A riffle in the South Llano River suggests a modest canoe trip. Deer and wild turkey abound at South Llano State Park and the adjacent Walter Buck Wildlife Management Area near Junction.

6. Angora goats, more curious than cautious, pose at the fence for the photographer.

high-jump and pole-vault pit in the backyard. Along the river bottom I cut yaupon vaulting poles and cane poles for crossbars. I fished the deep, dark pools for bass, sunfish, and catfish and hunted raccoon and opossum in the woods of the river bottoms at night by carbide lamp.

No one ran the rivers. A young man against whom I played high school football drowned in the Colorado at La Grange after a night of teenage drinking—and the river took the blame and the body. My mother spent a sleepless night when my father went night fishing with friends, sure that he would drown. Rivers were mainly forbidden territory for recreational use, but they were used as dumping grounds by farmers and ranchers as well as by municipalities and industries. Some of the evidence is still there along the shore—like the stretch of Neches River below Steinhagen Reservoir.

Roy Bedichek and J. Frank Dobie observed and recorded the abuse of rivers half a century ago. Dr. Larry McKinney, the Texas Parks and Wildlife Department's senior director for water resources, points out in a recent article titled "Troubled Waters" that, like the human circulatory system, rivers "carry away nutrients, sediments, and other [natural] byproducts that are redistributed throughout the system and eventually wash down to the estuaries, thence to the sea." When river systems—"the blood vessels of our Mother

Earth," to quote a 1987 remark of Nez Perce tribal councilman Allen Pinkham—are blocked, we face serious results, just as the human body does from a heart attack or stroke.

McKinney pulls no punches in his two-part article: he calls rivers and their associated natural communities "the most diverse of all terrestrial communities found in Texas. . . . They support a greater variety of plants and animals than any other biotic community." When we dam rivers, we alter landscapes, land values, and biotic communities. Are we saying we don't care about plants and animals, that they don't matter in our lives?

Can you think of anything that doesn't have an impact on rivers or isn't impacted by rivers and the quality and quantity of their water? So much depends upon them and in turn affects them, from the federal space program headquartered southeast of Houston to the use of herbicides, pesticides, and fertilizers on the high plains cotton fields; from the irrigation of crops in the Lower Rio Grande Valley to grazing patterns along the Brazos headwaters; from agricultural practices in the Hill Country to the Gulf Coast petrochemical industry; from using riverbanks for dumping grounds and rivers for sewage disposal to sport fishing in the state's numerous reservoirs.

McKinney clearly states the three primary threats to Texas rivers and streams and to the diversity they represent: "(1) diversion of water from them, especially out of the [river] basin; (2) reservoir construction and operation; and (3) water pollution." He further points out the "common dilemma of resource management": decision makers lack information or they chose short-term goals over "long-term sustainability of the resource providing the benefits." In other words, we have dammed the rivers and foreclosed on our futures. In economic terms, we have forgone long-term benefits for short-term gains, a short-sighted economic policy that will have disastrous long-term results.

There are glimmers of change, however. In an essay on the National Park system, based on a lecture given in 1972 at Colorado State University in Fort Collins, Colorado, and published in *Aspects of the American West,* Texas historian Joe B. Frantz wrote, "We have been groping toward cooperating with our environment instead of forever and inflexibly demanding its unconditional surrender to our short-tempered and temporary needs and demands." (44)

Texas has been slowly changing in public attitudes toward the natural world and environmental issues generally. Federal laws, and more recently state laws, have been passed and are being enforced to control abuses of rivers and estuaries to the benefit of all. Present state policies, many of them forced on Texas by federal legislation, have begun to turn the corner, but as McKinney sug-

7. Cypress trees line the Medina River, a tributary of the San Antonio in the Texas Hill Country.

8. Aransas National Wildlife Refuge on the Gulf Coast is the winter home for whooping cranes and other rare birds.

gests, "We have hard decisions before us and we must be ready to make wise ones." He cites the cleanup of the Trinity River and the Houston Ship Channel and anticipated improvements in Matagorda Bay and Sabine Lake as examples of movement in the appropriate direction toward a cleaner, more livable Texas through changing attitudes and priorities and through some hard management decisions and actions.

Having once been an independent nation, Texas lacks federal public lands because it came into the United States without any of the public lands that in most states, especially in the West, provide public access to rivers. Less than 2 percent of Texas belongs to the public (that is less land than is devoted to highways and freeways). Many miles of rivers, closed to the public because their banks are privately owned, remain private preserves, playgrounds and dumping grounds for wealthy landowners and their friends. Many of the state's rivers have been badly abused through irresponsible private ownership. Boaters have been run off the land at gunpoint, and picnickers have been charged high entrance fees or threatened with shotguns—even shot at.

In recent decades many riverfront lands have become public property as state parks and river access points have been provided by a variety of state and federal agencies and river authorities. Building of federally funded dams has also prompted federal agencies to provide more public access. The various Texas waterways now offer vast recreational opportunity. The reputation of the Guadalupe, which flows through the Texas Hill Country, has broken state boundaries to become a destination whitewater run that draws rafters, kayakers, and canoeists from several sister states. The deep Rio Grande canyons of the Big Bend along the Mexican border draw paddlers from all over the United States and Mexico.

The Brazos—setting of John Graves's fine book *Goodbye to a River,* still in print forty years after first publication—offers excellent paddling opportunities, for all its impoundments, and the much-dammed Colorado, which flows through my home county (Fayette), provides colorful miles of canoeable waters as it flows through bucolic south-central Texas.

Only one Texas river has been given protection under the National Wild and Scenic Rivers system, a 191.2-mile stretch of the Rio Grande that runs with Mexican water provided largely by the Río Conchos flowing north from Chihuahua. Oregon, by contrast, has protected half a hundred rivers under the federal system and has a powerful state river protection program as well. Texas has no state system for river protection, limited legal means of preventing abuse to waterways, no real program for protecting free-flowing rivers from dams, dewatering, or diversions. Texas is one of a double handful of states that have yet to provide the means for the public to say: "Rivers are important to me. Let's give them some protection from exploitation."

Rivers of Texas

PART I

Border Rivers

El Río Grande del Norte

LOCATION: *South and west border with Mexico from El Paso to the Gulf*
NAME: *Spanish for "big river of the north" (from Mexico's point of view); also known as the Río Bravo (brave, strong, powerful river)*
CITIES: *El Paso, Del Rio, Laredo, McAllen, Brownsville*
IMPOUNDMENTS: *Amistad (near Del Rio), Falcon (50 miles below Laredo)*
TRIBUTARIES: *Pecos and Devil's rivers in Texas, Río Conchos in Mexico*
RECREATION: *River running in Big Bend canyons and below, hiking, fishing*
WATERSHED: *40,000 square miles in Texas*
LENGTH: *1,896 miles; roughly 1,000 miles of international border*
PUBLIC LAND: *Big Bend Ranch State Park, Big Bend National Park, Rio Grande Wild and Scenic River, Seminole Canyon State Park, Amistad National Recreation Area, Falcon State Park, Lake Casa Blanca State Park, Bentsen–Rio Grande State Park, Santa Ana National Wildlife Refuge, Resaca de la Palma State Park*
FEATURES: *The Big Bend, Lower Valley, Boca Chica*

IS THE RIO GRANDE really a Texas river? It starts in Colorado, bisects New Mexico, then forms a thousand miles of the international boundary between Texas and Mexico, with shared jurisdiction. Different means of measuring the distance along the border result in variable figures of river mileage, between 889 and 1,254 miles. Wherever the Rio Grande touches Texas, except for a brief stretch north of El Paso where it separates Texas' westernmost corner from New Mexico, Mexico has as much claim to it as Texas has. Many believe that since most of the water in the Rio Grande on its trip along the Texas-Mexican border originates south of the border, Mexico has the stronger claim.

Still, the river does divide the United States from Mexico and Texas from four Mexican states: Chihuahua, Coahuila, Nuevo León, and Tamaulipas. We share the border even if we don't quite share the river's water or the bounty it provides. Therein lies the core of our border problems with Mexico: the disparity between the haves and the have-nots, between those who have economic opportunities and those who don't, between the happy and hopeful and the hapless and hopeless.

A seventeen-year-old Mexican girl, seven months pregnant, dies of dehydration in the desert, trying to provide her unborn child the opportunities that come with being born in the United States. An eighteen-year-old American citizen of Hispanic heritage, herding his family's goats near the Rio Grande, is shot dead by a U.S. marine on drug patrol near Redford, Texas (more on that story later). A canoeist, observing an obvious drug run across the Rio Grande, is warned off with automatic weapon fire. Rafters in the rugged Big Bend country are fired on by Mexican youths who have seen too many American western movies. The border can be a dangerous place.

The Rio Grande marks more than half the international boundary between Mexico and the United States. This river border that both separates and unites two different worlds marks a stark, rugged, hauntingly beautiful arena where drug trade flourishes, smuggling occurs daily, and "illegal aliens"—thus termed as though they were from another planet—enter the United States regularly. It serves as a catalyst for an evolving new culture that grows out of both countries but is unique to this borderland of a thousand miles from El Paso to Boca Chica.

El Paso is no more like Brownsville than Amarillo is like Beaumont. The lovely Spanish language is more common throughout this borderland than is English. In San Benito in the Lower Rio Grande Valley, 98 percent of the high school students have family background in the Hispanic culture. Language and culture are powerful uniting forces. So is the dollar, commonly used on both side of the border. Even as Mexican nationals continue to stream across this border river, searching for economic opportunity, American dollars flow south in ever greater numbers. Perhaps, like osmosis through a membrane, the movement of people and ideas, dollars and goods, will someday reach a positive equilibrium.

The Longest Border River

The Rio Grande served as the southern border of Texas when it was a nation—at least from Texans' point of view. Mexico challenged that boundary,

9. A sinuous Rio Grande marks the border between Texas and Mexico; this section is above the Big Bend.

claiming the Nueces River farther north and east as border, and frequently invaded the disputed territory, which became known as the Nueces Strip. Texas even considered the big river its western border, claiming all of New Mexico to the Rio Grande and north into Colorado and beyond.

The Rio Grande served as the southern border when Texas became one of the United States, after a war with Mexico to prove that point, and it serves as the border today; as such, it is only part of Texas from midriver. But even if the whole width of the river does not legally belong to Texas, Texans regard it as their own, as an important part of the Lone Star state, historically, geologically, and economically.

By the time the Rio Grande reaches El Paso, it is pretty well used up by farmers, ranchers, and municipalities in Colorado and New Mexico and by evaporation in the high desert atmosphere of the landscape through which it travels. As much as two-thirds of its volume, by some estimates, is lost to the atmosphere. By the time it reaches Fort Quitman southeast of El Paso, it is gone entirely except in high-water years or during sudden and heavy storms.

Fortunately the Río Conchos from Mexico flows into the Rio Grande just above Presidio to replenish the big river. Its flow through the Big Bend depends on rain and snowmelt in the Sierra Madre Occidental of Chihuahua and Durango in northern Mexico.

The canyons of the Big Bend National Park—where the river flows around the base of the Chisos Mountains—have an international reputation, but most local river runners prefer the Lower Canyons, once they've done the trio of gorges in the park: Santa Elena, twenty miles long and 1,516 feet deep; Mariscal, ten miles long and 1,700 feet deep; and Boquillas, thirty-three miles long and 1,640 feet deep. What we call the Big Bend country the Spanish knew as *el despoblado,* the empty or unpopulated region because it seemed so inhospitable. Running the major canyons of this empty region challenges and thrills hundreds of boaters every year.

A Brief Geology

Big Bend geology is varied and complex. As Darwin Spearing writes in *Roadside Geology of Texas,* "The geology controls the topography, which controls the local weather, which controls the local plants and animals" (24). He further points out that the kinds of rock and the patterns of weather constitute the two basic factors of topography. Weathering and erosion wear down mountains. Gravity and erosion then carry away the materials carved from the landscape. The Big Bend country certainly exhibits extreme topography, basic differences in elevation being more than a vertical mile (roughly 2,000 to 7,800 feet).

Rafting the river above Santa Elena Canyon one November, I observed the most massive sill that I'd ever seen, a layer of magma that had cooled and hardened before reaching the earth's surface. It lay many feet thick in places between layers of limestone and in formations on both sides of the river for miles, as far as I could see. Obviously volcanism participated in the geological story.

Briefly, volcanism, geological activity involving molten rock or magma, takes two forms: extrusive (external), in which magma reaches the surface in the form of a lava flow or more violent volcanic eruption, and intrusive (internal), in which magma flows into cracks and crevices beneath the earth's surface, then cools and hardens in existing rock. If it flows between layers, it is called a sill; if it crosses layers, it is known as a dike. Lava and basalt are extrusive rock; granite is intrusive. The Big Bend area is full of both extrusive and intrusive volcanism, but that's only part of the story.

Two other basic concepts of geology are that newer (more recent) layers of

10. Boquillas Canyon in Big Bend country yawns upstream as a Rio Grande rafting party enters a more open stretch.

11. Two canoes suggest the magnitude of Boquillas Canyon; the view is upstream, so that Mexico is on the left and the United States on the right.

rock normally lie above older layers, a logical observation, and that rocks intruded by magma must be older than the magma itself. Magma produces igneous (pyrogenic or fire-formed) rock. Rock altered by heat and pressure over time is called metamorphic (literally, changed in form), and rock that forms from deposits of sediments, no matter what size, becomes sedimentary rock: siltstone, sandstone, or conglomerate.

The sill that I observed had been pushed through layers of preexisting limestone and had spread out for miles in several directions. The heat and pressure generated had altered the adjacent rock, changing its form, so that all three basic rock types exist in the Big Bend. All of Texas' major mountains lie in the Trans-Pecos, where the greatest amount of volcanism has occurred.

Generally speaking, igneous rocks and metamorphic rocks are harder than sedimentary rocks, but some sedimentary rocks are harder than others, as we see in the Caprock country of the Llano Estacado, where harder rocks protect underlying strata from erosion to create voodoos and cliffs. Some rock layers are known as cliff-formers because they erode less readily than others or they form vertical patterns.

Since weather as well as the kind of rock impacts erosion, let us consider Big Bend weather patterns. The surrounding lower-elevation landscape receives between ten and fourteen inches of annual precipitation, but the higher elevations receive almost twice as much, up to eighteen or twenty inches. Further, at higher elevations more precipitation falls as snow because temperatures are lower at these altitudes. Rain and snow cause different patterns of erosion and different vegetational patterns; snow melts at different rates depending on whether it lies in sunlit or shady areas, and rates of snowmelt and evaporation depend on the patterns of sun and shadow.

Low temperatures cause frost wedging and heaving, which lead to exfoliation of certain rocks, all in a process known as weathering, which helps to break down mountains and create soil. Also, availability of moisture affects the growth of microorganisms that help turn rock into soil, and hundreds of microclimes occur in the contrasting shade, shadow, and open sunlight of eroded mountains, all of which affects the plant and animal life that can live in a given biome.

The river is a major factor of erosion, but where the river goes, where it cuts its course, has much to do with the kind of rock through which it flows and with the patterns of precipitation and weathering that help it cut through the landscape and deposit the debris from those processes. Wind as a weather factor plays a role in both erosion and deposition. Wind-deposited sediments known as loess erode easily and add to the turbidity of rivers. Plants and animals also participate in erosion as their roots penetrate rock or their borrows or trails help alter the landscape. Human activities generate even more profound patterns of erosion, increasing runoff rates through road building, destroying with the plow the protective ground-covering grasses that have prevailed for millenia, and wearing out the land with overgrazing.

We know that Cabeza de Vaca and his surviving companions were probably the first Europeans to cross the Rio Grande. Where? No one is quite certain, but we do know that the four men could not have gotten to where they were found from where they must have begun on the Gulf Coast without crossing the great river of the north. The year would have been 1535. A few years later Coronado, prompted by stories told by the survivors of the Narvaez Expedition and led by one of them, Estevánico the Moor, crossed the great river in central New Mexico, but the Texas segment of the Rio Grande soon became known to the European world.

12. A feral burro nibbles a morsel from the sand along the Mexican side of El Río Grande del Norte.

In fact, its mouth had been discovered in 1519 by Spanish explorer Alonso Alvarez de Piñeda, who named it El Río de las Palmas (river of palms) for the numerous palm trees that grew at its mouth (of an estimated 40,000 acres of palms at that time, only 47 acres remain today). In 1581 Franciscan missionary Fray Agustín Rodríguez and Francisco Sánchez Chamuscado led a joint expedition up the Río Conchos (northern Mexico) to the Rio Grande near what became Presidio, then northwest up the great river to El Paso and beyond. The following year Antonio de Espejo reached the Rio Grande by following the same route northward.

The river had several early names—Río San Buenaventura, Río Ganapetuan, Río Turbio—before Juan de Oñate, in the vicinity of El Paso on his way to settle New Mexico in 1598, named it El Río Grande del Norte (it was Oñate who cut off one foot of every Acoma warrior his army captured as a lesson to Pueblo Indians who resisted the Spanish invasion).

Numerous Spanish expeditions soon became familiar with the Rio Grande, for the two main roads into Texas both crossed the great river: El Camino Real (the royal road) crossed it near the Mission San Juan Bautista (established in 1699) and the nearby Presidio del Río Grande on the road to San

Antonio, and La Bahía Road (the low road) crossed at Laredo (established in 1755) on the way to La Bahía, which became Goliad. Several towns had grown up on the south bank of the Rio Grande by the middle of the eighteenth century: Reynosa, Camargo (at the head of navigation), Mier, and Revilla, which later became Guerrero, now under the waters of Falcon Reservoir.

As Texas and Mexico squabbled about the border and traded invasions during the days of the Texas republic, a Texas army invaded the town of Mier (in Mexico, downstream from modern Falcon Reservoir) and was defeated and captured, which in turn led to an infamous black-bean lottery in which Texas prisoners were executed. The Mier Expedition (1842), organized to counter several Mexican raids into Texas (San Antonio, Victoria, and Goliad), crossed the Rio Grande into Mexican Territory, where the Texans, outnumbered 10-1, were defeated on Christmas Day. After the captured Texans tried a mass escape, they were marched to Mexico City where Santa Anna, again in power, ordered their execution. When his officers refused to comply with his order, Santa Anna amended the order to executing every tenth prisoner. The Texans drew beans from a pot to determine which ones would be shot. Those who drew black beans from a mix of black and white ones were killed. Remains of the executed prisoners were returned to Texas in 1848. Their remains were buried at Monument Hill across the Colorado River from La Grange, a few miles from my hometown. The monument was dedicated in 1936, one of my earliest memories.

The idea of traveling on the river or up the river rather than merely crossing it must have occurred early, but the Spanish were not known for river travel. Many early entrepreneurs dreamed of commerce on the Rio Grande, but lack of a port at its mouth cost the Rio Grande access to overseas markets.

Henry Austin, a cousin of Stephen F. Austin's and a friend and former roommate of Robert Fulton (the man who invented the steamboat), had a try at steamboating on the Rio Grande. He explored it in the *Ariel,* his sidewheeler, for three hundred miles to the mouth of the Salado. Finding the river too shallow above that point, he plied it briefly between Matamoros and Camargo, but circumstances and timing turned against him. He left the Rio Grande for the Brazos, damaged the *Ariel* on the shallow Brazos Bar, and limped into Galveston Bay and thence up Buffalo Bayou, where she eventually rotted and sank.

Flatboat trade between Laredo and Reynosa developed, despite an island near the mouth of the Río Salado that created a shoal, the Great Ledge, several miles upriver from the Río Salado, and the Double Reef some miles above the ledge. The river was reported to be navigable by steamboat as far upstream as the mouth of Devil's River 575 miles from the Gulf, but that seems to have been more wishful thinking than reality, though occasional traffic did reach that far upstream in smaller craft.

Texas congressman Thomas Jefferson Green, a survivor of the 1842–43 Mier Expedition, saw the Rio Grande as similar to the Ohio River, but British consul-general Charles Elliott saw it as inappropriate for military transport because of its low water in the dry season and its rapids. Still, as a means of commerce, it interested Capt. Mizin Kenedy, a Florida river pilot, and Richard King, who eventually created the gigantic King Ranch in South Texas. Even though these two riverboat pilots hauled cotton on twenty steamboats on the lower river during the Civil War, steamboat success on the Rio Grande was always just around the next bend; it never really happened. It had its best chance in the late 1840s and early 1850s, just after the Mexican War. Railroads and irrigation put river transport out of business: the railroads could go where rivers did not, and increased irrigation along the river dropped water levels even lower.

Getting to Know the Great River

My first experience with the Rio Grande came in the spring of 1956, just after I'd gotten out of the army. While serving as director of the Andrews Youth Center in the Permian Basin, I took a group of high school boys on a camping trip into the Big Bend. The night we arrived we slept on the ground in the Chisos Basin in a fierce wind that threw sand and gravel at us all night. The next night we camped at the mouth of Santa Elena Canyon. In the shadows of late afternoon we hiked into the canyon for half a mile, marveling at the steep walls, enjoying the unique vegetation and the spectacular bird life. Settling in for the night, we scattered around the dying campfire. When I awoke near midnight, I heard a faint rustling, raised my head to look around, and observed a trio of skunks looking for leftovers. I didn't dare move for fear of frightening the skunks into taking defensive action—best simply to lie there quietly until I finally dropped into a restless sleep. In the morning, we swapped stories about what we had seen in the moonlight; all of us had observed the skunks parading through camp, sniffing at this tousled head or that protruding toe. We all had a good laugh.

The third night we camped across the river from the village of Boquillas. Wading across the river, we visited the tiny Mexican town, which could have been the set for a western movie: horses and burros tied to rails in front of a saloon, vaqueros drinking tequila while a lusty musician played the guitar. I recall stepping on a pricklypear cactus pad in the river mud—it was full of spines and stuck to the sole of my tennis shoe—as I recrossed the river to our camp.

One Thanksgiving in the mid-1980s I rafted Santa Elena Canyon with a group from the Adobe Whitewater Club in Albuquerque. The Rock Slide had created a bottleneck. A party of canoeists ahead of us took forever to negotiate the narrow maze among gigantic limestone boulders that had fallen from the canyon walls in prehistoric times. We waited our turn, scouting carefully, then made our run. The first raft had a flip-line tied around it to help right the craft if it flipped. When that flip-line caught a submerged rock and hung up, it took the crew a half hour to discover the problem, cut the line, and complete their run. The next boat missed the route, was swept to the left, and got hung up on another shallow rock for ten minutes. Learning from their mistakes, I made a clean run on the Mexican side, high-siding on a boulder on the right that narrowed the gap to a mere six feet—my raft was eight feet wide.

On a drive to the Big Bend country the fall of 1997 for a Thanksgiving run through Boquillas Canyon, I'd spent a few days researching and photographing the Pecos River, the major Rio Grande tributary in Texas. As I drove south from Fort Davis toward the Rio Grande, the landscape changed from the flat semiarid rangeland along the Pecos to rugged mountains with rich grassy slopes, then, south of Marfa, into real Chihuahuan desert. I drove to Presidio on the Rio Grande, a border town that frequently registers the hottest temperatures in the state or the nation.

The atmosphere was hazy with autumn, factory smoke, and fires burning south of the border in Mexico. I took the river road southeast and stopped briefly at Fort Leaton State Historical Park, where after the Mexican War (1846–48) Ben Leaton and three partners, all of them bounty hunters, terrorized the local population on both sides of the border until his death in 1851. He also farmed the floodplain and traded with local Indians, Apaches and Comanches. Descendants of the bounty hunters, who were involved in a number of murders, lived in the fort until 1926; eventually the ruins were donated to the State of Texas.

At Redford I stopped to visit Enrique Madrid, whom I'd never met, on the suggestion of a Yukon outfitter and paddling friend of mine, Dick Person. Enrique, a serious-minded, analytical, and outspoken product of the border culture, serves as an archeological steward, helping protect important sites in the area from vandalism. His home is full of books and his mind is full of ideas. He spoke of his family's roots in the area, going back to 1876 when the Apache leaders Victorio and Naña raided near here and befriended his ancestors. He spoke of his ancestors building low dams, a concept they learned from watching beaver along the Rio Grande, twelve-foot structures designed to help local farmers irrigate crops including corn, cotton, and melons. He also spoke of a killing on the border.

Esequiel Hernández, Jr., was an eighteen-year-old Texan, an American citizen of Hispanic background who was shot to death near Redford, Texas, on May 20, 1997, by a U.S. marine on border patrol duty. Armed with an eighty-year-old .22 caliber rifle, Esequiel was out on the range herding his family's goats and hunting rabbits. At this writing, the federal government has offered $1.9 million to settle a wrongful death lawsuit, but the case is far from over. It has stirred massive resentment along the Rio Grande border and drawn attention to the sorry situation that exists there.

I had first learned about the killing in the newspapers and on the evening news. It became more meaningful to me when I met Enrique in Redford a few months later. He had known the boy, who was a neighbor, and he was angry about the boy's death. Enrique's mother, Lucia Rede Madrid, had taught Esequiel to read. The boy's death sadddened her, and angered her too.

Enrique's mother, Esequiel's teacher, has been honored on both sides of the border for her work with children. A retired teacher since 1975, she has spent more than twenty years making books available to people in both Texas and Chihuahua and teaching people to read in an attempt to increase their literacy and improve their lives. A member of the Texas Woman's Hall of Fame, she has received the President's Volunteer Action Award from President George Bush and the President's Award for Volunteer Excellence from President Ronald Reagan. Her attitude about the border is best expressed in her words, quoted by Larry D. Hodge in his article "Rio Grande, Bond of Life": "The river is not there to divide us. It brings us together" (36).

Enrique expressed the same sentiment to me during my late-November visit. He sees the river as the heart of a vibrant new cultural revolution, drawing from both countries but stronger and more resilient than either. Extremely well read, Enrique kept shoving books at me, telling me how important each book is for helping people understand the border culture. He quoted from the *Utne Reader* and *National Geographic,* from special reports and erudite documents. I wish I'd had more time to spend with him, but I was heading for Boquillas Canyon to rendezvous with friends.

After leaving Redford, I drove past the recently acquired Big Bend Ranch

State Park, more than a quarter-million acres (269,714, to be precise) of Chihuahuan desert along the Rio Grande and the River Road, El Camino del Río, FM-170. What a beautiful drive! Dusty it is, and bumpy, and slow, but it forces you to take time to look at the country, which flanks Colorado Canyon and enhances nearby Big Bend National Park.

When I reached Rio Grande Village after a late-afternoon drive through the park, I met my party in the campground, where a herd of javelina rooted through the woods. Our three rafts and a kayak were ready to launch by midmorning the next day. We photographed several canoes on the four-day run, but for the most part we had the river to ourselves. I have never worked harder to get down a river in my life. We averaged only about eight miles a day on low water, a slow trip, but we enjoyed every minute of it, saw rare birds (peregrine falcon), javelina, and feral burros, and found several small candelilla operations and huge piles of candelilla stems from which the wax had been extracted.

Candelilla, a plant that grows abundantly in the Big Bend country, is able to live in the harsh climate by exuding a waxy protective coating. A valuable natural wax can be extracted from this waxy coating by boiling the plant and treating it with diluted sulfuric acid. After the crude candelilla wax (called cerote) has been skimmed off the surface, the plant residue is pitch-forked out of the vats and allowed to dry to become fuel for the next batch. The cerote is poured into molds, often merely holes dug into the sandy beach along the river. Purified candelilla wax may be used in cosmetics, chewing gum, inks, paints, and polishes.

Technically the production and distribution of candelilla wax is controlled by the government on both sides of the border for environmental and economic reasons, but from time to time a lively trade in black market wax has occurred to avoid the collection of custom fees and taxes. There is also the problem of campaisanos harvesting the plant in Big Bend National Park, a protected area, on the Texas side of the river, then hauling it across the river to be rendered of its wax. Most of the wax ultimately winds up in the United States, but some of it makes its way across the border without either government's gaining appropriate revenue.

Camping on a midriver island one night (were we in Mexico or Texas?), I was awakened by the sound of some large animal splashing across. I looked through my tent window and in the moonlight saw a light-colored animal, a horse or burro. At dawn another splashing animal crossed, followed a few minutes later by a man on horseback from the Mexican side. While we were breaking our overnight fast, two riders returned, one driving a white horse, the other leading a sorrel mare. Apparently the animals had escaped from a candelilla encampment in the middle of the night; the vaqueros were up early, missed the animals, and simply retrieved them. We were on the border.

Shorter or less spectacular river segments connect the canyon reaches, and Colorado and Madera canyons above Santa Elena offer scenic runs as well. However, it is the Lower Canyons below the Big Bend that attract most regional boaters in kayaks, rafts, and canoes. This stretch, protected as a National Wild and Scenic River, offers isolation, stunning scenery, and 191.2 miles of challenging river running.

Farther downstream I encountered the Rio Grande in a less dramatic setting. I drove through coastal prairie and marsh to its mouth at Boca Chica. Well, almost to its mouth, because the road doesn't go there. It reaches the Gulf about three miles north of Boca Chica, and you have to walk or drive along the beach to get to the river mouth. Since I arrived on a blustery day at high tide during a storm, I declined the opportunity to reach the mouth and began working my way upstream—by car.

No Border to the Birds

In the Lower Rio Grande Valley I visited my snowbird cousin from Wisconsin, Rosaline Brayer, and her husband Joe in Alamo. They've spent winters in Alamo for more than twenty years. Joe fell in love with the Texas winter climate during his basic training days in the army, stationed near Bastrop. I also visited nearby Santa Ana National Wildlife Refuge on the Rio Grande, famous for high bird counts because many tropical species occur here. I hiked several miles of trails and saw chachalacas, kiskadees, vermilion flycatchers, green jays, and grooved-billed anis, all rare birds to me.

That night I camped at Bentsen–Rio Grande State Park, another great birding area, and canoed the palm-lined *resaca* (oxbow lake) left when a bend of the Rio Grande was cut off from the river in its natural meandering. I missed Resaca de la Palma State Park, the 172-acre National Audubon Society protected area called Sabal Palm Grove Sanctuary, and Laguna Atascosa National Wildlife Refuge north of Brownsville and east of Harlingen, both excellent birding areas, because I was working my way upriver.

My next stop was Falcon State Park. Being a riverman, I was more impressed with the downstream view from the dam than with the reservoir itself, but both offer good wildlife-viewing possibilities. The five-mile-long dam has

13. Sand dunes near Boca Chica at the mouth of the Rio Grande on a cloudy day in January characterize much of the Texas Gulf Coast.

drowned sixty miles of river and flooded eighty-seven thousand acres. This impoundment has in a sense created a new wildlife habitat downstream providing instream flow in delivering irrigation water downstream. Steamboats once traveled up the Rio Grande as far as nearby Roma, a village settled in 1767. Across the Rio Grande in Mexico is the village of Mier, where the black-bean incident occurred as Santa Anna continued his anti-Texan actions. If access to the Rio Grande were developed as well as is access to Falcon Reservoir, the Rio Grande would see a great deal more river traffic, but that might make the Border Patrol's work more difficult—one reason it hasn't been done.

Vic Hines of Austin likes to paddle upstream in a small narrow canoe he built himself. He doesn't pole, as I've taught myself to do (I prefer it to paddling especially for canoeing upstream). He simply reads the currents and, like Lewis and Clark, finds the eddies and moves upstream by carefully reading the river and working its currents. With much effort he has paddled 370 miles of the Rio Grande from near its mouth to the base of Falcon Dam, then with a car portage, still farther upstream. It took him five weeks. He found superb wildlife habitat and a few border problems.

When Frederick Law Olmsted, creator of Central Park in New York City, crossed the Rio Grande at Eagle Pass to Piedras Negras in 1854, he found escaped slaves in Mexico, probably the ex-slave settlement near Eagle Pass established in 1849. As early as 1840, runaway slaves under Antonio Canales participated in an effort to establish the Republic of the Rio Grande, but even before that, in 1838, Vincent Córdova had led a group of Negros, Mexicans, and Indians in an abortive counterrevolt against the Republic of Texas government in far-away East Texas. Injustice has always been difficult to combat when people turn a blind eye to it.

A hundred and fifty years have imposed some ironic twists: people seeking a better life are still spurred toward border towns and across the border, but today we speak of the labor market, and the people now head north to find better-paying work, not south to escape forced labor. Serving as Texas' only international border, the Rio Grande divides more than two countries. It divides two peoples, two cultures, two sets of dreams that could be one. Will the border that has divided the two countries for a century and a half ever become a unifying force, as some argue it could? Is NAFTA a step in the right direction or a further deterrent?

Joel Garreau, in his 1981 book *The Nine Nations of North America,* outlines nine economic and cultural regions that would seem to make logical "nations." The one he calls MexAmerica begins at an imaginary line (what are borders anyway?) from Houston-Galveston-Austin westward, then north along the east side of the Sangre de Cristo Range in north-central New Mexico and going south into central Mexico. He suggests that logically, economically, culturally, and in several other ways, such a nation would make more sense than what we have today. It isn't going to happen any time soon, but I find it an intriguing idea—one that would indeed make of the Rio Grande not a boundary but a profoundly unifying force.

Sabine

LOCATION: *Northeast Texas, Louisiana-Texas state line to Gulf of Mexico*
NAME: *From the Spanish sabino, "cypress tree"*
CITIES: *Longview, Greenville, Marshall, Orange*
IMPOUNDMENTS: *Toledo Bend Reservoir, Lake Tawakoni, Lake Fork Reservoir*
TRIBUTARIES: *Cowleech forks, Lake Fork Creek, Big Sandy Creek, Big Cow Creek*
RECREATION: *Hunting, fishing, boating*
WATERSHED: *9,756 square miles (7,400 in Texas)*
DISCHARGE: *6.8 million acre feet*
LENGTH: *580 miles, 265 miles along state line (plus 20-mile length of Sabine lake and 10-mile length of Sabine Pass)*
PUBLIC LANDS: *Lake Tawakoni State Park, Martin Creek Lake State Park, Sabine National Forest, Indian Mounds Wilderness, Tony Houseman State Park, Sabine Pass Battleground State Historical Park, Sea Rim State Park*
FEATURES: *Sabine Pass*

IN THE SABINE RIVER, Texas shares with Louisiana roughly three hundred miles of swampy border. The Sabine produces more water than any other Texas river (6.8 million acre feet from a watershed of 9,756 square miles), a quarter of its volume flowing from the soggy state to the east. The Sabine begins near Greenville east of Dallas and flows southeast, becoming the state line near Logansport, Louisiana, then turning south toward its union with the Neches in Sabine Lake southwest of Orange. The combined flow of the Sabine and Neches rivers into Sabine Lake and ultimately into the Gulf of Mexico through Sabine Pass south of Port Arthur vaults the lower Sabine into nineteenth place among U.S. rivers producing the greatest flow, well ahead of the Colorado River of the West, which doesn't even rank among the top fifty.

The Sabine's entire watershed lies within an annual rainfall region of more than forty inches, most of it receiving between forty-five and fifty-six inches—one explanation for a watershed less than a quarter as large as that of the Brazos contributing considerably more flow to the Gulf than does the Brazos, which produces about 5.2 million acre feet. In its meandering course through East Texas the Sabine flows through three different physiographic regions: the blackland prairies, the East Texas timberlands, and the coastal prairies. While this detail may suggest a "prairie" nature to the terrain, few people along the river itself think of it as prairie. To them it is swampland, a maze of wetlands producing abundant fish, massive trees festooned with Spanish moss, dense vegetation that is home to alligators and water moccasins, and marshes harboring large, often loud, sometimes colorful birds and a variety of other wildlife that local residents can trap or hunt.

Such habitat certainly characterizes the lower Sabine, but its headwaters flow through the rich blackland prairie east of Dallas, fertile farm country where local residents raise wheat and grain sorghum, cotton and corn, beef and dairy cattle, sheep and poultry. As the river moves into the East Texas timberlands, logging activities and timber products become more important. In fact, 88 percent of the watershed is considered East Texas timberlands. Oil and gas production have boosted the local economy in the Sabine watershed. Cultivated farming has dropped off in recent decades due to low natural productivity, infertile soils, and worn-out eroded lands that in many areas have returned to livestock pasturing or timber production.

The Sabine and its tributaries promote hunting and fishing on both a subsistence and a recreational level and some commercial fishing and trapping in the farm lands, forests, and river bottoms. The understory includes hardwoods—oak, gum, elm, hickory, and dogwood—as well as azalea and other flowering shrubs and wildflowers thicken the woods. Two publicly owned segments of hardwood bottomland along the upper Sabine between Mineola and Tyler—the 3,000-acre Little Sandy National Wildlife Refuge (the Little Sandy Hunting and Fishing Refuge, formerly the Little Sandy Hunting and Fishing Club, is leased from private owners under an easement by the U.S. Fish and Wildlife Service) and the neighboring recently purchased 4,937-acre Anderson Tract (also known as the Old Sabine Bottom Wildlife Management Area owned by Texas Parks and Wildlife Deparment)—help protect natural habitat and native plant and animal species. Neither area offers public access, nor is either available for consumptive use, a response to an evolving

14. A small outboard motorboat negotiates a bend of the upper Sabine River at flood stage.

public attitude in Texas and elsewhere reflecting a nationwide respect for the unexploited natural world.

Exploitation had been the name of the game along the Sabine in past decades. Two major dams on the Sabine itself and one on its tributary Lake Fork Creek, plus a dozen minor ones on various tributaries, highlight Texans' traditional penchant for reservoirs rather than free-flowing rivers. Pollution from agricultural and logging practices and from the petrochemical industry has reduced water quality, to the detriment of many natural processes and recreational activities. Federal laws during recent decades, many of them implemented under state and local authority, have begun to clean up the mess, and state-initiated laws in the 1990s have helped.

The Texas Clean Rivers Act (1991), working through statewide river-basin authorities, has added to the solution through periodic water-quality assessments and more. In contrast to Louisiana, where, as noted, a quarter of the Sabine's water originates, Texas now has the Sabine River Authority (SRA) as the basin-wide planning agency for all Texas Clean River Program activities in the Sabine Basin. The SRA has moved "toward an integrated and systematic approach to protect the water resources of the Sabine River," claims the executive summary of the SRA's 1996 Assessment of Water Quality in the Sabine River drainage. Thus long-term planning, anathema to many exploiters and conservative politicians, has become part of the process.

Big Thicket Country

Leon C. Metz, in *Roadside History of Texas,* sets the boundaries of the Big Thicket as extending "from the Sabine River to as far west as the Brazos and as far south as the coastal prairie of South Texas" (172). J. Frank Dobie, in his delightful account of Ben Lilly, *The Ben Lilly Legend* (1950), points out that "the original Big Thicket of Texas lay for a hundred miles up and down the Sabine River with an average width of fifty miles" (104). Dobie writes that even by Ben Lilly's time in the Big Thicket, around 1906, "agriculture and lumbering had eaten deeply into it," but since then "oil and the ruthless paper mill industry have blackened and mutilated more of it" (104). At the turn of the century, for scientists studying the now extinct ivory-billed woodpecker, Ben Lilly collected two specimens of the rare bird in the Big Thicket on the Louisiana side of the Sabine, where several state and federally protected areas now lie within the Sabine watershed.

Was Dobie one of those terrible environmentalists so hated in much of Texas or merely an honest realist, a Texan who loved the land and the natural world it represented more than he felt the need to exploit its resources? Perhaps he was someone with respect for that natural world and its evolutionary processes, a man with the foresight to understand important ecological relationships and one who was willing to tell the truth as he saw it. He grew up on a South Texas ranch far from the Sabine in both distance and character, but as a man intimate with the land, he obviously understood relationships at which few modern city dwellers can even guess.

Another truth teller, Edward Hoagland, in his collection of essays entitled *Red Wolves and Black Bears,* wrote in the 1970s of the Big Thicket as the original home of the endangered red wolf, and of red wolf hybrids then still roaming the area. He found it strange that remnants of the species had been discovered in the salt marshes of Texas' most industrial and populated section—"instead of the pineywoods and hillbilly thickets always listed as their home" (133). He faulted Texas for allowing the poisoning of red wolves until

1966 and for doing nothing "to resurrect the wolves from unprotected varmint status" (136). An outsider looking in, he pointed out that "Texas encompasses considerably less state-owned park and recreation land than New Jersey" (144). But he wrote those words a quarter-century ago. Things have changed for the better since then, especially in actions of the state's Parks and Wildlife Department, which is evolving into a major force for the natural world.

As a young man growing up in south-central Texas, I remember the battle to save the Big Thicket, which I'd never seen at the time. Houston attorney Orrin H. Bonney and his wife Lorraine helped galvanize the Sierra Club into leading the effort to protect the area and its unique plant and animal life (see his "Big Thicket: Biological Crossroads of North America"). However, politicians who believed in exploitation kept protection at bay until what was left lay in several discrete segments. Today the Big Thicket National Preserve, established in 1974, exists along the nearby Neches River and some of its tributaries, but it scarcely compares to what once comprised the Big Thicket along the Sabine and Neches rivers. Metz has referred to it as "a string of pearls," a series of linear segments given protective designation, rather than the massive contiguous area it might have been before its exploitation.

A frequent contributor to *Texas Monthly,* naturalist Stephen Harrigan, in the preface to his collection of essays on Texas, *A Natural State,* notes that "Texas is an imperfect state . . . that still takes pride in its continuing triumph over the land" (xi). The exploiters, he suggests, are still in charge. In the final essay of the collection, "What Texas Means to Me," he writes of "the thick, suffocating Big Thicket forests, where you could find quicksand and wild orchids" (184), a different kind of American (or Texan) dream, one that respects the natural world and revels in its gifts and abundance in situ.

Houston freelancer Carol Barrington, on the other hand, says, in her 1995 *Texas Highways* article on the Sabine, "A River for All Reasons," that "the upper Sabine and its tributaries achieve genuine beauty only when their waters broaden out behind dams" (6). I liked her article and find her one of the best writers contributing to the magazine, but I disagree with her viewpoint. Dams kill rivers, turn them into a series of dying impoundments, destroy the natural processes that have evolved over geological time to drain the land and cleanse it, to recycle waste products and to create habitat for plants and animals that make human life possible and enhance its duration. Rivers both build and destroy land in a continuing natural process that dams disrupt and that humankind has a difficult time tolerating when it affects private property.

Dams don't prevent floods. They permanently flood many miles of rich bottomlands and often cause flooding elsewhere. Few dams have been designed to hold the water of hurricane-generated superstorms such as those that frequently hit the Gulf Coast, or the one that hit Del Rio on the Rio Grande in August, 1998, or the one that dumped up to two feet of rain in the headwaters areas of the Guadalupe in October, 1998. Dikes and levees also cause flooding upstream and down, especially when they break, and they encourage people to build in the floodplains where, by nature, they don't belong. Indigenous people including Native Americans learned to live with their natural conditions rather than trying to control them.

While recognizing the necessity of some dams, I prefer the beauty of biological diversity that results from free-flowing rivers. Texas may have overdone the dam building. Reservoirs may be pretty to look at and offer productive fishing and other recreational opportunities, but they also concentrate toxic substances by capturing surface runoff and atmospheric deposition of heavy metals and other contaminants. Many reservoirs, including several in the Sabine River Basin (particularly Toledo Bend Reservoir) have experienced fish consumption advisories.

Because of mercury contamination, concentrated by the act of impounding rivers, people have been advised to eat no more than two meals (eight ounces for adults, four ounces for children) per month of largemouth bass and freshwater drum combined. Eating contaminated fish can be a serious matter, as many Japanese people learned to their detriment in previous decades. Mercury poisoning can lead to serious neurological symptoms including blindness, comas, and death. Fortunately environmental controls have reduced the threat of many toxins. While few of the toxins pose a threat from contact recreation or to public water systems, high concentrations of many of these toxins do remain in many lake sediments.

Caddos, Spaniards, Frenchmen, and Confederates

Let's back up a few centuries and look at the Sabine River as it was in the days before European invasion. The Caddo Indians occupied the upper Sabine, Neches, Trinity, and their tributaries. They lived in permanent villages, were highly successful farmers, and achieved the highest level of cultural development of any Texas Indian tribe (279), according to W. W. Newcomb, Jr., an authority on Texas Indians and director for many years of the Texas Memorial Museum in Austin. Actually a confederation of more than two dozen smaller tribes, the Caddo shared a common language (linguistically related to neighboring tribes to the north and west) and a culture allied to tribes of the American southeast, most closely akin to the Natchez of the lower Mississippi Valley.

So closely were the various southeastern tribes culturally related that anthropologists believe a seaborne migration from the Caribbean occurred during prehistoric times along the Gulf Coast, resulting in the indigenous peopling of the mainland (282). The Caddo civilization had ancient roots going back more than a thousand years before written history, to a people who built flat-topped earthen temple mounds, primitive pyramids. Their culture spread west to the Trinity River and east to the Atlantic Coast, the entire physiographic region of low-lying, humid lands with a mild climate that we know today as the American southeast.

Since their traditional territory lay in an area claimed by both the French and the Spanish and later by Americans and Texans, the Caddos experienced early and frequent contact with European invaders. They first encountered Europeans in 1541 when the army of Hernando de Soto attacked them and plundered their granaries, a practice that the Spanish continued for more than a century. The Caddos next met the French under La Salle (1686), but shortly thereafter another Spanish expedition under Alonso de León (1689) appeared to uproot the French, who had already abandoned the area. The early eighteenth century saw continual expeditions into the Caddos' world by both Spanish and French and, before long, permanent settlements that changed the Caddos' life forever. Their civilization essentially collapsed, primarily due to epidemic diseases, before Texas became an independent nation.

But what was life like along the Sabine during the days of the Caddo culture? They grew two kinds of corn, half a dozen types of beans, numerous varieties of squash, sunflower seeds, and tobacco. They gathered nuts—pecans, acorns, chestnuts—and several kinds of wild fruit: blackberries, cherries, grapes, mulberries, and plums. They hunted small mammals, upland game birds, and waterfowl as well as bear and bison, taking the latter primarily during winter months when the seasonally migrating buffalo were nearby. They fished the Sabine and other streams, using spears, nets, and trotlines almost as these are used today. In fact, anthropologists believe modern methods of fishing along the Sabine and other East Texas rivers grew from native practices. The Caddo wove reed baskets and made "fascinating and varied" pottery. They lived in grass houses (such as those recently constructed at Caddoan Mounds State Historical Park near Alto). They made bows out of *bois d'arc* (Osage orange) and used dugout canoes for transportation and fishing. They are considered "the most productive, advanced, and populous [indigenous] peoples of Texas," according to W. W. Newcomb (313).

Other native tribes lived along the middle and lower Sabine. Several Atakapan-speaking tribes, Hais in what is now Texas and Adai in what is now Louisiana, occupied an area from central Louisiana west to the Trinity and San Jacinto rivers in Texas. The Atakapa, "cannibals" in the Choctaw tongue, lived in southwestern Louisiana across the Sabine and in the vicinity of Sabine Lake; in the middle of the eighteenth century two of their villages lay on opposite banks of the lower Nueces near present-day Beaumont. Because of the nature of the terrain, largely swampy land that precluded crop raising, they lived primarily by hunting, fishing, and gathering in an area rich in wild food plants, fish, and game. Like their neighbors the Caddo, they hunted buffalo when the huge shaggy beasts were in the neighborhood, mostly in midwinter, as well as deer, bears, alligators and turtles. These native people used alligator grease to repel insects, bear grease for numerous purposes, though some tribes revered the bear and did not kill it. They also gathered bird eggs, shellfish, and other wild food. Some historians think that Cabeza de Vaca may have lived with one of these coastal Atakapan tribes known as the Hans during his trek across Texas in the early 1530s.

Much of what is known about these tribes was gleaned from Simars de Bellisle (also spelled Belle-Isle), a French officer abandoned by his captain on Galveston Bay in 1719. He lived as a captive of one of the coastal tribes for almost two years, hunted and fished with them, gathered wild edibles, and learned their ways. The natives tattooed their bodies and faces, went barefooted, and wore only breech clouts most of the year. Skilled fishermen who used dugout canoes, they often visited offshore islands in their food-gathering quests, and they speared alligators through the eyes.

Reports of French presence led to a Spanish expedition into the area in 1745 led by Capt. Joaquín de Orobio Bazterra. Spanish missions were established among these primitive tribes during the latter half of the eighteenth century but abandoned because Spanish military and religious authorities were working at cross purposes and the Indians proved less than cooperative. Independence apparently suited these peoples better than the austere Spanish ways.

After the Spanish and French fought it out for decades, the French finally won, then sold to the United States what was called the Louisiana Territory (1803). Unfortunately no one knew its boundaries. President Thomas Jefferson thought the Rio Grande should be the western boundary, according to Dan L. Flores, and confusion reigned for decades over the matter. At one point

Jefferson proposed to the Spanish "a district of neutral territory" between the Sabine and the Colorado. Yet when the American Red River Expedition was turned back by a substantial Spanish army, the American government grew alarmed to find Spanish troops east of the Sabine. Gen. James Wilkinson, a controversial figure who had been implicated in plots to take Texas from the Spanish, stood down the Spanish army and negotiated a neutral buffer strip (the Neutral Ground Agreement of 1806), which in effect designated the Sabine River as the *western* boundary of the United States as enlarged by the Louisiana Purchase.

Thus the Sabine became the border dividing the United States from Spanish Texas, but few people paid much attention. Under the agreement both countries claimed the disputed territory but neither governed it, a situation that created a no-man's-land where fugitives from both countries found refuge. Philip Nolan had made forays into Texas in the 1790s, running guns into Spanish territory and bringing back horses, but he apparently also served as a spy for certain American interests—or at least interests planning to steal Texas from Spain. Aware of Nolan's devious ways, a Spanish cavalry unit under Lt. Miguel Musquiz attacked his party and killed Nolan the spring of 1801. Nolan's information would feed several American attempts, none successful but all involving crossing the Sabine, to grab Texas away from the Spanish during the first two decades of the nineteenth century.

In 1819 the United States and Spain signed a treaty designating the west bank of the Sabine from the Gulf of Mexico north to the thirty-second parallel as the official western boundary of the United States. But two years later Mexico won independence from Spain, and the boundary squabble began all over again. In 1848, after Texas had become a state and the United States had fought a war with Mexico over the annexation of Texas, Congress named the middle of the river the *eastern* boundary of Texas but left ownership of the islands in the river in limbo for another century.

To backtrack a little, in 1821 Stephen F. Austin turned his father's grant from the Spanish government into a grant from the Mexican government for the first legal settlement of American citizens into that part of Mexico that became Texas. The name Texas, Newcomb points out, came from the Caddoan word *tayshas,* meaning "allies" or "friends," a term the Indians applied to the Spanish as well as to other members of their own confederation. The Spanish quite likely pronounced the word "Taychas" and spelled it Tejas.

The Sabine, then, became the demarcation point between the United States and Texas, which remained a part of Mexico for only another decade and a half. Writing in 1831, Mary Austin Holley, a cousin of Stephen F. Austin, referred to the Sabine in these terms: "The Sabine takes its rise in the northern part of Texas ... and pursues a southeast direction for about 150 miles." She mentions Tancks Creek as the point at which the Sabine turns south and "forms the boundary between Texas and Louisiana." She described the Sabine, which she quite likely never saw, as watering "a fertile and well timbered country" and as being "navigable for about 70 miles from its entrance into Sabine Lake." She wrote from secondhand information, having reached the Brazos Valley by ship from New Orleans; she had not crossed the Sabine to enter Texas.

In 1836 when Texas won its independence from Mexico, the Sabine was well established as its eastern border, at least from the Gulf Coast for a couple of hundred miles inland. Beyond that, the border became indistinct. Not until well after the Texas War of Independence were the headwaters of the Sabine settled, in the early 1840s, and then largely by southerners from the southeastern states. While Texas became a part of the United States in 1846, such southern settlers led inevitably to Texas' secession from the United States only fifteen years later: fifteen years as part of Mexico, ten years as an independent nation, fifteen years as a state—hardly enough time or stability in any governmental form for Texas to mature and define itself. And then came the Civil War, the War between the States.

One of the most astonishing Confederate victories of that war occurred at Sabine Pass, which drains the combined waters of the Sabine and Neches rivers into the Gulf of Mexico. A major Union effort to split Texas away from the rest of the Confederacy occurred the summer of 1863 as a Union force of between fifteen hundred and five thousand men (accounts vary; Rupert N. Richardson gives the high number) in twenty-two ships, including four gunboats, prepared to attack the garrison guarding the narrow channel of Sabine Pass at a makeshift mud-and-log defense arrangement called Fort Griffin. An Irish saloon owner in Houston before the war, Lt. Richard W. Dowling, known as Dick, commanded an artillery battery of six cannons and forty-six Irishmen at the pass (perhaps as few as forty-two or as many as forty-eight Irishmen; again accounts vary). The crew had been practice firing at pilings in the water and had the range to various positions in the pass accurately determined. Ordered to abandon the position and spike the cannons (that is, to render them useless if they were captured), Lt. Dick Dowling disobeyed orders and prepared to defend the pass.

On September 6, 1863, the Union gunboats entered Sabine Pass, leading the attack. In a matter of minutes the Irish artillerymen disabled two of the gunships, disabled several troopships, and routed the entire Union force. With help from 150 infantrymen under Capt. F. M. Odlum, the Texas volunteers captured between 315 and 500 Union men (Richardson says "about 350") and sent the Union Navy into disorderly retreat in what the *Handbook of Texas* calls "the most spectacular military engagement in Texas during the Civil War."

Sabine Pass, annexed by Port Arthur in 1978, is now home to extensive petrochemical operations and offshore oil-rig construction activity as well as to a small shrimp boat fleet. Its route to the Gulf has been short-circuited by the Gulf Intracoastal Waterway (GIWW), but the battlefield has been commemorated by the 1936 establishment of a monument to Dowling and his men.

Paddling and Birding Upriver

Most recreational boating on the Sabine involves power boats, but canoeing has become increasingly popular along several reaches. The fifty-nine-mile stretch from the State Highway 271 boat ramp west of Gladewater to SH 43, between Marshall and Tatum, has a few natural and man-made hazards (log-

15. Petrochemical operations and offshore oil-rig construction dominate the economy at Port Arthur on Sabine Pass.

16. A small fleet of shrimp boats operates along the Sabine Pass outlet to the Gulf of Mexico.

jams, minor falls, low dams) but offers a scenic float broken into numerous shorter segments by crossing roads and highways. An eighteen-and-a-half-mile stretch from U.S. Highway 59 between Marshall and Carthage to SH 79 near River Hill (between Carthage and De Berry) is a popular run, though not recommended at high water due to natural hazards. In *Rivers and Rapids,* Ben M. Nolen and Bob Narramore note this segment as "a very scenic trip, boasting fantastic natural beauty and an abundance of wildlife" (84). If you canoe below SH 79, you stand a good chance of getting lost in the numerous channels and oxbows below FM 2517 and US 84 between Joaquin, Texas, and Logansport, Louisiana, at the head of Toledo Bend Reservoir.

Below Toledo Bend Reservoir lies "one of the most scenic trips in the state," in Nolen and Narramore's judgment, a stretch of more than fifty miles of stateline river flowing with reservoir-release water; only one road crosses, ten and a half miles below the dam (SH 63, becoming Louisiana SH 8 to Burr Ferry as it crosses the Sabine). Remote and natural, with slow-flowing current and lined with tall cypress trees, the stretch has a swamplike appearance with white-sand beaches and bars. Largemouth bass and catfish are the main attractions for fishermen. The put-in lies immediately below the Toledo Bend

Dam; the take-out for the longer run is at SH 363/US 190 between Bon Weir, Texas, and Merryville, Louisiana.

Big Cow Creek, which begins in northwestern Newton County and flows ninety miles southeast into the Sabine, offers an isolated and off-the-beaten-track canoe trip. For a week-long paddle through solitude, launch at SH 87 two miles southeast of Newton and take-out on the Sabine several miles southeast of Trout Creek, where a spur road reaches the mouth of Big Cow Creek. Or continue down the Sabine to Deweyville for ten days of the same.

A long isolated stretch on the main river runs for sixty miles between SH 363/US 190 and the SH 12 crossing at Deweyville in southeastern Newton County. Four primitive roads approach the river, which widens considerably in this segment, retains its swampy character, and provides numerous opportunities to explore adjacent bayous on both sides of the river, as a number of small creeks enter the Sabine in this well-watered area. Below Deweyville lies a thirty-seven-mile stretch to Sabine Lake, a deep, wide river (more than five hundred feet wide at Orange) that may see some ocean-going vessels. The Gulf Intracoastal Waterway enters the Sabine south of Orange at Pavell Island, an oxbow.

Pine Park Rest Area between Bronson and Hemphill (at the junction of FM 2024 and SH 184) is one of the best places along the middle Sabine watershed to find the red-cockaded woodpecker, along with several other deep-woods species, including other woodpeckers. South of Hemphill near the tiny community of Rogers (SH 87 at R 255), in Newton County south of Toledo Bend Reservoir, lies a major rockhound collecting area for both petrified wood and flint. Another good place to find petrified wood is on either side of the Sabine immediately below Toledo Bend Dam.

Indian Mounds Wilderness—a unique American beech, black hickory, and southern magnolia forest—rises above the west shoreline of Toledo Bend Reservoir within Sabine National Forest east of Hemphill. Four champion trees (largest of their species) grace this 11,946-acre wilderness: a little-hip hawthorn, a flatwoods plum, a Florida sugar maple, and an eastern hop hornbeam. The largest white oak and black cherry trees in Texas national forests are also to be found here, along with other rare and beautiful trees, shrubs, and flowers, including several rare native orchids. This is one of the truly special places in East Texas.

The upper Sabine touts bird-watching, especially for bluebirds and bald eagles. Rains County sponsors an annual Eagle Fest, usually the third weekend of January, and Wills Point holds an annual Bluebird Festival in mid-

April. Despite Carol Barrington's negative press for the riverine Sabine, I find it delightful, flowing through the pineywoods where dogwood and wild fruit trees bloom in spring and hardwood forests awaken the soul with vibrant autumn colors. The upper Sabine watershed includes several more state parks: Martin Creek Lake near Tatum, the Governor Hogg Shrine near Quitman, and Lake Tawakoni.

Lake Tawakoni, created by the Iron Bridge Dam completed in 1960, has a surface area of 36,700 acres and holds 927,440 acre feet of water. Five and a half miles long, the dam impounds the Sabine River below several important tributaries. Paired with Lake Fork Dam, arguably the best bass lake in Texas (it has produced all but sixteen of the top fifty state record bass), it captures water from the upper Sabine Basin, and together they control the river's flow to the Louisiana state line. With two hundred miles of shoreline, Lake Tawakoni boasts catfish and striped and white bass fishing and offers excellent bird-watching opportunities at certain seasons.

Toledo Bend, the biggest reservoir on the system, has drowned eighty-five miles of natural river to create a 1,250-mile shoreline. It is the largest man-made lake in the South, the fifth largest (in surface area) in the nation. Authorities claim three hundred pounds of game fish per acre, largely black, white, and Florida bass, stripers (up to forty pounds), crappie, bream, and catfish. In recent years the importance of bird-watching has become clear as bald eagles, coastal shorebirds, pelicans, egrets, cranes, ducks, and many migrating birds visit the reservoir. Wildlife species include armadillo, deer, fox, opossum, raccoon, coyote, possible red wolf hybrids, beaver, and feral hogs. Spring wildflowers include wild azalea, dogwood, wild fruit trees—peach, pear, plum—paintbrush, the pale pink primrose commonly called "buttercup," bluebonnet, feral crimson clover (a domestic plant gone wild), and numerous other forbs and weeds.

The Lower Sabine

The lower Sabine area has come to be known as the Golden Triangle, the points of the triangle being Orange (on the Sabine), Beaumont (on the Neches), and Port Arthur (on Sabine Lake), all three cities linked to the Gulf by the GIWW and all three dominated by oil refineries and petrochemical plants. Beaumont is addressed in more detail in the chapter on the Neches. Port Arthur began as a fishing village in the early 1840s. A deep-water canal constructed at the end of the nineteenth century turned the town into a seaport that soon became a major oil shipping center. As Acadians from Louisiana began moving to the area to find high-paying jobs and came to constitute up to 20 percent of the population, Port Arthur was dubbed the "Cajun Capital" of Texas.

Known in 1830 as Green Bluffs—though I can't imagine any bluffs in the neighborhood—Orange, named for a local orange grove, grew up as a lumber town, then nearly died when all the timber had been cut. Discovery of oil in 1913 gave it a new lease on life, and it was further stimulated during World War II by the ship-building industry. When I was a lad of twelve, my father worked in the shipyards, building landing craft for the invasion of the Pacific islands. The town grew from a population of twelve thousand to sixty thousand virtually overnight, with many people, my family included, living in government housing built on wetlands filled with various debris.

People disrupting the local wildlife had to put up with raiding raccoons and with alligators, but few really enjoyed the offerings of the Sabine River. There were bank fishermen, but many newcomers avoided the river marge—they were afraid of it. People who knew the area might have boated the river and its adjacent wetlands, but gasoline was scarce. I didn't visit Orange again until half a century later in the early 1990s, when I stopped to see my high school classmates who lived there, Ken and Pat Lorfing. Ken, who had spent a career working for one of the chemical companies in the area, gave me a tour of the town, pointing out the changes since I'd lived there. Much smaller than during the ship-building days of World War II, Orange had reverted to being a minor seaport and fishing center, a quieter town of twenty thousand with a less aggressive development mindset than some of her neighbors along the lower Sabine and Neches.

When I returned to Orange to research this book, I found everyone from bank fishermen and canoeists to power boaters and jet-skiers using the river, which rolled by high and fast in late March. My paddling partner Dave and I launched my canoe into the swift current beneath the Interstate 10 bridge over the Sabine, paddled upstream a short distance in a quiet backwater, then entered the Blue Elbow Swamp, one of the most beautiful places we paddled during a two-week early spring tour of Texas. Tall moss-draped cypress trees, for which the river is named, formed the backdrop, with dense vegetation of palmettos and arrowleaf decorating the shoreline. We soon left the freeway noise behind us as we paddled through the lush vegetation, following a man-made channel into the swamp, which had been logged a century earlier; but little evidence of the early desecration remained. We paddled through a natural world.

17. Tall cypresses draped with Spanish moss line this channel through Blue Elbow Swamp near Orange.

As noted, the lower Sabine is Cajun country, an area where land and water intermix and provide natural food, cultural diversity, and water-related recreation. One day a year, the Texas Parks and Wildlife Department sponsors a biologist-led tour of Blue Elbow Swamp for canoeists on the northeast edge of Orange, through the area Dave and I canoed in the spring of 1998. The lower Sabine boasts two state parks: Sea Rim State Park southwest of Port Arthur, and Sabine Pass Battlefield State Historical Park south of Port Arthur. The 13,264-acre J. D. Murphree Wildlife Management Area on Taylor Bayou, which flows into Sabine Lake from the west, offers a good place to watch wildlife, from alligator, river otter, beaver, nutria, and muskrat to white-faced ibis, anhinga, purple gallinule, and common snipe as well as the largest population of canvasback ducks in Texas. Boats tours are available, and private boats may launch at several ramps. Both Orange and Port Arthur have historical museums, and Orange has the Stark Museum of Art.

The Sabine River is many things to many people in both Texas and Louisiana. Although the river is the center of a common economy based largely on the timber and petrochemical industries, much of the Sabine Basin is rural and isolated, primitive and poor. Not a few residents live off the land and water, hunting, fishing, and trapping for their food and livelihood as much as for recreation.

A great many residents and visitors alike use the Sabine River and its watershed for a wide variety of recreational activities, and some still see it in terms of raw nature. The river serves as the natural boundary between Texas and Louisiana, has had a checkered history as a political boundary, and, like the Rio Grande, is the focus of cultural richness that grows out of its history. But unlike the Rio Grande, the Sabine already functions as a unifying and nurturing element in the landscape and is likely to continue that way.

Red River

LOCATION: *Texas Panhandle eastward, forming Texas' northern border*
NAME: *Comes from the color of the water*
CITIES: *Wichita Falls, Denison, Sherman, Texarkana*
IMPOUNDMENTS: *Lake Texoma, Wright Patman Lake (on the Sulphur River), Caddo Lake*
TRIBUTARIES: *Pease, Wichita, Little Wichita, Sulphur, Big Cypress Creek*
RECREATION: *Hunting, fishing, power boating, water-skiing, jet-skiing, canoeing*
LENGTH: *1,360 miles, second longest in Texas; 440 miles of border with Oklahoma, 40 miles with Arkansas*
PUBLIC LANDS: *Buffalo Lake National Wildlife Refuge, Lake McClellan, McClellan Creek National Grasslands, Palo Duro Canyon State Park, Caprock Canyons State Park, Matador National Wildlife Management Area, Copper Breaks State Park, Hagerman National Wildlife Refuge, Caddo National Grasslands, Atlanta State Park, Lake of the Pines (COE), Caddo Lake State Park*
FEATURES: *Chisholm Trail Crossing, Spanish Bluff*

THE RED RIVER, like the other border rivers, Texas shares with other states. The farthest fingers of its headwater streams reach into New Mexico. Several of its major tributaries that begin in the Texas Panhandle flow into Oklahoma before entering the Red from the north. The Red divides part of southwestern Arkansas from Texas and ultimately flows through Louisiana, the only Texas river that lies in the Mississippi Basin. It is a river of the South and of the southern plain.

Capt. Randolph B. Marcy, who explored the Red River in 1852 for the U.S. government, described what he called the two great geographical sections of the river: one extending from the Caprock eastward, "a prairie country almost entirely destitute of trees over a broad bed of light and shifting sands for a distance measured upon its sinuosity of some 500 miles" (136), and the other "a country covered with forest trees of gigantic dimensions, growing upon an alluvial soil of most preeminent fertility, which sustains a very diversified sylva" (136). He remarks further that "the entire face of the country, as if by the wand of a magician, suddenly changes its character" (140).

The point at which the character of the Red River changes so abruptly is, of course, the cross timbers, which Marcy saw as "a natural barrier between civilized man and the savage" (139). He also found the post oak and blackjack country forming a boundary line dividing "the country suitable for agriculture from the great prairies" (138). Ever the observant soldier, Marcy considered the "savages" through whose country they traveled, primarily Comanches and "Kioways," noting: "Vestiges of their camps were everywhere observed along the whole course of the valley" (141).

I found a first edition of his 1854 report to Secretary of War Jefferson Davis, *Adventures on Red River: Report on the Exploration of the Headwaters of the Red River,* in the library at Philmont Boy Scout Camp on upper Cimarron Creek in northeastern New Mexico, a tributary of the Canadian River. Here I did much of the background research for this book, using the personal library of Ernest Thompson Seton, which serves as the core for the Philmont collection; working through these old books was a thrilling experience for me.

The Red River, as Marcy discovered, begins in the Texas Panhandle, one of three major rivers with headwaters on the Llano Estacado or Staked Plain, which deserves a word because it dominates the region. A massive plateau, slightly tilted to the east and canted to the south by ancient geological forces, the Staked Plain lies high and dry in the Texas Panhandle and adjacent eastern New Mexico, an area commonly called Little Texas. Near Dalhart its elevation is four thousand feet above sea level; near Big Spring, twenty-four hundred feet. It constitutes one of Texas' most remarkable, yet subtle features.

Geologists refer to the Gangplank, a wedge of sediments stretching from Wyoming to Texas, as representing ancient sediments from the eastward erosion of the Rockies and their subsequent deposition. The Llano Estacado was cut off from its Rocky Mountain sources by the headward erosion of the Pecos River, which captured the streams flowing eastward from the Rockies and isolated the massive plateau. The water-storing Ogallala Aquifer is composed of stream-deposited sediments covered with wind-blown sand and silt topped with caliche layers, in effect sealed shut so that percolating surface waters have a difficult time penetrating the formation, which contains billions of acre feet of fresh but fossil water (more about that in the Canadian River chapter).

Darwin Spearing points out in his *Roadside Geology of Texas* that "rivers adjust their gradients in response to the volume of sediment load and water supplied to them, in balance with the distance they have to travel" (357). Consequently, many of the streams of the Llano Estacado, responding to heavy rainfall during Pleistocene times, cut massive canyons into the Llano. One of these is Palo Duro Canyon, carved by the Prairie Dog Town Fork of the Red River, which today seems incapable of such massive erosive power.

The several forks of the Red River—Elm, North, Salt, Prairie Dog Town—and its tributary the Wichita all head on the Llano Estacado. After leaving the Caprock country, the forks join to create the Red River, which forms roughly 440 miles of the state's northern boundary with Oklahoma and forty miles of its boundary with Arkansas. After leaving Texas it flows quietly through a corner of Arkansas, then into Louisiana before dumping its reddish silt into the Mississippi River, or occasionally (during flood stage) into the Atchafalaya, a turbid Mississippi distributary in western Louisiana.

The Red River drowned many a man during Texas cattle drives, most of which involved crossing it somewhere along their route. It drowned a few women and children too, when it went on the rampage, flooding throughout its alluvial valley, especially in the days before the dams, but it occasionally floods even today. In its flooding it creates the rich farmlands that characterize the Red River Valley of Oklahoma and Texas.

Whenever water slows, it drops its suspended load of sediments: sand, silt, and organic materials. As the river rises above its banks, it spreads out, losing its force, and slows down; the sediments remain as the floodwaters recede, enriching the riverside landscape. A natural levee develops from the sediments that settle on the floodplain near the river, and what I call "current shadows" form down-current from any obstacle that slows the flow of the current: trees, shrubs, fence posts, farm machinery.

From Buffalos and Indians to Farm Country

The Red marked the southern boundary of Indian country, where numerous tribes were relocated onto reservations. It once served as an isolated no-man's-land for criminals, as bad as—or worse than—the notorious Nueces Strip in South Texas. During the days surrounding the Civil War and during the war itself—when Kansas was "bloody" and Missouri not yet civilized—the Red

18. Prairie Dog Town Fork of the Red River flows past a bluff that an ancestral river created.

19. It is hard to believe that Palo Duro Canyon was carved by the water of the tiny Prairie Dog Town Fork of the Red River.

20. *Red River sands mark the river's bed at low water, as winter-bare riverside trees offer a barrier to winds that may blow it to another area.*

River marked the boundary between law and lawless, and North Texas suffered from marauding Indians as well as from a lawless element among the whites. Forrest Carter's novel *The Outlaw Josey Wales* paints a good picture of the era.

Coronado's expedition across the southern plains in his search for Quivira (Kansas) in 1541–42 without doubt traversed Red River headwater streams. Such sources as Palo Duro and Tierra Blanca creeks, which join to form the Prairie Dog Town Fork of the Red (its main branch), actually head in eastern New Mexico. McClellan Creek, which begins several miles east of Amarillo (north of Interstate 40), augments the flow of the North Fork of the Red, as does Sweetwater Creek east of Mobeetie, one of the most infamous cattle towns of the West. The Salt Fork of the Red, which heads a few miles east of Amarillo (south of I-40), drains an area between the North and Prairie Dog Town forks.

All the Red River headwater forks and tributaries lie in what was buffalo country, the land of the bison that so impressed early Spanish explorers. Because of the bison, this was also Indian country, the domain of some Apache tribes, the Comanche, Kiowa, and Southern Cheyenne. Before the horse expanded their range, the Indians of the southern plains had to work hard to make a living. Once they became equestrians, a new culture evolved, and the

Indians' lives became somewhat easier until Europeans began to settle in what had always been Indian territory. Soon the lands north of the Red became officially designated Indian Territory, a repository for eastern tribes, and later a concentration camp for all Indians whose land had been stolen by Europeans.

Both the North and Salt forks of the Red flow into Oklahoma before they join the main branch of the Red from the north. The Washita River, another Texas Panhandle stream that begins north of Mobeetie and on which Black Kettle's Southern Cheyenne village was wiped out by General Custer the fall of 1868, also joins the Red from the north. Fort Elliott southwest of Mobeetie was named for Maj. Joel H. Elliott—one of Custer's officers whom Custer simply abandoned, along with eighteen of his men—at the Battle of the Washita, in which Custer earned a reputation as an Indian fighter by killing many Cheyenne women and children in a peaceful winter village.

The Prairie Dog Town Fork of the Red officially becomes the Red at the hundredth meridian, which marks the north-south boundary between the Texas Panhandle and Oklahoma. The south bank of the Red serves as the boundary between Texas and Oklahoma from that point eastward.

Wallace Stegner, writing about John Wesley Powell, father of both the U.S. Geologic Survey and the Bureau of Reclamation, titled his biography *Beyond the Hundredth Meridian.* Powell, in his study of the arid regions of the West, determined that beyond (that is, west of) the 100th meridian, the land was too dry to farm, that there was too little rain, that farmers needed help, needed to irrigate if they were to farm successfully.

A geologic note seems appropriate here, for geologic factors create both the color and the taste of Red River water. Deep-red Permian sandstones, through which the river's founding forks and tributaries run, provide the color, evident in Palo Duro Canyon, the same layers of ancient sediments that color the Colorado and Brazos Rivers. Resistant white beds of anhydrite and gypsum, both calcium sulfates, cause the salinity that at lower water levels permeates the river's water. At high flows, the salty water is diluted enough to be less noticeable, but low flows, coupled with high rates of evaporation, increase the salinity.

Specific salinity levels have created unique biomes along the Red River. A proposed Army Corps of Engineers desalination project to "improve" the water for municipal and agricultural uses has been opposed by wildlife agencies in both Oklahoma and Texas, but increasing population continues to generate greater demands for more water in all its usable levels. While the Red River drains a vast area, its watershed lies largely west of the 100th meridian, an arid region that generates limited runoff and little usable water.

21. The broad Red River is bridged many times as it loops along, forming the northern boundary of the Lone Star state.

It may sound complex, but simply put, the Red River drains everything in the Texas Panhandle between the Canadian River watershed and the headwaters of the Brazos. Two other minor Texas river systems, the Pease (North, Middle, and South forks) and the Wichita (North, Middle, and South forks), plus the Little Wichita, drain the area east of the Caprock and south of the main Red; they flow into the Red from the south, east of the hundredth meridian, which corresponds to the isometric rainfall line west of which farming without irrigation is considered marginal. The upper, western Red River drainage is semiarid; the lower drainage farther east is watered well enough by rainfall and occasional snow to support farming—in most years. However, the Red River country lies at the heart of the 1930s Dust Bowl, which—after the summer of 1998—may be returning.

East of the hundredth meridian, farms theoretically function fine without irrigation. Going eastward, populations gradually increase and the distance between communities decreases. The song "Red River Valley," originally written in 1896 about the Mohawk Valley in New York State, seemed to fit this river valley of fertile farmland shared by Texas and Oklahoma. With a few word changes, it soon became a popular song celebrating the river and its surrounding land of opportunity.

The undulating border between the Lone Star and Sooner states represents the vagaries of the Red River's convoluted course: essentially eastward but with large loops, big bends, and numerous oxbows and abandoned meanders. No wonder the states fought so long and hard over the legal boundary, which kept changing with each new flood. The Texas Legislature, always trying to enlarge the state, claimed the North Fork as the boundary; Oklahoma claimed the Prairie Dog Town Fork.

The U.S. Supreme Court in theory settled the dispute in 1896, awarding Gregg County, which lay between the forks, to Oklahoma, and declaring the Main or Prairie Dog Town Fork the boundary. However, when oil was discovered in the riverbed during the second decade of the twentieth century, the dispute began anew. In 1921 the U.S. Supreme Court once again sided with Oklahoma, declaring the south bank of the Red as the official state line.

Lake Texoma, created in the mid-1940s, is the only impoundment on the main branch of the Red River. It substantially widens the apparent boundary between the two states, although the official state line describes a series of artificial midlake arcs and curves through the open water of the eighty-nine-thousand-acre reservoir, tenth largest in the United States. It has more than five million acre feet of storage capacity, a little over half of which is Texas' share. With 580 miles of shoreline, the reservoir boasts forty-two boat ramps, more than two dozen marinas, and numerous campgrounds.

The extreme northeast corner of Texas borders southwestern Arkansas as the Red River swings widely through a series of major loops, river milage being almost three times the crow-route distance. After leaving Texas north of Texarkana, the Red heads almost due south through Arkansas and Louisiana to Shreveport, capturing the runoff from such north Texas stream systems as the Sulphur River and the Big Cypress Creek–Little Cypress Bayou system and Caddo Lake, part of which lies in Louisiana. The Red then takes a southeasterly direction to its confluence with the Mississippi east of Alexandria—though as noted, at flood stages, some of the Red's turbid waters may enter the Atchafalaya Basin.

The Great Raft and Caddo Lake

Although rumors and legends suggest that Caddo Lake may have resulted from the New Madrid earthquake of 1811, geological evidence fails to support such a theory. Early in the nineteenth century, a major logjam many miles long on the Red River in western Louisiana created Caddo Lake on what has

22. The Sulphur River, seen at low water, is a Red River tributary in northeast Texas.

become the Texas-Louisiana state line. Known as the Great Raft, the logjam blocked Big Cypress Creek and formed the lake with a mass of durable cypress and cedar debris that also blocked much of the river. So compact was the Great Raft that "horsemen could ride over it not knowing that they were passing over the water of a river," reported one early observer, and cattle herds crossed it on their way to Texas or leaving Texas for New Orleans markets.

Capt. Henry Miller Shreve led the effort to remove the raft. The city at the head of navigation was named Shreveport for the man who had cleared the Great Raft. During one period in the mid-1830s, Shreve cleared nearly a mile a day, seventy miles in two and a half months. Shreve, a keelboatman and river pilot, designed the shallow-draft steamboat by moving the boiler out of the hold and onto the deck. He then invented the snagboat, a catamaran steamboat with a powerful wench and crane arrangement suspended between the craft's double hulls. Appointed by Congress as superintendent of Western River Improvements, Shreve cleared stretches of the Ohio, Missouri, Mississippi, Arkansas, and Red Rivers by blasting bedrock and boulders, snatching sawyers and sleepers from the river, and leveraging planters and stumps from the muck. When federal funds ran out, he set up at the head of navigation on the Red River at Shreveport, his namesake. Once the Great Raft was cleared to Shreveport, the Red River and the outflow from Caddo Lake (Big Cypress Creek) changed enough to open a channel that allowed steamboats to run all the way up to Jefferson, which soon became the second most important seaport in the state, after Galveston. Steamboat traffic continued on the Red River above Shreveport for decades, even in the face of growing railroad routes in the region. A disastrous fire on the steamboat *Mittie Stephens* on Caddo Lake in 1869 cost more than sixty lives.

When the raft was finally cleared in the 1870s, Caddo Lake drained, leaving a swampy bayou. Modern Caddo Lake resulted from oil industry political pressure in the 1920s to have an artificial barrier erected at the lake's natural outlet by the Army Corps of Engineers to reconstitute the lake and thus make it possible to drill for oil. The oil companies could not manage to drill in the muddy marsh left by the draining of Caddo Lake, but they knew how to drill from floating platforms.

Hans Weichsel, Jr., grand master of the Texas canoeing community, to whom the current edition of *Rivers and Rapids* by Ben M. Nolen and Bob Narramore is dedicated, once told me that Caddo Lake is his favorite paddling trip in the entire state. Massive cypress trees with drooping Spanish moss dominate the thirty-two-thousand-acre lake, which also supports American lotus and picturesque lily pads. It serves as a sanctuary for many forms of wildlife, from alligators and armadillos to white-tailed deer, including seventy-one species of fish and numerous waterfowl species. Fishing is good and both bird-watching and scenery are superb.

Canyon Country

Caddo Lake may lie in the Red River watershed, but it represents a substantial contrast to the Staked Plain sources of the Red. Just as human activities have altered the nature of Caddo Lake, so we have altered the Red River headwaters, which once flowed steady and pure. Early accounts of the rivers that head on the Llano Estacado—the Red, Brazos, and Colorado—suggest permanent water in most of their source streams, not the draws and dry arroyos we know today, and we read too of the lush grasses that originally fattened the bison herds.

Human activity since European invasion has lowered the water table and allowed overgrazing of the range. With the pumping of groundwater from the Ogallala Aquifer beneath the Staked Plain for the past half-century, the water table of the high plains has dropped considerably, and natural springs that once fed the Red River source streams have dried up, providing less water to the river. Native Americans say that by splitting open the breast of Mother Earth, we have allowed the land to blow and wash away; we have even changed the climate and certainly the patterns of land use, to the detriment of the rivers that carved the land, that watered the land and its creatures.

Dr. Larry McKinney, the Texas Parks and Wildlife Department's senior director for water resources, points out the important link between groundwater and surface flow. He found that by 1973, sixty-three of Texas' 281 major springs had failed; that only seventeen of thirty-one large springs remained active; and that of the four largest springs in the state, only two continued to flow. "None of those springs stopped flowing because of natural causes," he warned in a recent two-part article in *Texas Parks and Wildlife* titled "Troubled Waters."

Moving upriver, are Copper Breaks, Caprock Canyons, and Palo Duro Canyon state parks, all in the area Marcy described as "a prairie country almost entirely destitute of trees." Copper Breaks State Park lies on a small (sixty acres) impoundment of the Pease River. Near here in 1860 Texas Ranger Capt. Sul Ross, for whom a West Texas university is named, "rescued" Cynthia Ann Parker from Comanches who had captured her twenty-four years earlier. The breaks exhibit colorful layers of shale, clay, and gypsum, sediments deposited during Permian times (250 million years ago), with distant views of the surrounding flat terrain.

Caprock Canyons State Park east of Silverton marks the breaks of the Staked Plain, its eastern edge where the land drops several hundred feet to the lower plain. The home of the Texas Parks and Wildlife Department bison herd, this park has miles of hiking and biking trails and is linked to other public lands by an equestrian trail. There's even a special equestrian campsite. The park lands are part of the acreage that cattleman Charles Goodnight purchased in 1882 as agent for John G. Adair, to form the nucleus for the J. A. Ranch, one of the largest in the eastern Panhandle. The North Prong and the South Prong of the Little Red River flow through Caprock Canyons.

The oldest and most famous Panhandle park is Palo Duro Canyon State Park southeast of Amarillo, which I first visited in the late 1950s. At 16,402 acres, Palo Duro is one of the state's largest parks. It too marks the descent of the land from the high plains to the lower plains in a series of breaks. When you see the tiny stream at the bottom of the eight-hundred-foot-deep canyon, it seems impossible that the diminutive Prairie Dog Town Fork of the Red River could have carved so impressive a gorge through the colorful layers of ancient rock and unconsolidated sediments. Much of the year, its course is narrow enough to jump across. But when the snow melts or the summer rains come, it flows with amazing ferocity, a rumbling red rage across the green riparian landscape at the bottom of the canyon.

Other Recreational Boating and Parks

The Red River offers many miles of boating possibilities and numerous boat ramps in both Oklahoma and Texas. *Rivers and Rapids* lists three main segments, all of them below Wichita Falls: the forty-seven-mile stretch from U.S. Highway 81 north of Ringgold and west of Nocona to the Bulcher Motorcycle Park at Mountain Creek, northeast of St. Joe (this stretch passes historic Spanish Bluff, which lies on a loop a few miles north of Boston); a sixty-eight-mile stretch from the Bulcher Motorcycle Park past Gainsville to Lake Texoma; and a 32.5-mile run below Lake Texoma through Hendrix, Oklahoma, to a bridge take-out on State Highway 78 north of Bonham, Texas, near Karma, Oklahoma.

There's also an excellent river access point on U.S. 59/71 a few miles north of Texarkana, at a State of Arkansas facility where I stopped one day to study the river. Most of the major segments can be broken into shorter runs by launching or taking out at alternate access points where roads and bridges cross the river. Study local maps and check with local fishing shops, canoe rental outfits, or shuttle drivers, and check *Rivers and Rapids* for relatively up-to-date information, as the book is revised every few years. Local paddling clubs can also provide basic information. Since some of the access points involve private property, expect to pay a modest fee.

Paddling the Red will depend on water level: at low water it may be mostly sandbars, quicksand, and mud; at high water it can be downright dangerous. Major hazards include sunburn and windblast; snakes, poison ivy, and insects; strong wind, low water, and high water. Below Lake Texoma the water is clear; above the lake it is likely to be muddy but generally unpolluted. Above the lake the fish of the day will likely be some form of catfish: flathead, channel, blue—a 148-pound catfish has been reported. Some bass may be present above the lake, but the clear water below the lake offers much better bass possibilities: white, spotted, striped, hybrids, and largemouth.

Few towns lie along the river itself, and those that do remain small. The land near the river seems ideal for such public lands as Caddo National Grasslands near Bonham and Hagerman National Wildlife Refuge west of Denison.

At Caddo, a mix of grasslands and scattered woods with several small lakes provides habitat for a variety of wildlife and wildflowers in nearly eighteen thousand acres of federal land. Wildlife at Hagerman includes thousands of wintering ducks and geese and spring migration of warblers and other songbirds.

The Eisenhower Birthplace State Historical Park and Eisenhower State Park also lie near the Red, as does Bonham State Park. The first, a small historic park near Denton, only six acres, obviously commemorates the location of our former president's birth (October 14, 1890). The 457-acre park that bears his name lies on Lake Texoma in the cross timbers, the geographical feature described by Marcy in 1854. Located on a limestone bluff overlooking the lake, the park lies near the former crossings of the Chisholm and Shawnee cattle trails.

Caddo Lake State Park and Atlanta State Park both lie on Red River tributaries that flow into Louisiana before joining the main river. Texas' most northeasterly park is Atlanta, a 1,475-acre unit on Wright Patman Lake, formed by the impoundment of the Sulphur River. The park's name comes from the nearby town of Atlanta, which was named by settlers from Georgia. Caddo Lake State Park lies on Big Cypress Bayou above the lake. The first time I canoed it, I became confused, didn't know which way to go to find the famous lake, and paddled for an hour downstream before I finally found it, but the view was worth the effort.

Women of the Red River

The story of people living along the Red River adds to its meaning as a giver of life. Sherrie S. McLeRoy's *Red River Women* is well worth reading if you have an interest in the history of the Red River country and the people it has nurtured. The book profiles the lives of eight women who lived in the area between 1815 and 1990. Several had multiple last names, indicating that they either survived husbands and remarried or were divorced in an era when this was rare.

Sophia Suttonfield Auginbaugh Coffee Butt Porter, who moved to Texas in 1935, was caught up in the Runaway Scrape. Perhaps a prostitute at one time, she was granted a divorce by an act of the Texas Legislature. She knew Sam Houston, but some of her stories about him may be less than the whole truth. Lydia Starr Hunter McPherson was a writer for the Sherman *Democrat,* then became the first woman publisher in Oklahoma, later returning to

Texas to write and publish; she was a true woman of the Red River, who lived on its banks for twenty-nine years.

Lucy Petway Holcombe Pickens, a great beauty who lived briefly in Marshall, married a wealthy U.S. senator from South Carolina. When her husband became ambassador to Russia, she became a favorite at the Russian Court of Czar Alexander II. She was active in the Confederate cause during the Civil War, and her face graced the Confederate hundred-dollar bill.

One of the most famous Indian captive stories in the history of the American West, along with the Cynthia Ann Parker story, involved Olive Ann Oatman Fairchild, who was thirteen in 1851 when she and her younger sister Mary Ann were captured by Yavapai Indians in the Mojave Desert. While held captive for six years, she was ritualistically tattooed but not sexually molested. After her rescue she dictated her memoirs, *The Captivity of the Oatman Girls,* to Royal Byron Stratton, who published them in 1857. Olivia traveled throughout the country giving lectures on her experience. She became a Red River woman when she moved to Sherman several years after marrying John Brant Fairchild.

The book also includes accounts of Lucy Ann Thornton Kidd-Key, educator; Ela Hockaday, who founded the Hockaday School; Edna Browning Kahly Gladney, who championed children's rights; and Enid Mae Justin, who founded the Justin Boot Company—all women of the Red River. McLeRoy's book adds a decidedly human touch to the Red River story. It is people who have made it what it is today.

What is it today? Because it flows from a region of low precipitation, it generates relatively little runoff; only one reservoir graces its main stem, a rarity in modern Texas. Because so many of its tributaries flow through Oklahoma and because the Sooner state owns the river and its riverbed, Texas does not have much to say about how its waters are used. Although it collects waters from such Texas rivers as Big Cypress Bayou and the Sulphur, these flow out of the state before they join the Red, their waters again largely out of Texan control.

In the middle section of the Red, a region of much heavier rainfall than the headwaters area, the issue is often too much water rather than not enough. For all the dams on tributary streams and despite the considerable size of Lake Texoma, the Red River still floods. To look at it north of New Boston much of the year is to wonder what all the fuss is about and where the name came from: the river is a wide sandy streambed laced with trickles of clear water, too low for paddling a canoe and many feet below the bridges that cross it.

But when the heavy rainfall comes, the water turns the color of the rusty railroad bridges and rises many feet in a few hours. The sandy streambed disappears beneath a raging torrent that sometimes kisses the bridges. Humankind still does not control nature, especially in an El Niño year; drought still follows flood, and flood follows drought. Much like along the Nile of North Africa, Red River floods enrich the soil of the valley, adding fertile silt and nutrients even as they wash away topsoil and crops.

The thirteen-hundred-mile-long Red River—longest in the nation among those that don't begin in the mountains—has seen the prehistoric peoples who hunted the Llano Estacado before it had its Spanish name. It welcomed the first Spanish explorers with fresh water and wild fruit and bison galore. It witnessed first the decimation, then the demise of the buffalo, the coming of civilization in the form of plow and six-gun and barbed wire, of drilling for water and oil and gas, of irrigated farming and pesticide poisoning.

Floods and drought have visited it; cattle trails and railroads, country roads and interstate highways have crossed it; steamboats and canoes have negotiated its waters. It has been dammed, but it still flows to the Gulf, still drains and waters the fertile valley it created, still separates Texas from Oklahoma and Arkansas. Texas may not legally own the Red River, its bed, or the oil beneath it, but this long border river is firmly ensconced in the Texan heritage.

PART 2

Heartland

The Texas Colorado

LOCATION: *Base of the Panhandle southeast to the Gulf of Mexico*
NAME: *Spanish for the color red, one of several red rivers in Texas*
CITIES: *Big Spring, San Angelo, San Saba, Austin, Bastrop, Smithville, La Grange, Columbus, Wharton, Bay City*
IMPOUNDMENTS: *Lake Buchanan, Inks Lake, Lake Lyndon B. Johnson, Lake Marble Falls, Lake Travis, Lake Austin, Town Lake*
TRIBUTARIES: *Concho, Pecan Bayou, San Saba, Llano, Pedernales*
RECREATION: *Sailing, water-skiing, boating, fishing, windsurfing, jet-skiing*
WATERSHED: *39,900 square miles*
DISCHARGE: *2 million acre feet*
LENGTH: *831 miles*
PUBLIC LANDS: *Big Spring State Park, Lake Colorado City State Park, Colorado Bend State Park, Fort McKavett State Historical Park, Enchanted Rock State Park, South Llano State Park, Walter Buck Wildlife Management Area, Inks Lake State Park, Longhorn Cavern State Park, Lyndon B. Johnson State Historical Park, Lyndon B. Johnson National Historical Park, Pedernales Falls State Park, Bright Leaf State Park, Balcones Canyonlands National Wildlife Refuge, McKinney Falls State Park, Lake Bastrop State Park, Bastrop State Park, Buescher State Park, Monument Hill–Kreischer Brewery State Historical parks.*
FEATURES: *Highland Lakes, Kingsland Archeological Center, State Capitol (Austin), Monument Hill (La Grange)*

THE COLORADO RIVER of Texas—not to be confused with the Colorado River of the West, which carved the Grand Canyon—bisects the state from the base of the Panhandle to the Gulf of Mexico. Only in Texas does the distinction need to be made. When you talk about the Colorado River in Texas, people generally know you mean the river that heads on the high, dry Llano Estacado, the Staked Plain. Outside Texas few people know of the Texas Colorado, and that is their loss, for it epitomizes the Lone Star state from the oil-rich Permian Basin and historic ranchlands of the high plains through the Hill Country and its Highland Lakes to its coastal wetlands on Matagorda Bay.

Its source, its tributaries, and its different personalities make this a river that typifies Texas. The Texas Colorado is often called the largest river wholly within Texas, but like that of the adjacent Brazos, its watershed claims New Mexican arroyos. Headwater springs, snowmelt from the high plains, and rainfall throughout its course provide its water. Far-reaching tributaries augment its flow, widen its watershed, and expand its reputation as an important river. It courses through terrain so varied as to feature nearly every landscape the state offers.

Second in area only to the adjacent Brazos among Texas watersheds, the Colorado River drainage divides the state into two almost equal segments, one lying north and east, the other south and west. The wetter northeast segment includes the Panhandle, North Texas, East Texas, and the southeast. The drier southwest segment includes all of South Texas, southwest Texas, and the Trans-Pecos country. In its own watershed and in the areas it divides, following a pattern typical of Texas, the farther west you go, the drier it becomes until the land is semiarid, even a desert in the far west; and the nearer the coast, the wetter the region, especially during hurricane season, which greatly impacts precipitation along the Gulf.

This pattern of increasing rainfall eastward and coastward and increasing aridity inland and westward has an important effect upon rivers: those that head in the dry western part of the state produce less discharge to the Gulf than those heading in the eastern part of Texas, where rainfall is abundant. By the same logic, as these rivers originating in drier country flow south and east into wetter areas, their character changes with the increased rainfall, until at the Gulf Coast many of them have marshy mouths, due in part to the terrain through which they flow.

Their damp deltas are also influenced by their geology. The coastal plain along the Gulf is composed of massive layers of sediments from the weathering Rockies, sands and silts laid down by millions of years of erosion and deposition. The lower Colorado in the coastal plain flows slowly and peacefully, its lowest reaches responsive to Gulf tides. The headwater region of the Colorado, by contrast, lies at the juncture of the Llano Estacado and the Edwards Plateau, which is composed of thick beds of Cretaceous limestone formed under the ancient sea that once covered much of Texas. The southern Llano Estacado, where the headwater draws of the Colorado begin, lies at lower elevations than the northern end where the Red River heads, but the Colorado qualifies as one of the three rivers spawned by the Staked Plain.

Deep in the Heart of Texas

If, from one perspective, the Colorado defines Texas in dividing it, from another standpoint this river is the pivot of the Lone Star state, historically, geographically, culturally, and economically, much as is the Brazos. The area between the Brazos and the Colorado includes the Austin land grant on which the Old Three Hundred settled in the 1820s, a part of Mexico at the time. The same year that Austin's first colony arrived in Texas (1821), the Santa Fe Trail opened between St. Louis and Santa Fe and Mexico won independence from Spain. The following year, with a teenage Jim Bridger in tow, the first major brigade of fur trappers left St. Louis for the Upper Missouri, to seek their fortunes in lands opened to them by the Louisiana Purchase less than twenty years earlier.

Thus Texas pioneers were settling the rich Colorado River bottomlands as the mountain man era began in the Rocky Mountains—decades before anyone even thought about settlement in that high cold region far to the west and north. While land sold for $1.25 an acre in the eastern United States, Texas land along the Colorado went for a tenth as much—12.5 cents an acre. Only fifteen years after Lewis and Clark returned from the Pacific, pioneers were establishing homes along the Colorado. Only a decade after the end of the War of 1812, Americans were settling Central Texas.

Like so many Texas rivers, the Colorado flows through several physiographic regions. From its headwaters on the Staked Plain, it trickles through the rolling prairies of the north-central plains, gushes with renewing spring water into the Burnet-Llano uplift of the Hill Country, and flows through the blacklands and post oak belt to the coastal plains. Some authorities even consider it to pass through the edge of the cross timbers.

The Colorado flows for more than 650 miles (more than 800 if you consider its New Mexican drainage) from its source to the Gulf, the basin narrowing as it approaches the coast, where adjacent river systems compete for space. Draining nearly forty thousand square miles of the Lone Star state—an area the size of Kentucky—the Colorado generates more than two million acre feet of water, most of it impounded by no fewer than twenty dams in its watershed. In recent decades irrigation has become common in areas along the Colorado that historically practiced dryland farming, part of the reason that crops have changed over the years. Much of the former cotton-growing acreage in the lower Colorado Basin has been converted to grain and other food crops, while cotton has moved north and west to the high plains, where irrigation based on mining Ogallala water threatens the aquifer.

Starting in extreme West Texas—Cochran, Yoakum, Gaines, and Andrews counties—with Seminole Draw and Mustang Draw, the drainage of the Colorado actually reaches into New Mexico, but the low precipitation of that region generates little runoff water except in rare periods of sudden but brief heavy rainfall known as male rain to some Native Americans because it is produced by masculine thunderstorms. Real flow begins with springs northwest of Lamesa in Dawson County and with the big spring at Big Spring, a prehistoric watering hole for bison, pronghorn, paleo-Indians, and later for wild horses and historic Indian tribes.

Three ecological regions meet near Big Spring, where the Colorado barely begins to acquire the status of a river: the high plains, the rolling plains, and the Hill Country. The eye of the spring for which the town and nearby state park are named lies in Comanche Trail Park just southwest of town. This area may not have been the heart of Comanche Country, but it certainly knew the thunder of Comanche warhorses, for the spring was a major watering hole along the Comanche Trail to Mexico.

The Texas Colorado knew numerous Indian tribes: the Comanches at its headwaters, and raiding throughout its length; the Lipan Apaches along its west-reaching tributaries; the Tonkawas along the main river and several tributaries in the Edwards Plateau; and several Karankawan tribes where it courses the coastal plain.

The Comanches were related to the Shoshones of the Northern Rockies (Sacajawea's people, of Lewis and Clark fame), who considered the Comanches a rather backward but distantly related tribe: the universal Plains Indian sign-language symbol for Shoshone was a sinuous hand motion away from the body (snake), while the sign for Comanche was the same, except that the movement was toward the body (backward snake). One of the first groups to acquire the horse, the Comanches soon became the most powerful tribe of the southern plains. Lucia St. Clair Robson's novel *Ride the Wind* artfully re-creates the last decades of the Comanches.

According to J. G. McAllister, who studied these peoples in the 1930s and was later a professor of mine, the Lipan Apaches were related to the Tonkawas of Texas, the Kiowa Apaches of Oklahoma, and the Jicarilla Apaches of New Mexico, and were similar in many ways to the Mescalero Apaches of New Mexico. The Lipans generally got along well with the Texans, fighting alongside them against the Comanches, but after most of these Apaches had died of European diseases, the remnants were lumped with the Tonkawas, later to be expelled from Texas.

Composed of a number of autonomous bands, the Tonkawas, whose name in the Waco language meant "they all stay together," lived in Central Texas in an area through which the Colorado flowed. The numerous Tonkawa subtribes ranged from the Edwards Plateau to the Brazos but definitely lived along the central Colorado. They too enjoyed peaceful relations with the settlers, for the most part, and often scouted for the Texans during counterattacks against the raiding Comanches. To thank them for their help, the Texans created a reservation for them on the upper Brazos; but the reservation was soon dissolved, and the surviving Tonkawas were sent to Indian Territory.

The Colorado does not actually become a significant river until it reaches its confluence with the Concho east of San Angelo in O. H. Ivie Reservoir (Concho County). Less than a decade old at this writing, the nineteen-thousand-acre impoundment is one of the most recent "water development" projects on the high plains, once more exhibiting Texas' penchant for flatwater lakes in preference to free-flowing rivers.

The Concho forks meet at San Angelo, home of Elmer Kelton, one of our best and most prolific western writers, whose novels with Texas settings have won several Western Writers' Silver Spur awards. Kelton has also received the Distinguished Writers Award from the Western Literature Association. I stopped in San Angelo to interview Kelton about rivers in January 1997. He'd answered my letter asking for the interview, saying, "I don't know what I can add to your knowledge about Texas rivers. I grew up a long way from any kind of water except the narrow and salty Pecos River. I never learned to fish or to do any kind of boating."

But he does know rivers; indeed, he treats them in his novels and features their impacts: drowned livestock and cowboys at crossings, alkaline water, ambushes, and water supply. He wrote further, "My perception of the rivers relates primarily to their function in the state's early history and their function today as a source of water for agriculture, industry and the urban population. Unfortunately we are straining that resource severely."

Concho means "shell" in Spanish, and the Concho River is famous for its mussels and their freshwater pearls. The historic cattle trail up the Concho's

Middle Fork leads through Castle Gap to Horsehead Crossing on the Pecos. The Concho flows through the heart of San Angelo, enhancing its character and beauty. Like many Texas communities, San Angelo in recent years has used its river as the core of an urban beautification program. San Antonio, after all, didn't invent the concept nor did it begin using its river as a showpiece until 1939. The very rivers that sometimes flooded communities because they were built in the floodplain have become the center of urban development as dams have helped control flooding.

With the inflow from Pecan Bayou and the San Saba and Llano rivers downstream, the Colorado becomes a major water resource. Each of its primary tributaries is a major river system in its own right. The San Saba has a long and fascinating history. J. Frank Dobie details the story of the Lost San Saba Mine in *Coronado's Children,* but an equally interesting story concerns the San Saba Mission and its tragic history.

In 1749 a delegation of Lipan Apaches asked for a mission. When the Spanish accommodated them, by establishing both a mission and a presidio on the San Saba in 1757, the Comanches objected. On March 16, 1758, a force estimated at two thousand Comanches and Wichitas attacked and essentially destroyed the mission and presidio. A year later a Spanish army of six hundred followed the Comanches to the Red River, where on October 7, 1759, the Indians routed the Spanish. Although only nineteen Spaniards were killed and fourteen wounded, the Europeans were soundly defeated and demoralized, an excellent example of why the Spanish failed to colonize Texas.

Several miles below the confluence of the San Saba with the Colorado lies Colorado Bend State Park, near the head of Lake Buchanan, when the reservoir is full. Gorman Falls and Gorman Cave are part of the five-thousand-acre park, off the beaten track but well used by fishermen, especially on weekends. The Saturday night I camped there, I was kept awake half the night by power-boat traffic and groups of partying fishermen. Canoeists can run a thirty-mile stretch of the Colorado from U.S. Highway 190 between San Saba and Lomita or a fifteen-mile stretch from Flat Rock just west of Bend to the park, but neither run is recommended during deer season because of heavy hunting in the vicinity.

The North and South Llano join near Junction to create the Llano, a favorite of mine. After paddling a stretch of the South Llano one winter, I camped at South Llano State Park in the midst of the greatest concentration of wild turkeys and white-tailed deer I'd ever seen. From a launch site below the dam in Junction City Park, the main Llano offers a twenty-mile canoe

23. Three old friends are commemorated in a statue at Barton Springs near the Colorado River: Naturalist Roy Bedichek, writer J. Frank Dobie, and historian Walter Prescott Webb.

run to a private take-out on the river immediately below State Highway 385 at Yates Crossing, south of London. The river courses through solid limestone, with shoals at low water levels and plenty of rock outcrops showing.

On another research trip I visited the town of Llano, not far from the Llano's confluence with the Colorado at the head of Lake LBJ. Llano, which experienced a major flood in the late 1990s, has a wonderful historical museum where I spent a morning exploring the area's past and photographing its present. I met the present in the form of an engineer surveying the river for a new bridge planned to replace the present structure, which was damaged by the recent flood. I also photographed an old log cabin that rests in retirement on the bank of Llano behind the admission-free museum.

The Upper Colorado and the Pedernales

The next tributary to augment the Colorado's flow, the Pedernales, became famous worldwide during the presidency of Lyndon B. Johnson. LBJ and Lady Bird hosted numerous Texas-style barbecues on its banks during his

24. A low dam on the Llano River above the condemned bridge in Llano gives the river momentary peace.

political career. Pedernales Falls State Park features a series of sliding falls that drop a total of more than fifty vertical feet in two hundred yards over 300-million-year-old Marble Falls limestone. Lyndon B. Johnson State Historical Park and Lyndon B. Johnson National Historical Park both lie along the Pedernales, which flows into the Colorado at the head of Lake Travis.

Pedernales Falls State Park near Johnson City features both the rare green kingfisher and the belted kingfisher as well as the endangered golden-cheeked warbler and wild turkeys. The falls form an impressive natural feature at any water level, and the cypress-lined river belies the harsh surrounding landscape. A few miles west of Johnson City lies Lyndon B. Johnson State Historical Park, the best place in Texas to be sure of seeing bison, but the herd is small and confined. Red fox also frequent the area, along with armadillo and the ubiquitous white-tailed deer. The state park lies across the river from the national park. The Sauer-Beckmann Living History Farm on the state park site functions as a 1915 farm. The national park includes the LBJ ranch and house, the turn-of-the-century schoolhouse where Johnson attended school, the family cemetery as well as a reconstruction of Johnson's birthplace.

Tributaries entering the Colorado from the west—the Concho, San Saba, Llano, and Pedernales—originate in the Edwards Plateau, where, despite the relative arid climate, limestone-bottomed streams generate more runoff than do areas with soil deep enough to hold rain water and rare snowmelt. Streams that enter from the east bank head in a slightly more humid area of deeper soil and greater water-holding capacity and therefore, even though they may receive more precipitation, generate less runoff to augment the main river's flow. Pecan Bayou, which drains an area southeast of Abilene and enters the Colorado a few miles west of Goldthwaite, is the only significant tributary flowing into the Colorado from the east side.

The adjacent Brazos River drains lands close to the Colorado through such streams as the Lampasas and San Gabriel tributaries of Little River. For the most part, the Colorado River flows near the eastern edge of its watershed, its western tributaries reaching far westward to drain a much drier region. The

25. A pioneer cabin at Llano Historical Museum graces the bank of the Llano River.

26. A low-water bridge across the Pedernales River near LBJ's ranch was built to withstand floods.

watershed of the Colorado seems strangely lopsided because the tributaries entering from the west have such extended drainage basins and the few entering from the east, with the single exception of Pecan Bayou, have such modest ones.

The upper reaches of the main watershed course the Caprock country, a high (for Texas), dry land where range cattle and Permian Basin oil and gas have dominated the economy for decades, as they did when I moved to Andrews in the 1950s to serve as the first director of a new youth center and to head the county's summer recreation program. In recent years, with irrigation, the area has begun to produce cotton, pecans, and sorghum, but already the draw-down of the Ogallala Aquifer is reducing the economic feasibility of such agricultural ventures. During winter months sandhill cranes and ducks populate the ponds and lakes of the high plains drained by the upper Colorado.

Beginning in this rather drab, monochromatic country, where cresote bush and mesquite prevail and quail, jackrabbits, coyotes, and raptors constitute the most obvious native fauna, the Colorado is not as red as its name implies. In fact, many people, as far back as Santa Fe trader Josiah Gregg in 1841, believed that the Brazos and Colorado swapped names through the vagrant waves of history; even the Canadian River, when it flows, runs redder than the Colorado.

Big Spring State Park (near Big Spring) and Lake Colorado City State Park (near Colorado City) offer two of the best places in the upper Colorado River watershed to watch wildlife: gray fox, coyotes, striped skunks, ringtails and raccoons, occasional white-tailed deer, both cottontails and jackrabbits, and many small rodents, including prairie dogs. Songbirds including such spectacular species as painted buntings and blue grosbeaks nest here or stop by during migration. You might also see great horned and burrowing owls, scaled quail, roadrunners, towhees, and numerous species of waterfowl and shorebirds.

Highland Lakes and Nearby Parks

The Colorado River drainage contains the state's most highly developed series of impoundments, which provide hydroelectric power and water for much of the state. Although not the first river development agency established in Texas, the Lower Colorado River Authority (LCRA) nonetheless helped pioneer hydro power and brought it to its highest achievement. Texas has numerous impoundments but none so well coordinated as the six mainstem dams on the Colorado: Buchanan Dam and Lake, Inks Dam and Lake, Wirtz Dam and LBJ Lake, Starcke Dam and Lake Marble Falls, Mansfield Dam and Lake Travis, and Tom Miller Dam and Lake Austin.

My experience with the Highland Lakes began during my Schulenburg boyhood when one of our neighbors, Oscar Brown, the father of my friend Tommy Brown, took Tommy and me on a fishing trip to Lake Buchanan. We caught a few fish, but I was more impressed with the black squirrels running all over the bedrock banks. I was just a kid, perhaps eight or ten. During my college days at the University of Texas, I learned to water-ski on Lake Austin and occasionally went to parties at friends' cabins on Lake Travis. The day after I returned to Austin following my discharge from the army, I got the worst sunburn of my life by spending the entire day in a swimsuit paddling a rented canoe on Lake Austin.

Between Big Spring and Austin, half a dozen state parks and wildlife preserves offer major recreational opportunities for wildlife watching: Colorado Bend State Park (near Bend), Hamilton Pool and Westcave Preserve (near Bee Cave), South Llano State Park and Walter Buck Wildlife Management Area (near Junction), Pedernales Falls State Park (near Johnson City), and Lyndon B. Johnson State Historical Park (near Stonewall).

South Llano State Park and Walter Buck Wildlife Management Area lie northwest of Kerrville, far west of the Colorado itself but well within its watershed. The North and South forks of the Llano meet near Junction and feed the mainstream Colorado. Colorful wood ducks and painted buntings and the endangered black-capped vireos are found here. The area contains one of the state's largest historic turkey roosts, used for centuries where hundreds of wild turkeys roost every night in an area of a few acres. When I camped at South Llano State Park one winter evening after paddling a short segment of the river, dozens of wild turkeys trooped right through my campsite as I fixed dinner. From the same campsite I counted more than two hundred white-tailed deer at dusk. Mammals of the area also include fox, bobcat, beaver, raccoon, ringtail, armadillo, and other small creatures.

You may find both the endangered golden-cheeked warbler and the black-capped vireo at Colorado Bend State Park, thirty miles west of Lampasas, along with other songbirds, hawks, and bald eagles. When I camped there one Saturday night, the relatively isolated park teemed with life, largely fishermen and their families, many of them using power boats on the river well into the night and again early the next morning to access Lake Buchanan. During midweek, however, the river offers excellent canoeing opportunities and less crowded camping.

A personal favorite of mine, Hamilton Pool, now part of a Travis County preserve, was once a privately owned swimming hole. When I took a weekend visit to the pool with the aforementioned Tommy Brown and his girlfriend Gerrie, now his wife, they were amazed that so lovely a place existed within a hundred miles of home. I'm pleased that it has been preserved, along with nearby Westcave (LCRA). Both parks embrace the Pedernales River west of Austin. Texas has finally begun to protect some of its unique features at public expense, rather than seeing them exploited as commercial enterprises or remaining purely private playgrounds.

The Colorado River watershed includes Austin, the state capital and only major city in the entire watershed. When I was a boy growing up in south central Texas, bats were generally considered pests. There were old wives' tales of bats getting tangled in women's hair, of their biting toes sticking out of cowboys' blankets, of their carrying rabies. As bat behavior became better known, people's attitudes began to change. When the South Congress Bridge over the Colorado River in Austin was reconstructed in 1980, bats began to move into narrow vertical crevices beneath the bridge. Today the colony that lives there is estimated at a million and a half. Their evening forays to feed on insects (they consume up to fifteen tons each summer night) attract hundreds of bat watchers thrilled at the sight of the smokelike spirals emerging from their summer homes beneath the nearly thousand-foot-long bridge across the Colorado.

Most of the Colorado River Basin remains rural, depending upon farming and ranching as it did a century ago. Crops have changed, and livestock species vary as exotic species have come to be raised in many parts of the state, but the landscape, for the most part, remains bucolic. Farming methods have become much more energy-intensive and farms have become bigger, but agriculture remains dominant. The *Texas Almanac* now lists "agribusiness" under economy, rather than farming and ranching, a reflection of the nature of modern agriculture.

To be sure, the Texas Colorado has had its Hispanic influences, but since so few people lived in the drier upper portions of the basin in the early days, so many of the early settlers in the wetter areas downstream came from the southern United States, and so many later settlers came from central Europe, Hispanic influence in the watershed remained minimal until recent years. This is, after all, the area settled by many of the Old Three Hundred.

With relatively few Hispanic place names downstream from the mouth of the Concho (San Saba, Llano, El Campo) and so many northern European names—Johnson City, Austin, Webberville, Smithville, La Grange, Wharton, Bay City—Hispanic influence in the Colorado River Basin has been moderate, compared to much of the rest of the state, though the Colorado does enter the Gulf of Mexico by way of Matagorda Bay. The Lower watershed abound in Czech, German, even Polish architecture such as the famous painted churches, and agricultural practices for generations reflected European roots.

Paddling and Birding Lower on the Colorado

I grew up near the Colorado, played high school football against teams from Bastrop, Smithville, La Grange, and Columbus, all on the Colorado, and Eagle Lake not far away from the river. Later, attending the University of Texas, I'd cross the Colorado six times on my way to Austin, but in those days we never considered canoeing the river, and crew racing was an Eastern sport.

Not until the winter of 1995–96 did I canoe the Colorado, participating in the Alamo City Rivermen's annual Freeze Trip held in mid-January. We paddled (I poled) a sixteen-mile segment near Bastrop, camping overnight on an island and enjoying a Dutch-oven cookout. True to form, it froze that night, but with tents and good cold-weather sleeping bags, we fared well.

The Colorado almost always has enough water for canoeing, and the weather, even in midwinter, rarely interferes. In 1999 when I again participated in the Freeze Trip, temperatures never got below 47°.

In the spring of 1998 I canoed a slower stretch of the Colorado, where the river makes a huge loop near Columbus. Using a bicycle shuttle of only a mile, I paddled the seven-mile loop through pecan bottomland used mostly for livestock grazing. Only twenty miles from my hometown, this stretch of river offered me a new three-hour experience, placid paddling on a sluggish river on a bright sunny day decorated with wildflowers and bird songs, especially the cardinal's cheery notes.

Suggesting the presence and importance of the natural world during Texas' naming days, numerous place names along the Colorado refer to natural features or phenomena: Big Spring, Water Valley, Granite Shoals, Marble Falls, Dripping Springs, Bee Cave, Mustang Ridge, Red Rock, Round Top, Rock Island, Eagle Lake. Early settlers lived closer to the natural world than we do, though they may not have appreciated it as we have come to do in recent decades, now that we have lost so much of it through development and progress. The pioneers were wresting a living from the land. They cut trees to clear land and build homes, hunted and fished for food, trapped for furs to wear and to sell. The Colorado country had much to offer.

And it still does. Just downstream from our island campsite but above the river, Bastrop State Park protects thirty-five hundred acres of the "lost pines of Texas," a swath of loblolly pine isolated from the northeast Texas pineywoods area by almost two hundred miles. Nearby Buescher State Park also lies in this isoloted swath of piney woods. Lake Bastrop, created when LCRA dammed Spicer Creek, became one of Texas' newest state parks in the late '90s, a third lost pines park. A few miles to the southeast (ten miles northeast of La Grange on the Colorado) lies Rice-Osborne Bird and Nature Trail, in twenty-acre Oak Thicket Park, which is jointly operated by LCRA and the La Grange Chamber of Commerce. Here you may find the spectacular scissor-tailed flycatcher, painted bunting, hermit thrush, tricolored heron, and red-winged blackbird.

Closer to the coast two more wildlife areas offer rare opportunities to see unusual birds: Attwater's Prairie Chicken National Wildlife Refuge and Eagle Lake, one more LCRA establishment, both near Eagle Lake. Here you may find the endangered Attwater's race of greater prairie-chicken, white-tailed hawks, crested caracaras, roseate spoonbills, and in winter, thousands of ducks and geese, perhaps even bald eagles and white pelicans.

27. Despite having three rods, this fisherman did not seem to be having much luck at Eagle Lake.

People throughout the South know fire ants, which reached Texas a generation ago. My brother Paul in Schulenburg tells me that chiggers and redbugs, tiny insects that once made summers miserable with their itchy bites, have essentially disappeared. The fire ants have wiped them out. Quail no longer nest successfully because the fire ants kill and devour the nestlings as they do all ground-nesting birds, including the Attwater's prairie-chicken, one reason the endangered species has not made a successful recovery. At Eagle Lake, where I enjoyed seeing thousands of wintering birds as well as nutria and water moccasin, the fire-ant mounds made the strongest impression on me. I was careful not to disturb any of them.

On the coast itself, lying athwart the mouth of the Colorado is the protective Matagorda Peninsula, where you might find whooping cranes and eighteen other threatened and endangered species, including white-faced ibis, reddish egret, peregrine falcons, piping plovers, brown pelicans, white-tailed hawks, and wood storks; four species of sea turtles; and thirty-seven species of shorebirds.

The sounds of these shorebirds on the Gulf Coast are a far cry from that of wintering sandhill cranes on the Staked Plain hundreds of miles upstream.

These two landscapes, so far apart and so very different, are linked together by the Colorado River in its gradual change from high plains arroyo to coastal plain sedge flats, just as the river has seen the slow change of Texas from the long centuries of prehistory through the buffalo days of the Comanche to the twenty-first century.

The Colorado River provides water for irrigating croplands and watering livestock, for producing hydroelectric power and diluting pollution, for municipal consumption and industrial processes, for fish and wildlife habitat and a wide variety of recreational activities. It is the living heart of Texas, beating with ancient rhythms and modern reservoir releases. It offers hundreds of miles of canoe paddling and fishing possibilities and more than a dozen reservoirs for power boaters, sailors, windsurfers, jet-skiers, water-skiers, and flatwater anglers.

It's not so different from other Texas rivers. It's longer than most and more controlled by humankind, the most frequently dammed major river in the Lone Star state. Perhaps its many impoundments result in less frequent and less severe flooding, but it still floods as it did in October, 1998, especially in the coastal plain. It did serious damage to low-lying areas in Wharton.

Because I grew up near it and have traveled extensively in its watershed, and especially because I've canoed its waters, this river that flows through the heart of Texas has a special place in my heart.

Brazos de Díos

LOCATION: *West-central Panhandle southeast to Gulf of Mexico*
NAME: *In Spanish, Brazos de Díos, the "arms of God"*
CITIES: *Lubbock, Abilene, Waco, Temple, Bryan–College Station*
IMPOUNDMENTS: *Possum Kingdom Lake, Lake Granbury, Lake Whitney*
TRIBUTARIES: *Salt and Clear forks, Palo Pinto Creek, Paluxy River, Bosque River, Cowhouse Creek, Leon River, Little River, San Gabriel River, Yegua Creek, Navasota River*
RECREATION: *Swimming, boating, fishing, water-skiing, jet-skiing, canoeing*
WATERSHED: *42,800 square miles*
DISCHARGE: *5.2 million acre feet*
LENGTH: *942 miles*
PUBLIC LANDS: *Muleshoe National Wildlife Refuge, Fort Griffin State Park, Abilene State Park, Action State Historic Park, Possum Kingdom State Park, Lake Mineral Wells State Park, Dinosaur Valley State Park, Lake Whitney State Park, Meridian State Park, Mother Neff State Park, Fort Hood Military Reservation, Belton Lake (COE), Fort Parker State Park, Lake Somerville State Park, Washington-on-the-Brazos, Stephen F. Austin State Park, Brazos Bend State Park, Brazoria National Wildlife Refuge*
FEATURES: *Blanco Canyon (Coronado's Cona, staging area in his search for Quivira), Fossil Rim Wildlife Center, setting of John Graves's* Goodbye to a River

THERE'S A SONG, "The Rivers of Texas," also known as "The Brazos River," that catalogues fourteen rivers in the Lone Star state but mentions the Brazos River six times. It first appeared in Vance Randolph's *Ozark Folksongs.* According to Mason Williams, who has collected more than eight hundred river songs, Randolph got the song from a woman in Fayetteville,

Arkansas, who had learned it from a hired hand from Texas in 1921. Williams includes the song in his 1984 tape and record, *Of Time and Rivers Flowing*, Skookum Records, 1984.

We crossed the broad Pecos and we crossed the Nueces,
Swam the Guadalupe and followed the Brazos;
Red River runs rusty, the Wichita clear.
Down by the Brazos I courted my dear.

She hugged me and kissed me, and she called me her dandy;
The Trinity is muddy, and the Brazos quick-sandy.
I hugged her and kissed her and called her my own,
But down by the Brazos she left me alone.

The sweet Angelina runs glossy and glidey;
The crooked Colorado flows weaving and winding.
The slow San Antonio courses the plain.
I never will walk by the Brazos again.

The girls of Little River: they're plump and they're pretty.
The Sulphur and Sabine have many a beauty.
Down by the Neches there's girls by the score;
But I never will walk by the Brazos no more.

Its chorus ends with the line: "There's many a river that water the land."

The longest river in Texas between the Red and the Rio Grande, the Brazos ranks third in size among Lone Star state rivers and, with its New Mexican arroyo headwaters, rates as having the largest watershed of any heartland river. In many ways it epitomizes the Lone Star State, for its history, culture, geography, and economy represent Texas as completely as any major stream in the state. From the many forks of its forming headwaters on the Llano Estacado west of Amarillo and Lubbock to its tidal marshland mouth south of Houston, the Brazos says Texas in every way.

The Brazos brackets Texas history from Cabeza de Vaca to the Space Age. A survivor of the ill-fated Narvaez expedition, Cabeza de Vaca was among the first Europeans to set foot on what would become Texas. He is thought to have made landfall near the mouth of the Brazos, perhaps on Galveston Island. Whether or not he actually crossed the Brazos near its mouth, he certainly saw it during his wanderings between 1528 and 1536. On the coastal plains it is a substantial river with a wide mouth. He must have crossed it on the high plains. We know he had a bison robe, which he might have acquired by trade. Several early Spanish and French explorers found the lower Brazos a significant hazard to cross, even though it missed appearing on several early maps.

Spanish coastal explorers named it the Brazos de Díos (arms of God) for some reason lost in antiquity (there are several theories), but they failed to explore inland. Noted French mapmaker Guillaume Delisle included the Brazos on a map published in 1703, but subsequent Spanish cartographers continued to ignore its existence for almost a century. Father José María Puelles, a Franciscan friar at Nacogdoches, an early Spanish settlement in East Texas, accurately located the Brazos and indicated its course and relative size on his 1807 map, though that map lacked coastal veracity. The overland explorers and the sailors seem not to have communicated very well.

The Brazos has many faces in Texas. Like its flanking river systems, the Red and the Colorado, the Brazos heads on the Llano Estacado, the famous Staked Plain, homeland of the Comanche and route of numerous expeditions to explore this high, dry corner of the Southwest. Coronado's expedition doubtless crossed the Brazos headwaters in 1541 in the search for Quivira and the seven cities of Cibola. Several Spanish and a handful of French expeditions explored areas north of the Brazos headwaters during the next 250 years, but few found the Brazos until José Mares (1787) crossed it on his way from Santa Fe to the Texas Hill Country and San Antonio. On his way back to Santa Fe, he wintered on the Double Mountain Fork of the Brazos. Pierre Vial, "a mysterious Frenchman" who became a peace emissary to the Comanches (1785) and a Panhandle trailblazer (1786–87), also came to know the Brazos headwaters, traveling along the Salt Fork, then finding fresh water where the White River emerges from Blanco Canyon, Coronado's Cona, a series of Native American "rancherios," which served the Spanish commander as a staging area for his further explorations.

One of the most thoroughly researched books ever written about these early explorations and a rewarding account for any serious historian is *El Llano Estacado* by John Miller Morris, covering the years between 1536 (Cabeza de Vaca) and 1860 (the eve of the Civil War). He calls Cona "the most important geographical place-name in Texas connected to the expedition." (66) It is required reading for anyone who would know and understand the Staked Plain. In his introduction, Morris refers to the book as "a meditation on the role of human imagination in the discovery—or creation—of environmental meaning" (4). He offers excellent background for understanding the Red, Brazos, and Colorado rivers as well as the Canadian and Pecos, the five Texas rivers associated with the Staked Plain.

Earlier history of the lower Brazos has a French connection. La Salle probably saw its coastal reaches in 1687 after settling French families near Lavaca Bay. This colony did not last much longer than La Salle himself. Few Spaniards settled in what became Texas except as a reaction to foreign interests, largely French, and then only with massive external incentive. Not many people wanted to live in the vast Indian country north of the Rio Grande, especially after the Comanches acquired the horse.

Forks of the Brazos run all the way into New Mexico: Running Water Draw becomes the White River flowing through Blanco Canyon, the most likely location of Coronado's base of operations at what he called Cona. It then becomes the Salt Fork; Blackwater Draw and Yellow House Draw join to form the North Fork of the Double Mountain Fork, which joins Double Mountain Fork southeast of Lubbock; finally the Clear Fork, which begins near Rotan and flows eastward north of Abilene, turns north, then east again to join the other forks near Graham a few miles northwest of Possum Kingdom Lake. The various forks of the Brazos drain much of the southern Panhandle and West Texas north of Interstate 20 and west of Fort Worth, a vast dry region with few towns and plenty of cattle range, oil, and gas. This was traditional Comanche country.

Mary Austin Holley, author of *Texas,* wrote of several rivers she hadn't seen. The Brazos, at least near its mouth, she knew from personal experience, having descended it below Brazoria to Quintana. She describes it as "the largest in the province [taking] its rise near the source of the Red river." She also mentions its Salt Fork (Salt Branch, she calls it) as so salty that it "renders the whole river, for a while, brackish; and its waters deposit a fine red clay, as slippery as soap and as sticky as putty" (31). The color of the Brazos, she says, "varies from a deep red to almost chocolate."

Holley devotes more space to the Brazos than to any other river, the greater part of three pages. Listing its length as 750 miles, she comes closer in her estimate than she does for several other rivers, based on modern calculations. Writing in the 1830s, she describes the Brazos as she finds it in full flood, a condition she learns "is to be recorded as an exception and not as a rule" (32). She mentions a narrow bank of sand at the mouth of the Brazos, where "vessels are towed over the bar," that "the harbor within is perfectly safe," and that "three steamboats are in operation on the Brazos" (32–33). She also notes the Gulf's "blue mud" and "blue clay" bottom at the Brazos mouth. Where does this color originate?

The headwaters forks flow through a high, monochromatic landscape parched by hot wind and searing sun in summer, by sudden northers and blasting blizzards in winter. In her novel *Ride the Wind,* the story of Cynthia Ann Parker and the last days of the Comanches, Lucia St. Clair Robson writes of "a world where colors hadn't been invented yet," an excellent description of the region the Comanches called home. According to Robson, they called the Brazos Tohopt Pah-e-hona (28), "blue water river," and they used it as a major travel route. In its upper reaches it flows with red sand and silt from ancient sediments beneath the Llano Estacado, materials originating in the ancient Rockies. The blue mud and clay at its mouth result from the Gulf's water level rising over many millennia, drowning the mouths of all Texas coastal rivers. The blue muck Holley observed is characteristic of several rivers in the vicinity.

Downriver the Brazos broadens as several major tributaries augment its flow: the Paluxy River at Glen Rose, the Bosque River at Waco, the Little River (composed of the Leon, Lampasas, and San Gabriel rivers, Cowhouse Creek, and Brushy Creek) west of Hearne, Yegua Creek between College

28. Brazos River sandbanks suggest the falling water level and deep mud of a large river.

Station and Brenham, and the Navasota west of Navasota near Washington-on-the-Brazos, the very heart of Texas.

Cradle of the Texas Republic

At this point the Brazos is big, a wide river that once accommodated steamboat traffic. The Brazos served as a major site for the earliest Anglo-American settlement, the center of Stephen F. Austin's colony in the 1820s, with several early Texas villages located on the river. Andrew Robinson built a ferry for crossing the Brazos at the place where Washington-on-the-Brazos soon came into existence. San Felipe de Austin was established in 1823 and Columbia farther downstream, founded by Josiah Bell, in 1824.

A cotton economy evolved, with slaves accounting for half the population of the region. Immigrants from the United States, mostly from the South, had brought their slaves along when they began to settle the Brazos River bottomlands, which they soon turned into a replica of the Old South. These early Anglo settlers located their first capital, Washington-on-the-Brazos, on this important river transportation route, which also created an obstacle to overland transport.

Texas subsequently declared its independence from Mexico at Washington-on-the-Brazos, and the Runaway Scrape, the exodus of Texan civilians during the brief War of Independence, found the Brazos a major obstacle to escaping the attacking Mexican army, which threatened to kill all Anglos and had made a good start at the Alamo and Goliad. General Sam Houston and the remnants of the Texas army crossed the Brazos by steamboat while the flooding river delayed the Mexican army. After the Battle of San Jacinto, the treaty that ended the War for Texas Independence was signed at Velasco near the Brazos' mouth.

Raiding Comanches used the Brazos Valley as a travel route from their high plains home range to the early Texas settlements; the well-documented attack on the Parker compound in 1836 occurred near the Navasota River, a tributary of the Brazos, and the raiders almost certainly followed the Brazos to their headwaters homeland. Robson's *Ride the Wind* provides a vivid though fictionalized account of that raid and Cynthia Ann Parker's subsequent life with the Comanches.

Culturally, the Brazos reflects Spanish place names from such important sites as El Llano Estacado and Blanco Canyon northeast of Lubbock, which

29. An early ferry crossed the Brazos River at Washington-on-the Brazos (below the state park).

most likely served as Coronado's base camp for his 1541 quest for Quivira, to Velasco on the Gulf Coast. Today a largely Hispanic population along the Brazos headwaters in the southern plains works the land and operates the irrigation systems. As noted, the lower Brazos was settled in the 1830s and 1840s by farmers from the southern United States. In the 1840s and 1850s German immigrants, many of whom died because they were unprepared for the rigors of pioneering, began to arrive on the Gulf Coast. Later, in the 1870s and 1880s, more European immigrants arrived. Today the Brazos River valley reflects this cultural mix, also including many African Americans descended from those brought into Texas as slaves before the Civil War.

Although modern times have brought irrigated agriculture to the upper Brazos, much of its headwater landscape, as mentioned, remains cattle country, but also seeing extraction of oil and gas. This is the home of Dean Smith, not the basketball coach but the track star who did all of Texas proud in the 1952 Summer Olympic Games, where he won a gold medal in the sprint relay. After starring in track and football at the University of Texas, Dean went to Hollywood and became a stuntman, then worked his way into a few movies as an actor. He played Kit Carson in one Disney film. Dean grew up on a ranch along the Clear Fork, which he calls "my river," southwest of Graham near the tiny community of Eliasville. I visited him there the spring of 1998, got a tour of part of the ranch he inherited, and saw his Longhorn cattle, the Texas "grasshoppers" pumping oil, and the ancient dam across the Clear Fork, behind which he learned to swim.

Dean, whom I hadn't seen in forty years, is a modest man, still trim and well-conditioned, relaxed now that he has left Hollywood, though he retains numerous contacts and occasionally gets involved in a western, his specialty. "I'm not one of those environmentalists," he told me, an unnecessary apology for his next statement, "but I make these oil people toe the mark." He didn't want his ranch—or his river—despoiled by careless spills and toxic substances. I suggested to him that that's really all that most environmentalists want for public lands: an end to the careless use and thoughtless abuse of the public domain that an out-of-sight, out-of-mind philosophy creates for the rivers that flow through the land, spreading any pollution downstream.

My brief visit with Dean gave me new insights into the conservative West Texas mentality and a refreshing view of the Clear Fork, where cattle grazed on both side of the river as it meandered slowly through low rolling hills covered with sparse woods and lush early April grass. I'd intended to push the idea of raising Longhorns, but Dean was way ahead of me: he already has

30. Dean Smith sits on the banks of the Clear Fork of the Brazos River, which flows through his ranch. Dean, a Hollywood stuntman, won fame as a track star and football player at the University of Texas in the early 1950s and won an Olympic Gold Medal in 1952.

them on his ranch, as much for practical worth as in a bow to his having been a Longhorn himself at the University of Texas.

John Graves's River

Downstream the forming branches of the Brazos—Clear Fork, Salt Fork, Double Mountain Fork—finally unite to flow as one in Young County just above Possum Kingdom Lake. Here the Brazos takes on a brighter face. Below the dam in Palo Pinto County, it flows through a better-watered land, the stretch that John Graves wrote about in *Goodbye to a River.* In this area not far from Fort Worth, the Brazos is infinitely canoeable between reservoirs as it flows through rich farmland, pecan bottoms, and the history revealed so well by Graves.

Probably the most significant book about any Texas river, *Goodbye to a River* pivots upon a canoe trip down a portion of the Brazos to tell a story rich in Texas history, sound in literary merit, and full of folklore and homespun philosophy. Never out of print since it first appeared in 1959, the book serves as a protest against our building of dams with little consideration of the cumulative consequences. It is a paean to the natural river and the history this evokes. Generally considered one of Texas' most significant writers, Graves still lives not far from his beloved Brazos near Glen Rose, southwest of Fort Worth.

During my field research for this book, I visited him briefly, almost by accident. After spending a few hours at the Amon Carter Museum in Fort Worth, I had been driving downstream along the Brazos, crossing it by every bridge, occasionally testing its waters briefly by canoe (since I often pole my canoe, I don't need a shuttle), as I worked my way toward the coast. I wanted to see the Brazos from every approach, every crossing, every possible access. Near Brazos Point I noticed a sign that read "Glen Rose." Without being fully aware of where I was, I suddenly found myself in John Graves's country, only a few miles from Glen Rose. I turned west, located a pay phone at the next gas station, found his listing, and called him.

I'd used the opening chapter of *Goodbye to a River* in an anthology of river literature I'd edited some years before, *River Reflections.* In obtaining permission to use the excerpt, I'd corresponded with Graves. I thought he might remember me, and he did. He invited me out to his "hardscrabble farm" not far from Dinosaur Valley State Park on the Paluxy River, a Brazos tributary. He showed me around his place, where I spent an hour or two with the man whom I consider one of Texas' greatest men of letters.

During the time we spent together in his work room, lined with well-filled bookshelves, his desks and tables stacked high with books, we talked about literature, writers, and Texas rivers. He shook his head about the continuing degradation of the natural environment, but he found hope in the writings of Wallace Stegner, still alive at the time, and in such young writers as Rick Bass and Terry Tempest Williams. The time passed rapidly. I hated to leave, but it was getting on toward dusk. He had chores to do, and I had to get downriver.

I recently heard a story about Graves from conservation writer Charles Little, author of *Discovery America: The Smithsonian Book of the National Parks* and *The Dying of the Trees.* Little had been at a literary conference in which Graves participated. Asked, "Do you like to write?" Graves thought for a moment, shook his head, and said, "No, I hate writing"; then after a brief pause and with a sly grin, he added "but I like to have written."

Also author of *Hard Scrabble* (1973) and *From a Limestone Ledge* (1980), Graves continues to write. His latest book, *A John Graves Reader,* appeared in 1996 shortly before I heard him read from the collection at the San Antonio Public Library (January 23, 1997) and got his inscription in my copy.

Recreation Upriver and Down

The Brazos flows through several physiographic regions of the state, from the high plains of the Panhandle and the rolling plains of lower West Texas to the Gulf coastal plains, and with more than a dozen significant reservoirs within its watershed, it provides a wide range of recreational opportunities, from such motorized pursuits as power boating and jet-skiing to aeolian activities like sailing and windsurfing. Arm-powered gravity sports—paddling a canoe or kayak downstream—certainly offer additional possibilities on many miles of the Brazos. In *Rivers and Rapids,* Nolen and Narramore cover 163 miles of the more popular stretches of the Brazos, but there are many other seasonal possibilities.

In its long course through Texas, the Brazos is many things to many people. Its headwaters forks form one kind of Brazos, a high, dry, seemingly waterless plain that includes Muleshoe National Wildlife Refuge, where I have seen tens of thousands of lesser sandhill cranes wintering in this tallgrass prairie refuge. At dusk you can see flight after flight of the big birds flapping toward lake shores to spend the night. Ducks and geese as well as shorebirds winter on the ponds, and golden eagles seek the sick, lame, and lazy. Badger, bobcat, porcupine, and coyote are also resident.

The Brazos forks drop off the Caprock to a lower plain, just as dry, just as flat, but punctuated with buttes and towers and, to the west, with distant palisades that mark the Caprock. Here in cattle and oil country lies Abilene State Park, on the very edge of the Brazos watershed, a product of the Civilian Conservation Corps. Often confused with Abilene, Kansas, the Texas city of Abilene, where I earned my master's degree at Hardin-Simmons University, also lies in the Brazos watershed. The official state Longhorn herd lives at Fort Griffin along the Clear Fork of the Brazos, where beaver find suitable habitat as well. Remnants of the old fort, which served as one of the most important military outposts against marauding Indians (1867 to 1881), have been stabilized.

Once the Brazos forks join up, the main river is dammed to create three flatwater reservoirs: Possum Kingdom, Granbury, and Whitney. Possum Kingdom Lake, impounded behind Morris Sheppard Dam, is the crown jewel of the upper Brazos. With a storage capacity of more than half a million acre feet of water, Possum Kingdom, a Brazos River Authority project completed in 1941, has a 310-mile shoreline and a 17,700-acre surface when filled. Possum Kingdom State Park lies on the Cedar Creek Arm of the reservoir south of the westernmost portion. Bass fishing is reported to be good in the lake, but it is the river below the dam that interests me with its nearly thirty-nine miles of free-flowing reservoir-release water, part of the section that Graves canoed with his dog in the late 1950s.

Nearby Lake Mineral Wells State Park has hiking, biking, and horseback trails as well as Lake Mineral Wells, created by the Works Progress Administration (WPA) as part of the New Deal during the 1930s. It offers fishing and boating—and canoeing if you enjoy flatwater paddling among power boats. Its outflow joins the Brazos. Palo Pinto Creek then enters from the west. The next reservoir on the Brazos itself is Lake Granbury, named for a Civil War general and popular with the Fort Worth crowd only a few miles away.

Downriver near Glen Rose lie Fossil Rim Wildlife Center, a private ranch for exotic and endangered wildlife as well as native species, and Dinosaur Valley State Park, where you can walk in the footprints of dinosaurs in the Paluxy River. The next reservoir downstream is the state's fourth largest impoundment, Lake Whitney, which covers thirty-seven square miles and has a flood pool of two million acre feet, a 225-mile shoreline, and a state park. Highlights here are fishing, wintering bald eagles, wild turkeys, waterfowl, and shorebirds in a mix of grasslands and cross timbers on the site of an early Hainai Indian village now drowned by the reservoir. Nearby Meridian State Park, a Civilian Conservation Corps (CCC) project of the early 1930s, offers a modest out-of-the-way retreat for fishing, swimming, biking, hiking, and wildlife watching.

Below Lake Whitney, still 442 miles from the Gulf, the river flows relatively freely to the coast, its final miles meandering through coastal wetlands. Here lie Lake Fort Parker on the Navasota River, where a beaver swam past my lakefront campsite one evening, and Fort Parker State Park, where Cynthia Ann Parker was captured during the famous Comanche attack in 1836. Robson's *Ride the Wind* opens with a vivid account of that attack and follows with the Comanche side of the story.

Near Waco Dave Green and I launched my blue canoe, *Poseidon,* on the turbid waters of the Brazos after I'd done the three-mile shuttle from the junior college campus by bike. The wide river reflected the streamside vegetation and muted the freeway traffic. We heard a turkey gobble, surely not a wild Texas turkey this close to the city. As we drifted quietly along with the slow current, we heard it again and again; then we saw it, cresting the natural riverside dike left by frequent floods. The big wild tom gave us a puzzled look, then turned away from the river, and we heard him no more.

We paddled downstream to the confluence of the Bosque River with the Brazos, where a boat ramp at a Waco city park on the left (east) bank gave power boats access. We hugged the right bank and turned up the Bosque, where a bluff showed on our left as we paddled upstream. Turtles sunned on logs. A few small boats with outboard motors chugged along the quiet water. We passed the limestone bluff and paddled to our take-out, where a family fished in a peaceful parklike atmosphere at the edge of the campus. We were content.

Belton Lake, an Army Corps of Engineers impoundment on the Leon River and a Brazos tributary, offers swimming, boating, and fishing opportunities to local residents as well as military personnel at Fort Hood. A retired army friend of mine, Gilbert Gutierrez of Albuquerque Academy's security staff, shared with me a fish story that occurred on an arm of Belton Lake. He and his wife had fished until dusk, throwing the crappie they caught into a plastic laundry basket, the kind with lots of small holes around the sides. As it grew dark, they pulled in the basket of fish, which had been set in the shallow water and tied with a stout cord to a tree. A great thrashing in the basket prompted Gil to shine a flashlight at the basket. What he saw startled then frightened him: red beady eyes of several water moccasins that had been feeding on the fish in the basket. Tying the cord to the trailer hitch ball, Gil drove down the road toward home, but Gil swears the snakes followed the fish basket half a mile down the road.

Downstream Washington-on-the-Brazos, though bypassed by the railroad during the middle of the nineteenth century, has been remembered for its historic significance by means of a state park, which has recently undergone a six-million-dollar facelift. When I visited the park before the renovation, I found it full of Texas school children on a field trip, learning about their state's history. In my wanderings around the park, I found a beaver lodge on a small lake near the river, part of the returning natural aspect of so many Texas parks. When I visited it again after the renovation, it was full of picnicking people enjoying a Sunday outing on the high banks overlooking the river.

Not far downstream lies Stephen F. Austin State Historical Park, a 667-acre plot on the Brazos commemorating the Father of Texas, who lived here

31. A small power boat cruises the lower Bosque River near Waco.

and administered early Anglo-American colonization from this site. The state's first English newspaper, the *Texas Gazette,* began publishing here in 1829, and both the Texas postal system and the Texas Rangers originated here.

Farther downstream but not on the Brazos River itself, the Varner-Hogg Plantation State Historical Park honors Old-Three-Hundreder Martin Varner and one of Texas' most popular governors, James Stephen Hogg, who bought the property as a vacation home and to help preserve a historic Texas cotton plantation. Hogg's daughter Ima gave it to the State of Texas in 1956. There are those who object to commemorating plantation life because it was based on slave labor, but like it or not, it was part of Texas history.

Brazos Bend and Brazoria

The lower Brazos with all of its parks and natural areas remains much as it was in the early days of Texas history. Few towns have grown up along the river itself, perhaps because it floods periodically. I recall spending a delightful day hunting in the woods surrounding an ancient oxbow lake near Brookshire in the Brazos River bottom west of Houston. It had been raining, and the wet woods soon drenched me and my companion, but we trudged on through the mud toward the sound of distant thunder. We soon found ourselves on the edge of the bank-full river at high flood. It moved along fast and muddy, carrying trees, chicken coops, outhouses, and debris of every sort. The thunder we'd heard came from big chunks of riverbank sloughing off into the river with almost explosive force—like glacial ice calving into the ocean.

Brazos Bend State Park and Brazoria National Wildlife Refuge on the coastal plain offer excellent birding and are among the best areas in the state to see wildlife. Their presence so close to a major population center is commendable. This state park southwest of Houston—a mix of river and tributary creeks, marsh and low-lying oak savannas, ponds and lakes—offers an excellent opportunity to see alligators less than fifty miles from the skyscrapers of the state's largest city (although, of course, alligators can be found a lot closer to downtown Houston than that).

Brazos Bend State Park also serves as habitat for raccoon, white-tailed deer, bobcat (rare), swamp rabbit and cottontail, nutria (exotic); several species of snakes, including all of Texas' venomous ones; and, in season, numerous colorful songbirds, including indigo and painted buntings, and wintering shorebirds and waterfowl. A wide variety of wildflowers also inhabit the park.

I'll never forget my late January visit to Brazos Bend. The day was short, and storm clouds further shortened it, darkening the sky before six. Dozens of white-tailed deer wandered about as I settled in for a long night in the camper shell on the back of my pickup truck. I'd just driven through a fierce thunderstorm, and cloudy skies threatened more rain. I didn't have to wait long: lightning flashed, thunder roared, and the wind began to blow; acorns

32. A white-tailed deer buck cautiously approaches an open area in Brazos Bend State Park on the lower Brazos.

from the oaks overhead began pelting the camper shell. Then rain began to fall, sporadically at first, then in torrents, and before long the pellets hitting the thin metal shell became hailstones that began to play staccato tunes.

I couldn't sleep. It was too early, too noisy, and I was too worried. The wind must have gusted to fifty, sixty, seventy miles an hour, and the rain poured down, thundering on the camper shell. Lightning continued to flash every few seconds, and the thunder rolled as Mark Twain reported in *Huckleberry Finn*: "You'd hear the thunder go with an awful crash and then go rumbling, grumbling, tumbling down the sky towards the under side of the world, like rolling empty barrels down stairs, where it's long stairs and they bounce a good deal, you know." It kept up until well past midnight.

When I did finally fall asleep, I had bad dreams: I was trapped in the camper by oak trees felled by the strong wind, their root systems soaked and the trees' grip on the earth loosened. Then the water rose and, caught like a 'coon in a heavy wire cage (the camper), I couldn't get out, and I was about to drown. I'd wake up, look outside, feel around inside—nothing was wet, the roof sound, no trees clutching the camper. I slept little, left the campsite at first light after taking a few shots of the swollen streams, and headed for civilization. I bought a paper while breakfasting in Alvin and learned that Pasadena (southeast Houston, less than thirty-five miles away), had experienced a tornado the previous evening—in the middle of winter.

Brazos Bend State Park has more to offer than all-night thunderstorms in midwinter. In 1994 *National Geographic Traveler* magazine listed Brazos Bend as one of America's top ten state parks, and shortly thereafter it was featured on *This Morning* on CBS. Despite its national recognition, it hasn't been crowded when I've been there, and it offers such a wide variety of activities and wildlife that I go there whenever I'm in the neighborhood. Not only is it one of the best places in Texas to see big and abundant alligators, but it is a mecca for butterflies.

Just as the National Audubon Society holds an annual Christmas Bird Count to determine bird populations, so it holds an annual Fourth of July Butterfly Count, a one-day survey of total numbers and numbers of species. A recent count here found 464 individual butterflies and thirty-eight species. The park checklist runs to fifty species of butterflies and 277 species of birds, including the rare masked duck, a pale chestnut-colored bird usually found in the West Indies and Mexico.

Although Brazoria was an important seaport during Texas' days as an independent nation, today it is more a chamber-of-commerce and public-relations ploy than a real town. The name refers to an area encompassing the mouth of the Brazos, a loose-knit conglomeration of communities and tourist centers including Surfside, Quintana, and the Freeport complex of Chute, Jones Creek, Lake Jackson, and Oyster Creek. For all its faunal and floral features, Brazoria has a skyline marked by chemical plants and plagued by the odors of aerial emissions that sometimes spoil an otherwise outstanding fishing trip or estuarian experience.

Formerly a major shrimping center, until overfishing and pollution destroyed its capacity to produce the pink crustaceans, the "Port of the Brazos" has become something of a bird-watchers' paradise. The National Audubon Society conducts its series of Christmas bird counts nationwide during a two-week period at the end of each year. Birders count individual birds and bird species in a 7.5-mile radius for a twenty-four-hour period. Freeport often wins the unofficial competition for the most species seen, usually well over two hundred (the record is 226).

The Brazos is a mighty river near its coastal terminus. Its originating arms, its Brazos de Díos, fling widely across the Staked Plain. Between the two, the Brazos flows many miles through a changing landscape that the river has both carved and decorated, a magnificent display of natural processes and geologic forces. The Brazos watershed is Texas incarnate, in all the various meanings of the term: human in its form (it has a head, a mouth, many tongues), personified (it speaks), red or rosy (with silt or reflecting sunrise or sunset), giving form to Texas landscape and history. It even delves into prehistoric times, dredging up mastodon bones during its high-water rampages. It certainly has known the crossings of the Comanche war parties that so profoundly shaped Texas' human history, the pattern of which continues to unfold as the Brazos flows from the Staked Plain to the Gulf.

It holds many secrets and much joy that we can discover in and on its salty-silty waters if we seek with understanding and a mind, heart, and soul open to its many gifts.

Trinity River

LOCATION: *Dallas–Fort Worth south-southeast to Gulf of Mexico southeast of Houston*
NAME: *In Spanish La Santisima Trinidad (the Most Holy Trinity)*
CITIES: *Denton, Dallas, Fort Worth, Waxahachie, Corsicana, Crockett, Liberty*
IMPOUNDMENTS: *Lake Ray Roberts, Lake Lewisville, Lake Lavon, Lake Ray Hubbard, Cedar Creek Reservoir, Richland–Chambers Creek Reservoir, Lake Livingston*
TRIBUTARIES: *Denton Creek, Richland Creek, Cedar Creek, many small creeks*
RECREATION: *Fishing, hunting, power boating, water-skiing, jet-skiing, canoeing*
WATERSHED: *17,969 square miles*
DISCHARGE: *5,800,000 acre feet annually; ranks fourth among Texas rivers*
LENGTH: *715 miles; longest river entirely within Texas*
PUBLIC LANDS: *Lake Ray Roberts (COE), Lyndon B. Johnson National Grassland, Fort Worth Nature Center and Refuge, Dallas Nature Center, Benbrook Lake (COE), Parker Hill Prairie Preserve, Lake Ray Hubbard, Richland Creek Wildlife Management Area, Gus A. Engeling Wildlife Management Area, Fairfield Lake State Park, Lake Livingston State Park, Fort Boggy State Park, Anahuac National Wildlife Refuge*
FEATURES: *Heard Natural Science Museum and Wildlife Sanctuary*

THE FOUR MAJOR BRANCHES that create the Trinity River have historically been prone to flooding. The "wild and unpredictable" upper Trinity experienced major floods in 1915, 1922, 1957, 1962, 1964, 1966, 1979, 1981, 1991, and 1994. The flood of 1922 was a monster, but several more recent floods have also been severe. With a river as long as the Trinity, weather patterns that cause flooding at one end don't necessarily cause high water at the other.

33. A flooding Trinity River near Trinidad suggests the river's power.

Because of the combined storage capacity of the reservoirs on the Trinity, floods in the upper watershed may not wreak havoc along the lower river, which flows into Trinity Bay on the Gulf Coast. It joins the industrial world of Galveston Bay near Baytown, its mouth wide enough to constitute a massive network of highly productive wetlands. Even with so many dams in place and with massive storage capacity in its upper reservoirs, the lower Trinity has flooded extensively during the past decade, often inundating flood plain areas for extended periods, further proof that building within the flood plain makes little sense. Structural "flood control" answers don't always solve the problem.

Elm Fork begins so near the Red River north of the Dallas–FortWorth area that it drains land less than five miles from the Red on Texas' northern boundary. The Trinity thus flows almost the entire length of Texas, a course of more than seven hundred miles, counting all the loops and meanders. The lower fifty miles of it are especially convoluted, occasionally traveling three times its cross-country distance and leaving numerous oxbows behind.

Where does the Trinity fit geographically into the pattern of Texas rivers? It might be considered an East Texas River, but its headwaters flow through the heart of North Texas. Yet it can't be considered a North Texas river when it flows into Trinity Bay on the Gulf of Mexico within sight of Houston. It's too long to be classified as a coastal river; its headwaters are simply too far from the Gulf. So where does it fit?

In a sense it is in a class by itself (although, admittedly, there are those who feel this way about every Texas river). I consider the Trinity a heartland river, despite the fact that it flows well east of the state's geographic heartland, because it does encompass the heart of Texas' population: roughly a third of the people in Texas live within its drainage. Even though much of its watershed is rural farmland, the Trinity River basin includes major urban areas, making it the most highly populated watershed in the state. The Dallas–Fort Worth area, which lies entirely within the Trinity River drainage, has more people than Greater Houston, and even part of the Greater Houston population lives along the lower Trinity. With 70 percent of the water stored in Lake Livingston on the mainstem Trinity owned by the City of Houston, the Trinity River basin supplies much of the water that makes Houston viable. The Trinity Valley has more industrial development and more cities than any other Texas river basin.

Ever heard of the Trinity Barge Canal? In the 1970s the U.S. Army Corps of Engineers proposed a major "water development" and navigational scheme that would have made Dallas a seaport and the Trinity River a major waterway comparable to the Columbia in the Pacific Northwest or the Tennessee-Tombigbee in the South, a taxpayer-funded corporate-welfare program. Fortunately this proposal arrived just as the environmental movement began to gain momentum and as Congress began to question federal funding for such boondoggles. Chambers of Commerce along the Trinity still dream of creating an Inland Empire in Texas, but Texas taxpayers have begun to question the need for more dams and for inland seaports.

Like so many of Texas' longer rivers, the Trinity flows through several physiographic areas in its 715-mile trip to the sea: it heads in the cross timbers, grand prairie, and blackland belt, flows through the post oak belt and pineywoods, then courses the coastal prairies to its rendezvous with the Gulf. Its geology involves relatively recent sediments of Mesozoic and Cenozoic age, deposited since the age of dinosaurs. The entire watershed enjoys an annual rainfall average of about forty inches, the main reason that the Trinity's discharge into the Gulf ranks fourth in the state and that the watershed has so many reservoirs, more than twenty.

Its founding forks—West, Clear, Elm, and East forks—encompass a dozen counties from Archer and Young on the west to Fannin on the east, and five counties that lie along the Red River. The Trinity proper begins where the Elm and West forks, the longest, meet in Dallas a few miles southwest of Love Field. Each branch is impounded twice before it reaches the city: Elm Fork to form Lake Ray Roberts and Lake Lewisville north of Dallas, and the West Fork to create Lake Bridgeport and Eagle Mountain Lake northwest of Fort Worth. Denton Creek, a tributary of Elm Fork, is also dammed northeast of Fort Worth to form Lake Grapevine. An eleven-and-a-half-mile stretch of Denton Creek below the reservoir is a popular canoeing stream and among the favorites of the aforementioned Hans Weichsel, who has been paddling Texas rivers for almost fifty years.

The Clear Fork, which begins north of Weatherford, is dammed east of that city to form Lake Weatherford; it is dammed again, after it swings to the northeast, to form Benbrook Lake southwest of Fort Worth, and joins the West Fork near downtown Fort Worth. Although all three of these forks originate in rural areas, each is dammed twice before it reaches the urban heart of Dallas–Fort Worth. Are these streams rural or urban rivers? A little bit of both.

The East Fork, which never really enters the city scene, heads in southwestern Fannin and southern Grayson counties. It too is dammed twice, to form Lake Lavon and Lake Ray Hubbard northeast of Dallas. It joins the river's main branch between Ferris (Ellis County) and Oak Grove (Kaufman County) southeast of Dallas, where I found it flooding the spring of 1998 when I planned to canoe it with a friend from Indiana.

Settlement and Steamboats

Mary Austin Holley did not ignore the Trinity in her 1836 book *Texas,* though she greatly underestimated its length. She writes, "The Trinity rises near the Red River in its great western bend, and running southeastwardly discharges itself, after a course of three hundred and fifty miles, into the northeastern corner of Galveston Bay. It is navigable for steamboats about two hundred miles above its mouth. This stream is remarkably deep with high, steep banks, and is from forty to sixty yards in width" (33). She also mentions "a rich luxuriant soil covered with a fine growth of timber."

Landscape architect Frederick Law Olmsted wrote a book about his travels through Texas in 1854. He mentioned the Trinity as the most navigable river in Texas but found it too low for regular traffic. He crossed it on his way west to Houston, using a questionable ferry at a bluff on a fast-moving muddy river at low water level. He wrote of canebrakes and grapevines, of rich bottomlands, and "of an almost tropical aspect" to the riverbank vegetation.

Steamboat and flatboat transportation on the lower Trinity River greatly enhanced the importance of Galveston near the Trinity's mouth as a commercial center. In May of 1838, steamboats began regular trips as far as Cincinnati (well above present-day Trinidad, fifty miles due north of Huntsville). A traveler on one of the steamboats in 1843 reported seeing "enormous numbers of wild geese, swan, duck, brant, cranes, and pelicans, as well as fish, turtles, and alligators" at the mouth of the Trinity. A half-century later—on May 24, 1893—a 113-foot steamboat, the *H. A. Harvey, Jr.*, actually reached Dallas; but that was a rarity, for like many Texas rivers, the Trinity rose and fell so suddenly with the vagaries of weather that steamboating on the upper reaches was generally impractical, as Olmsted had noted.

Anglo-Americans had settled the upper Trinity in the 1840s, after Texas had become an independent nation but before it was part of the United States. Originally peopled by the Caddo Indians, then the Cherokees, the area had been cleared of these "obstacles to progress" in 1839. Comanches and Kiowas, of course, still haunted the area, raiding settlements and farms when the moon ripened to full in the fall in what was commonly called the Comanche Moon. One of the earliest settlers, John Neely Bryan from Tennessee, built his cabin in 1841 near the convergence of three forks of the Trinity. Dallas evolved around the Bryan homestead.

The region of the lower Trinity had been settled by the Spanish, who established Nuestra Senora de la Luz Mission in 1756 along with the town of Atascosito, near Wallisville, northeast of Anahuac. The first African Americans to appear along the Trinity were two slaves of three Frenchmen who settled on the Trinity in 1751 to trade with the Indians, but soon the Spanish authorities arrested them and expelled them from the territory. Louisiana settlers began moving into the region in the second decade of the nineteenth century. Anglo Americans began moving in during the 1820s and 1830s. A major Cajun influx occurred in the 1840s along the coastal Trinity; European immigrants began arriving in the 1850s. The lower Trinity has a well-mixed population.

Texas naturalist Roy Bedichek observed in *Adventures with a Texas Naturalist* that "hardly a scratch" of Indian picture writing is found east of the Trinity, an indication of either lack of cultural development or lack of surfaces appropriate for leaving them. Whatever the case, the Trinity seems to have served as a boundary of some kind to indigenous people. Most resident Indians of the upper Trinity either died of European diseases or were shipped across the Red River to Indian Territory. The Comanches continued to raid for a third of a century after the Trinity headwaters began to be settled, but they too were eventually sent north of the Red River.

Such river towns as Alabama, Cairo, Cincinnati, Drew's Landing, Hog Pen, Taos, and Tuscaloosa, established on the Trinity in the early 1840s when river traffic was at its peak, began to disappear after the railroads came to Texas. They reflect the origin of the population that settled the middle and lower Trinity. Hog Pen, for example, seems to suggest the southern practice of turning hogs and cattle loose to forage in the river bottoms. The owners would periodically pen the animals to work them, mark them, castrate the boars and bulls, and butcher or market what they needed—as settlers on the nearby Neches did, according to Thad Sitton in *Backwoodsmen*. Many southerners settled East Texas, which remains part of the Deep South even today and certainly had much to do with Texas' secession from the Union to participate in the Civil War as part of the Confederate States of America.

Both ends of the Trinity developed; the major midsection did not. One of the earliest settlements on the Gulf Coast of eastern Texas, the Spanish Mission Nuestra Senora de la Luz, was established in 1756 but abandoned in 1771. A French colony settled in the vicinity but failed (1818). James Taylor White, who became the first Anglo cattleman in Texas, settled on Turtle Bayou near the Trinity mouth. Anahuac, established in 1821 as a port of entry for American colonists, was known as Perry's Point until 1825. It became a hotbed of anti-Mexican sentiment, and in June, 1835, William Travis here led a rebellion often considered the spark that led to Texas independence. After Anglo settlement began in earnest, the lower Trinity grew as a shipping center, and steamboats ran many miles up the deep river.

From John Neely Bryan's 1841 cabin, Dallas grew as a trade center. In 1855 three hundred and fifty French colonists settled on the Trinity Forks. After surviving the Civil War, Dallas mushroomed with the coming of the railroads (1870s) and later the oil industry, to evolve into a banking and insurance center. In the mid-nineteenth century, Fort Worth started as a military post and grew up after the Civil War as a cowtown on the major cattle trails heading north to Kansas railheads. Pretty wild in its infancy—the famous photograph of Butch Cassidy with the Sundance Kid and the Wild Bunch was taken in Fort Worth—it evolved into a cultural center, home to Texas Christian University, the Kimball Art Museum, the Amon Carter Museum, and several others.

A Spring Visit

Driving to Dallas-Fort Worth from Albuquerque to pick up my river-running buddy Dave Green, who was flying in from Indiana to join me for a week's canoeing in East Texas, I crossed several Red River tributaries, camped at Copper Breaks State Park on the Pease River, paused for coffee with photographer-writer Wyman Minzner in Benjamin, and briefly explored the upper reaches of the Trinity Forks. Dave and I camped at the KOA campground in Hickory Creek (too close to the freeway for my taste.)

The next morning we found the East Fork of the Trinity, just east of Dallas, bank-full and carrying debris. Over breakfast we had picked the brain of river runner, writer, and Dallas attorney Cecil Kuhne, an old friend, and he'd suggested that we not try the rivers at high water. We took his advice. After shooting a few photos of the flooding East Fork, we headed toward the Sabine, returning to the Trinity several days later when the river level had dropped.

When rivers rise, they pick up debris along the bank, undercut the bank, and wash new soil and vegetation into the current, increasing its turbidity and suspended load and leaving behind a new riverscape of snags and sweepers. They also tend to bulge in the center and drag along the edges. When river levels drop, debris is deposited wherever it happens to be when the water runs out from under it, whether it be an undercut tree or bush or a dumped tire or washing machine. Dropping rivers also sag in the middle, the water along the edges remaining higher than the center of the river. During our drive south to explore the lower Sabine and Neches rivers, we had noticed these patterns, which Mark Twain wrote about in his 1884 book, *Life on the Mississippi,* and which I've observed during forty years of river running.

Later in the week we drove north again from the Neches after paddling several segments of the lower rivers. Even though skies were gray, the woods were bright with redbud and dogwood, the towns bright with azaleas, the landscape bright with buttercups, bluebonnets, paintbrush, claret cups, and crimson clover during our late-March tour. We saw numerous cardinals, "redbirds" in the local vernacular. It was their mating season, for dozens of male cardinals flew across the road or sang from roadside vegetation when we stopped at a park for lunch. Only during their mating season do cardinals display as obviously. We also saw mockingbirds, blue jays, wood peewees, grackles, red-winged blackbirds, meadowlarks, shrikes, and turkey vultures, the latter attracted by numerous roadkills and lakeside debris on several impoundments.

We stopped at a Trinity River crossing on U.S. 287, where the boat ramp was packed with camping fishermen cooking a breakfast of wild-hog sausage and scrambled eggs. Talking to the motley assemblage, we learned that they spent most weekends hunting, fishing, drinking, and literally eating high on the hog. One fisherman loaded a shotgun into his small boat powered by an outboard motor. I asked what he was going to shoot. "Snakes," he replied, as he motored upstream to check his trotlines.

Observing roadkills to catalogue the wildlife along the Trinity, we found 'possums, skunks, armadillos, domestic dogs and cats, nutrias, one coyote, a couple of foxes, several raccoons, and turtles. We also found old cemeteries—all well marked by signs, and good places for insights into local history—and old homesteads marked by exotic trees the pioneers had planted, by stone ruins and foundations, or by heaps of junk.

There is a general air of decay. Many of the small towns of rural Texas are crumbling into their past, the kids mostly gone elsewhere to find jobs, and only the oldtimers hanging on. In some areas, this means reversing a historic trend: at one time most of the poorer people lived in the country, farming or sharecropping, while those with more resources lived in towns. Now townsfolk who can manage it have moved to country estates and ranchettes, many businesses have moved to shopping malls along the interstate highways, and often the poor are left in the bankrupt towns, a sad situation evident in many small places along the Trinity River.

Once out of the urban atmosphere, the Trinity takes on a bucolic character, flowing through a tree-lined corridor between livestock pastures, hay fields, croplands, and orchards. Its course meanders south-southeast between Corsicana and Athens, between Fairfield and Palestine, between Centerville and Crockett. Dammed between Livingston and Cleveland to form Lake Livingston, the Trinity is blocked for the last time, largely to provide water for an ever-expanding Houston to the south. Below this final man-made obstacle, the Trinity enters its swampy stage, an area similar to the lower Sabine and Neches, a region of slow-moving water spreading through coastal wetlands, the domain of snake and alligator, nutria and beaver, waterfowl and shorebirds.

Birding and Other Wildlife

For all of its dense population and its citified upper reaches (as noted, about a third of all Texans live in its watershed), the Trinity has much of the natural world to offer. Even the impoundments near the Dallas–Fort Worth area—especially Lake Benbrook southwest of Fort Worth and Lake Ray Hubbard northeast of Dallas—attract many species of birds, including wintering bald eagles, colorful passerines, shorebirds, and waterfowl. The headwaters mix of cross timbers, grand prairie, and blackland belt guarantees a diversity of plant and animal life. Nature centers in both Dallas and Fort Worth provide educational opportunities as well as the chance to see wildlife within the Trinity watershed, if not on the river forks themselves.

Outside the cities, the Heard Natural Science Museum and Wildlife Sanctuary near McKinney boasts 270 species of birds, including a concentration of raptors and a number of small mammals. Near Merit northeast of Farmersville lies Collin County's Parkhill Prairie Preserve, a remnant of the tallgrass prairie and a wonderful place to see North Texas wildflowers. One of my favorites is the gayfeather, sometimes called blazing star, a flower that I first came to know while researching this book in the Philmont Boy Scout Ranch Library in northeastern New Mexico.

Ernest Thompson Seton's collection of books forms the core of the Philmont Library, where I discovered a sketch of the gayfeather in an 1854 edition of Captain Randolph B. Marcy's *Adventures on Red River: Report on the Exploration of the Headwaters of the Red River.* The sketch showed a flower that I'd seen at Philmont, a flower common in the tallgrass prairies of North Texas (see photograph by David J. Sams of a cluster of gayfeathers (45) in "At Play on Ray Roberts Lake" by Tracy Peeters and Richard Bedard in the July, 1997, *Texas Highways*).

Fifty miles east of Dallas, on the very edge of the Trinity watershed boundary shared with the Sabine, lies Wills Point. This pleasant little town bills itself as the "bluebird capital of Texas"—the state legislature actually declared it so on February 7, 1995—and celebrates that distinction with an annual Bluebird Festival in mid-April. Wills Point lies so close to the Sabine watershed that it also claims to be the "Gateway to Lake Tawakoni," which lies nearby on the upper Sabine.

At Richland Creek Wildlife Management Area near the dam creating Richland Creek Reservoir, you may see wintering bald eagles and ospreys as well as numerous species of shorebirds, waterfowl, and songbirds during warmer months. Nearby Gus A. Engeling Wildlife Management Area, a pristine 10,941-acre wetland-and-upland combination, is one of my personal favorites, perhaps because of the story behind the name, but also because of the interesting activities going on there.

This Wildlife Management Area (WMA), one of ten in the state dedicated to wildlife research, commemorates wildlife biologist Gus A. Engeling, who died in 1951 before the gun of a poacher trying to feed his family, a tragic conflict of values. The tragedy occurred the year after the State of Texas closed the open range, slamming the door in the faces of hundreds of families who had subsisted on the open range for generations.

While regulated public hunting is allowed in the WMA for deer, feral hogs, and turkeys, numerous species of wildlife are totally protected in the WMA. I visited during deer hunting season and saw half a dozen carcasses hanging in the shed. The area was open to hunting but not to me, a casual visitor looking for wildlife. Hunting is carefully regulated and parts of the area are closed to non-hunters when hunters are afield. I'd simply stumbled into the wrong area at the wrong time.

A stretch of Catfish Creek, a Trinity tributary that runs through the WMA, has received recognition as a National Natural Landmark. An example of the post oak savanna, it contains one of the last unspoiled peat bogs in the state and provides habitat for alligators, beaver, bullfrogs, and many waterfowl, from teal to anhingas and shorebirds. Beaver themselves create habitat by damming streams and raising water tables; several beaver colonies inhabit the watershed. The Texas Parks and Wildlife Department manages this unique area primarily by leaving it alone, letting it revert to a natural state after the extensive wood cutting it suffered (mostly for local firewood) in past decades.

Ray C. Telfair of the Texas Parks and Wildlife Department writes of the Catfish Creek ecosystem as "one of the few remaining relatively undisturbed spring-fed riparian wetlands of the western Gulf Plain natural regions." He points out that Catfish Creek's "twenty-four branches and small creeks maintain a free-flowing meandering bottomland" that is home to at least 471 plant species: "83 woody plants, 80 grasses, 46 legumes, 63 composite forbs [flowering plants], 172 other forbs, and 27 sedges, rushes, and bulrushes." The faunal species include "88 fishes, 18 toads and frogs, 15 turtles, 12 lizards, 30 snakes, 194 birds, and 45 mammals," plus the American alligator—a rich, diverse habitat indeed.

The Catfish Creek bottomlands, which were historically free of underbrush, had been used by several Indian tribes, who were little disturbed until about 1830. As settlers moved into the area, they began changing its very nature by burning and overgrazing (cattle, horses, hogs). By 1846 the last Indians had been removed. Prior to 1860, Catfish Creek bottomlands abounded in a variety of wildlife. However, by 1900 the passenger pigeon had been exterminated, and by 1920 few deer or turkeys remained. Livestock was removed from the drainage in 1951 to allow the range to recover. Wildlife has recovered as well; a cougar was noted there in 1984.

Just southeast of Engeling lies the community of Tennessee Colony, named for a group of settlers from that state. Much of Texas was settled by folks from Tennessee, including Sam Houston himself, who had once been governor there. Southwest of Engeling across the Trinity, Fairfield Lake, a state recreation area, impounds the waters of Big Brown Creek, which flows into Tehuocana Creek and ultimately into the Trinity. Bald eagles and ospreys winter here, and three species of owls frequent the surrounding hardwood bottomland. Fort Boggy State Park, an 1847-acre wetland southeast of Centerville, lies on Boggy Creek, the core of a bottomland hardwood forest where beaver and white-tailed deer abound.

Downstream, the U.S. 191 causeway across Lake Livingston is the next wildlife watching area. Here, at sunset during the summer months, you may see some of the estimated twenty-five thousand purple martins; in winter there are gulls, terns, and a variety of waterfowl. At the U.S. Forest Service Big Spring Scenic Area, northeast of Cleveland (just west of Shepherd) below Lake Livingston, bird-watchers may hear and see the prothonotary and Swainson's warblers, the pileated woodpecker and white-breasted nuthatch, and many other forest dwellers. Just south of Coldspring the Double Lake Recreation Area, also operated by the Forest Service, features a beaver pond and a boardwalk through the marshy upper end of the lake.

The Trinity River ends in Trinity Bay, the northeastern arm of Galveston Bay in Chambers County, a vast and varied landscape of low-lying land and water marked by marshes and landfills. The Trinity flows into its bay through a massive marsh south of Liberty, its meandering lower reaches creating wetlands that harbor numerous species of water-loving birds, mammals, and aquatic creatures such as fish, amphibians, certain reptiles (including alligators and several snakes), and crabs in the midst of a major modern industrial area.

The east shore of Trinity Bay south of Anahuac abounds in watchable wildlife sites. Anahuac National Wildlife Refuge to the east of Smith Point offers 27,506 acres of tidal marshlands in two adjacent units at the mouth of Oyster Bayou. Here you can see white-faced and glossy ibises, roseate spoon-

34. Jet skis, an intrusion on the river's solitude, are used on many Texas rivers. This scene shows a personal watercraft being loaded after an outing on the Trinity River near Trinity.

bills, both black-crowned and yellow-crowned night herons, twenty-two species of ducks, and four species of geese as well as raptors and songbirds. You might see alligators and bobcats too.

The Houston Audubon Society's small wooded birding sanctuaries at High Island southeast of Anahuac are famous for the migrating songbird "fallouts" that occur during spring migration across the Gulf of Mexico. Exhausted by the long over-water flight, dozens of species and thousands of individual birds land to rest in the woods: twenty to thirty species of warblers plus scarlet tanagers, rose-breasted grosbeaks, gray catbirds, and others.

Candy Abshier Wildlife Management Area near Smith Point south of Anahuac is another fallout area to see numerous birds of many species during spring migration, and thousands of raptors, which use the area as a staging ground for fall migrations. Like all estuaries, the one at the mouth of the Trinity offers an exotic mix of terrestrial and aquatic wildlife. One more viewing area is Atkinson Island, accessible only by boat, off Morgan's Point across the Houston Ship Channel from Baytown. For all the dewatering and industrial development in the area and the pollution of both air and water, tidal flushing and sea breezes ameliorate the negative and accentuate the positive.

From head to mouth, the Trinity varies as much as any river in Texas, especially for one that has such abundant rainfall throughout its course. It flows through highly populated urban and high-tech industrial areas, through pineywoods and southern swamps, through Texas history and modern America. It marks the boundary of East Texas as surely as the Pecos marks West Texas. Yet, even if nothing west of the Trinity fully qualifies as East Texas, this is not entirely an East Texas river, for it flows through the state's population centers where people use the rivers in a wider variety of ways simply because there are so many more people.

PART 3

Some Regional Specialties

The Neches of East Texas

LOCATION: *East Texas from Van Zandt County southeast to the Beaumont area*
NAME: *From the word meaning "white" or "snowy" among the Hasanai Indian tribe who lived along the river*
CITIES: *Tyler, Jacksonville, Rusk, Nacogdoches, Lufkin, Beaumont*
IMPOUNDMENTS: *Lake Palestine, Sam Rayburn Reservoir, Steinhagen Lake*
TRIBUTARIES: *Angelina, Attoyac Bayou, Village Creek, Pine Island Bayou*
RECREATION: *Fishing, hunting, trapping, power boating, canoeing*
WATERSHED: *10,011 square miles*
DISCHARGE: *5.6 to 6.0 million acre feet*
LENGTH: *416 miles*
PUBLIC LANDS: *Big Thicket National Preserve, Angelina and Davy Crockett National forests, Texas Point National Wildlife Refuge, Jim Hogg State Historical Park, Caddoan Mounds State Historical Park, Mission Tejas State Historical Park, Casselles-Boykin State Park, Village Creek State Park, two state wilderness areas, several state wildlife management areas*
FEATURES: *Forks of the River*

MORE THAN ANY OTHER watershed in Texas, the Neches River and its tributaries represent East Texas, a combination of pineywoods and bayou country where the southern hardwood forests of low swamplands meet well-drained sandy soils to create a unique environment characterized by the Big Thicket. The Neches flows right through the center of East Texas, not along its edge like the Sabine, nor all the way from North Texas to the Gulf like the Trinity, nor draining only the state's northeastern corner like the Sulphur, but through the living heart of East Texas.

In a land often noted for poverty and prejudice with roots in the Deep South, it stands alone in its wealth of native plants and wildlife and for opportunities to practice subsistence farming, a way of life dating to its earliest settlers and uninterrupted until 1950 when the state of Texas closed the open range. To the aboriginal residents it was known simply as the Big Woods. To early invaders it became known as the Neutral Ground, a no-man's land claimed by several governments but ruled by none.

Its rich bottomlands, fertilized naturally by the river's annual flooding, produce a wide variety of food and shelter for numerous species of wildlife and domesticated animals as well—hogs fatten nicely on the forest mast. The fecund vegetation, varied and vital to the natural scene, includes many plants that grow nowhere else, one of the reasons 86,000 acres of the watershed has been set aside for protection as the Big Thicket National Preserve established in 1974. This special area lies at a "biological crossroads of North America," and it has been designated an "International Biosphere Reserve" by the United Nations Educational, Scientific and Cultural Organization (UNESCO).

In his insightful book about the people of the Neches River watershed, *Backwoodsmen: Stockmen and Hunters along a Big Thicket River Valley,* Thad Sitton writes of the traditional southern lifestyle based on "feral livestock, subsistence farming, and free use of the 'open woods'" and of "people who made their own rules" (xii). Settled by poor farmers from the South who came not to conquer the land but to wrest a living from it, the Neches Valley remained a relatively unspoiled part of the pineywoods South—at least until the mid-twentieth century, when the open range closed as a result of stock law enforcement. This concept serves as the theme for Sitton's vital book, alive with oral tradition and important because it helps explain why this part of East Texas is as it is.

Quintessential River of the Pineywoods

Sitton describes the Neches as "a typical silt-laden, slow-moving southern lowland stream, which flows in its shallow, heavily-timbered valley" (16). And so I found it in the spring of 1998, a turbid river, sluggish with suspended silt, its banks lined with southern hardwoods: oak, ash, hickory, beech, gums, magnolia. Only beaver cuttings indicated timber harvest along the river itself, but clearcuts were evident along some of the roads, and numerous logging trucks roared along the back roads and highways. Sitton writes, "At a time when so many southern bottomlands have been drowned by reservoirs or drained and converted to soybean fields or slash pine plantations, much of

35. When the Neches River tickles the toes of trees along its shore, the river is up, as here seen in April.

the Neches bottoms remains in old-growth hardwood forest" (16). In some areas it's going fast, much of it used to produce wood fiber, one of the best reasons I know to recycle paper products.

Essentially the Neches watershed has poor soil fertility, but the river bottoms, enriched by frequent floods that leave a layer of silt and nutrients behind when the water level drops, enjoy greater fertility than surrounding higher ground. They also experience a greater diversity of plant life because seeds from the entire watershed gravitate to the river bottoms, increasing the variety of vegetation by adding exotics to the native flora.

Geologically speaking, the entire Neches watershed flows through Tertiary (primarily Cenozoic) and Quaternary sediments. They represent the age of mammals, the last sixty-six million years, relatively recent. Composed of materials that began filling the Gulf of Mexico after the dinosaurs disappeared, the region is known to geologists as the East Texas embayment. The lower Neches flows through the Gulf Coast Basin, deposits of more recent sediments.

36. Pines grow tall along the Neches River and right to the water's edge at high water levels.

The first paleo-Indians are thought to have arrived some thirty-seven thousand years ago. When the Spanish and French arrived, they found three groups of people: the Caddos, a peaceful farming and fishing people, and the Karankawas and Atakapas. The latter two tribes were known to have engaged in ritualistic cannibalism, a practice that is all most people know about them today. For more background on the native people found by early explorers in what became East Texas, see *The Indians of Texas* by W. W. Newcomb, Jr.

European exploration of the region probably began with Cabeza de Vaca, who may have visited Indian villages along the Neches in the 1530s. Hernando de Soto almost certainly crossed the Neches in late 1541 or early 1542, the same time that Coronado traversed what later became the Texas Panhandle. French explorers led by La Salle penetrated the Neches River country in 1685. The Spanish established the Mission San Francisco de los Tejas on San Pedro Creek (at the northwestern boundary of Davy Crockett National Forest), a Neches tributary near present-day Weches northeast of Crockett, on May 24,

1690. There were Spanish settlements on the Neches and Angelina and some of their tributaries in the early eighteenth century, but such settlements were sporadic and short-lived.

By the eighteenth century both France and Spain had weakened as colonial powers. Neither had successfully settled the area along the Neches, nor had they consolidated their territory. The Spanish military captain Domingo Ramón founded the East Texas mission of Nuestra Señora de Guadalupe de los Nacogdoches in the spring of 1716. But it didn't last long. Most other missions established in Texas fared as poorly, but in 1779, while the American Revolution was busy creating the United States of America, the Louisiana-born Hispanic rancher and impresario Gil Antonio Ybarvo resettled Nacogdoches (named for a local Caddoan tribe).

When the settlers of Los Adaes, the Spanish capital east of the Sabine, were ordered by the king of Spain to abandon their homes (1773), Ybarvo obtained authority to remove them to the Trinity, where he established the town of Bucareli. Here Ybarvo employed the first African American recorded in Texas history, a black weaver hired to teach settlers his trade. Alicia Vidaurreta Tjarks reported that "twice as many Africans as in the rest of Texas in the same period, lived in the town of Bucareli, and later in Nacogdoches, where the inhabitants of Bucareli were transferred." Most slaves were bought in New Orleans, often as an alternative to carrying cash back through the lawless borderlands. Human beings were safer to transport than was gold or silver.

Ybarvo constructed the Old Stone Fort (1779) that today serves as a museum on the campus of Stephen F. Austin State University. The structure, part trading post and part defensive military fort, became Ybarvo's headquarters. He may have been as much a fomenter of revolution as an impresario, for several attempts to wrest Texas from Spain all seem to have centered around his stone fort in Nacogdoches, which became a major gateway into Texas. In 1819 Dr. James Long at the head of an army of American filibusters took Nacogdoches, but the Spanish drove them out in short order.

In any case, Nacogdoches was the end of the line for Spanish authority, both geographically and historically. The American governor of lower Louisiana, Gen. James Wilkinson, seems to have played a devious game, allowing many Americans to cross into the "neutral ground" west of the Sabine. In 1819 the Adams-Onís Treaty (also known as the Florida Treaty because through it, the Spanish ceded Florida to the United States) temporarily resolved the boundary dispute and dissolved the neutral territory. Even though the treaty set the western boundary of the United States at the Sabine River, Americans continued moving into East Texas, many settling along the Neches and other East Texas rivers. They arrived by two routes: one across the Red River through the extreme northeast corner of the future Texas, and the other through Nacogdoches, which was the terminus of the Old San Antonio Road.

A trip down modern State Highway 21, which closely follows the Old San Antonio Road, is a trip through Texas history. It actually begins at Natchitoches, Louisiana, crosses the state line passing over Toledo Bend Reservoir, and runs westward through East Texas, crossing Attoyac Bayou and both the Angelina and the Neches rivers before taking a more southwesterly course at Alto. It is strewn with Texas historical sites, including Caddoan Mounds State Park and Mission Tejas State Historical Park, both near the Neches. One of Texas' rare designated wilderness areas, the Big Slough Wilderness, lies nearby on the Neches fifteen miles south of Alto and about five miles west of Wells. Here an eight-mile canoe loop including the Neches and the Big Slough offer the best way to see this tiny piece of preserved paradise.

In one sense the Texas War of Independence began in Nacogdoches in an August, 1835, dispute over recognition of Antonio López de Santa Anna as president of Mexico. Citizens' resistance to Mexican authority may have been precipitated by the Battle of Velasco near the mouth of the Brazos a few weeks earlier, in which Texans first spilled Mexican blood. Ordered by the Mexican commandant at Nacogdoches to give up their arms, the local citizenry, including many Mexicans, rebelled and drove Mexican authorities out of East Texas. Howard Peacock, writing about the Neches and Angelina rivers in *Texas Highways,* considers this conflict one of the most important battles in Texas history as it "made possible the organization of the Texas Revolution" (54).

The Indian Presence

About the time that Austin's colony began to settle Central Texas, Cherokee people displaced from the southeastern United States began moving into East Texas. They had been promised land between the Neches and Angelina rivers, first by the Mexicans, then by leaders of the Texas Revolution including their blood-brother Sam Houston, and finally by the Republic of Texas. However, in 1839, under Indian-hating president Mirabeau B. Lamar, the Texas (federal) legislature voided a treaty giving the Cherokees title to their land. After a brief but bloody war known as the Battle of the Neches, the Cherokees were removed to Indian Territory north of the Red River, another Trail of Tears. According to one account, their heroic eighty-three-year-old leader, Chief Bowles, was shot in the back as he limped off the battlefield with a leg wound; another report said he was executed by a pistol shot to the head.

Two decades later (1859) Caddo, Anadarko, Waco, and Tonkawa people—all belonging to groups who had taken to farming and often scouted for American and European settlers battling the raiding Comanches—were removed from their reservation on the upper Brazos and sent to Indian Territory north of the Red River. Texas' record for dealing with native peoples was no better than that of the United States or Spain. Only tiny remnants of aboriginal groups remain in Texas today.

An interesting note concerning the Alabama-Coushatta Indians, who now live in the Neches River watershed, is worth mentioning here. Toward the close of the French and Indian War, which ended in 1763, the Alabama Indians began migrating to the Neches River of East Texas. A few decades later their neighbors the Coushattas followed (1807) and established two villages on the adjacent Trinity River. Tribal historians suggest that the Coushatta Tribe arrived after 1795 and that a thousand Alabama Indians came in 1805. The Texas Congress granted each tribe two leagues of land on the nearby Trinity River, but white settlers soon began taking Indian lands. On Sam Houston's recommendation, the State of Texas purchased 1,280 acres (two sections) of land for the Alabamas, but somehow the Coushattas were left out.

For decades the Coushattas wrested a living from the Big Thicket; some married into the Alabama Tribe, and others got special permission to live on the reservation, tribal ties being close. Not until the 1920s did the federal government bail out the Coushattas—and the State of Texas—by purchasing more than three thousand acres of land adjacent to the reservation, where the two tribes now live in relative harmony. Of all the tribes that once lived in East Texas, only the Alabama-Coushattas retain a presence. Ironically all Indian tribes with reservations in Texas are migrants from other areas, either the Deep South or New Mexico, the Alabama-Coushatta in the Neches watershed and the Isleta along the Rio Grande.

One of the most famous Indians of the region was Angelina, for whom the river is named. Her background is lost in history and myth, but she may have been born in Mexico and probably grew up along the Rio Grande, perhaps at Eagle Pass but she lived her adult life in East Texas. She spoke fluent Spanish and first appeared in the journals of André Penicaut, a French explorer, in 1712; he reported finding "a woman named Angelique, who had been baptized by Spanish priests." She served as interpreter for an expedition led by M. de St. Denis and treated Simars de Belle-Isle with kindness when he was the captive of cruel coastal Indians. Both the Spanish and the French, political enemies, valued her services and used them extensively. She was a Texas version of Sacajawea. Angelina County is the only one of the 254 counties in Texas named for an Indian.

The Angelina River, likewise named for her, begins southwest of Henderson in Rusk County, formed by three creeks: Barnhardt, Scoober, and Shawnee. It flows many quiet miles before being swallowed up by Sam Rayburn Reservoir, one of Texas' famous fishing impoundments, then another eighteen miles between reservoirs, a favorite canoeing stretch. Below Rayburn the Angelina joins the Neches at the head of A. B. Steinhagen Lake (also known as Dam B Reservoir).

The Forks of the River, a marshy meeting of the Angelina with the Neches, is relatively unknown to most people. Few roads penetrate the vicinity, and most of them remain unpaved. You've really got to want to get there, and you need to use a boat. Much more accessible since the reservoir came into being, the Forks of the River is well described in *Land of Bears and Honey* by Joe C. Truett and Daniel W. Lay. I haven't been there, but I want to go, especially after hearing about it from Thad Sitton, who also writes about this famous de facto wilderness confluence and its people in *Backwoodsmen*.

Sitton writes poetically about the Neches, its rise in late winter and early spring and, like the Nile, its leaving a fresh layer of silt and nutrients along its floodplain. He writes of its flow through two national forests, along two of the state's six wilderness areas, and through the eighty-mile-long corridor of the Big Thicket National Preserve. When Texas failed to protect its wild heritage from loggers, dam builders, the extractive industry, and other exploiters of natural resources, the whole country finally got behind the effort. Some Texans led, others followed, but the state is now on the right track toward conserving larger segments of Texas as it once was for present and future generations.

Below Sam Rayburn Reservoir, the Angelina flows swift, deep and clear for another twenty-five miles to join the Neches near the head of A. B. Steinhagen Lake. Town Bluff Dam, known in the planning stage as Dam B, was the first major impoundment on the lower Neches. Completed in 1951, it dams the Neches between Jasper and Woodville, creating the 13,700-acre A. B. Steinhagen Lake, which has storage capacity of 94,200 acre feet. Blackburn Crossing Dam impounds the Upper Neches, forming Lake Pales-

37. The Angelina River is a major tributary of the Neches.

tine with a surface area of 25,560 acres, a 135-mile shoreline, and storage capacity of 411,300 acre feet. By far the largest impoundment within the Neches watershed is Sam Rayburn Reservoir, created by a dam at McGee Bend on the Angelina. Rayburn Reservoir has 114,500 surface acres and a storage capacity of 2,876,300 acre feet.

Near the southwest shores of Sam Rayburn Reservoir lies another of Texas' special places, Upland Island Wilderness, a few miles southeast of Zavalla in Angelina National Forest. One of the best articles I've read about the Neches is Thad Sitton's "The Enduring Neches," in which he makes the same point I've been trying to make in several of these chapters: "Big reservoirs halt floods, trap the life-giving sediments and destroy the natural ecology of the river for many miles below them" (16). He sees rivers as I do, by canoe and through an understanding of and a respect for natural systems, which we both believe in preserving.

Sitton's delightful *Backwoodsmen* is an excellent account of life along the Neches through the decades, constituting an environmental history of the region. In a similar vein, Texas naturalist Roy Bedichek, in a 1937 notebook entry published in his 1947 *Adventures with a Texas Naturalist,* describes a piece of Neches River bottomland as "an island of life in the midst of a weary land devastated by unscientific cultivation which followed in the wake of insatiable sawmills" (67). He notes that the fourteen-thousand-acre Lufkin Club west of Lufkin on the Neches, intended to provide protection for wildlife "which furnishes meat for the table and sports afield" (67), incidentally protected thousands of other forms of life.

But protection can have its drawbacks. Members of one East Texas rod and gun club decided to destroy all the skunks in the neighborhood to protect game birds from having their nests robbed of eggs, forgetting that skunks also eat snapping turtle eggs. The skunk-eradication program almost resulted in the end of fishing at the club because the snapping turtle population exploded, and the turtles fed on fish. The Neches River abounds in alligator snapping turtles, some weighing over a hundred pounds. One 150-pounder has been reported with a head as big as a human head; it scared the wits out of a noodler or grabber (someone who tries to catch catfish by hand by reaching into holes along the riverbank) and cured him of the practice.

Paddling on the Neches

Until doing the research for this book, my own acquaintance with the Neches consisted merely of seeing it from bridges. I'd never met the river on its own terms until I visited the Big Thicket National Preserve, hiked the Kirby Nature Trail along Village Creek, and, crossing the creek on a small footbridge, vowed to canoe it someday. Now I have done so, though not the section along which I hiked. It was too narrow, too shallow, too frequently blocked by fallen trees.

I hiked the trail in mid-January, saw the twisted vines and hollow-hearted trees, smelled the decaying vegetation, and heard the bird songs—not many in midwinter but enough to pique my curiosity so that I planned to return in spring when the warblers would be there. I saw the cypress trees and knees, heard the woodpeckers' staccato hammering and the barred owls' mournful "Who cooks for you?"

This first conscious experience with the Big Thicket recalled my Boy Scout days at a camp somewhere nearby, perhaps on another tributary of the Neches. My folks had moved to Orange when they both got jobs there during the World War II, but I'd been living with a friend's family in our old hometown for four months to finish the school year. I'd been in Orange for only a week when I went to scout camp at thirteen, not ready to be away from my parents again so soon. At camp, with a bunch of total strangers, I was so homesick

38. Village Creek offers a few obstacles to canoe paddlers, but with the current so slow, such problems are easy to circumvent: just paddle around them or stop to portage or line the craft around the obstacle, like leading a well-trained dog.

that I hardly remember the surroundings; about all I remember was taking a fourteen-mile hike and loving every sweaty minute of it.

Following up the vow made during my hike along the Kirby Nature Trail, I camped for three nights in the spring of 1998 at Village Creek State Park near Lumberton, just north of Beaumont, and canoed three different segments of the lower Neches and its tributaries. Village Creek came first, an early-morning trip with mist rising from the stream as my Indiana buddy Dave and I launched. We'd awakened before dawn, stopped for breakfast in Lumberton, then driven north a few miles on U.S. Highway 96 to the bridge crossing Village Creek. I dropped off Dave and the canoe, drove back to our campsite to leave the truck there, and rode back to the launch site on my bike, which then went into the canoe with us.

The highway sounds, muffed by the fog and heavy vegetation, soon fell behind us as we drifted silently along the still surface of the stream, which reflected perfectly everything we saw, from cardinals to cypress trees. An approaching train whistle startled us momentarily. Having just passed beneath the railroad bridge, we turned upstream to watch the slow freight train cross, the surface of the creek reflecting every car as it passed. The mist gradually lifted, but even so we could see only a little way into the woods because of the thick foliage. The muddy creek banks, tracked by raccoons, drifted quietly past as we paddled only enough to avoid sweepers and snags. What an idyllic experience! Fish jumped, squirrels chattered, birds called and flew across the creek: blue jays, kingfishers, cardinals. Before we realized we'd come that far, we reached our take-out just as three busloads of school children arrived. Fortunately their teachers called them to listen to a naturalist talk just as we landed, and we regained our solitude as we unloaded the canoe, hauled it out of the water, and lashed it onto my canoe rack for our next venture.

That afternoon we tried a stretch of the Neches from the left bank (east side) near Four Oaks Ranch. We'd planned to use the bike routine again, but as I was unchaining my bike from a tree for the ride upstream, a fisherman loading his boat onto a trailer offered me a ride. I locked the bike in my camper and accepted his friendly offer. We drove north to our access several miles upstream, where he left me after showing off the fish he'd caught. We launched and paddled into the middle of a big muddy river with a strong current, the Neches at high water. Rounding bend after bend, we found precious little dry land anywhere, and began to wonder if we'd gotten lost in a backwater—as Francis E. "Ab" Abernethy and his buddy Hubert Mott did during Easter week of 1947 on their six-day float down the Neches.

If you haven't read *The Bounty of Texas,* a Texas Folklore Society collection of stories edited by Abernethy, you have a delightful treat coming. In his preface to the book, Abernethy relates details of that river trip more than half a century ago. Intending to live off the land, they launched their homemade boat from U.S. 59 south of Diboll and floated to U.S. 69 near Rockland, essentially the stretch of river between Davy Crockett and Angelina national forests. They didn't do badly, except for one whole day going in a circle, but they had a once-in-a-lifetime experience.

Dave and I hadn't intended to live off the land. We had water along and a few snacks, but we certainly didn't plan to spend the night on the river. As the sun began to sink below the tops of the trees on the right bank, we wondered where our take-out was. Had we missed it? Were we in some backwater? No, there was too much current for that. Perhaps we'd somehow taken a wrong channel, but neither of us could remember leaving the main current. Finally, as sunset colors began to play across the horizon, we found our take-out across from the mouth of Pine Island Bayou. We hadn't allowed for the major meanders the big rivers takes as it swings from bank to bank. We'd had a pleasant float with just enough worry to make it an adventure.

We'd hired a shuttle driver for the next day. We planned to run from FM 1746 at Town Bluff east of Woodville below A. B. Steinhagen Lake about sixteen miles to a take-out on private land just below FM 1013, between Spurger and Kirbyville. The weather didn't look too good when our shuttle driver dropped us off to launch, and before we'd been on the river ten minutes, it began to rain. Old river guides on the Snake in Jackson Hole, we both had our wet-weather gear along, and we used it. However, the rain didn't last more than an hour, and when it stopped, the sun came out hot and muggy. We stowed our gear and paddled downriver, keeping an eye out for beaver sign and trotlines. We didn't expect to see beaver during daylight hours, but we wanted proof that they lived here—and they do: we found numerous beaver cuts and a few bank lodges.

We were both amazed at the junky banks of the river. Numerous weekend fishing shacks and a few permanent homes lined the bank, and while some looked really nice, others were dumps. The riverbank had been used as a not-so-sanitary landfill for years at some sites, and I'm not sure all the cabins had approved septic systems. Some Texans seem to think rivers are for dumping. The out-of-sight, out-of-mind philosophy is alive and well along this stretch of the Neches.

When people act irresponsibly, dumping trash on the riverbank or running sewer lines into the river, they're asking for local government to intervene and take responsibility, to raise taxes and increase public services. When local government doesn't do the responsible thing, it in turn is inviting the next level of government to take action, and so on all the way up. Irresponsible people have no right to complain about higher taxes or bigger government because they create both. Through irresponsibility, we tend to build bigger government by expanding governmental responsibility and services and increasing taxes for services we should be providing ourselves and for actions we should be taking ourselves.

Also alive and well in the area is racial prejudice, as I found in Nacogdoches when I stopped at an auto supply store near the campus of Stephen F. Austin State University. When I asked directions to the Old Stone Fort, I was told how to find it on campus and was then advised, "Look out for those black kids; they don't know how to drive too good." I know plenty of white kids who don't "drive too good" either. That slur soured my day. My first reaction was to get out of town and never go back, but that would reveal another kind of prejudice: judging the place from one person's thoughtless comment.

The Neches transcends all that. I camped one night at Boykin Springs in Angelina National Forest, and early the next morning, as I followed the Sawmill Trail, I began to notice pale gray blotches along the trail. At first I thought they were campers' ash disposal sites; then I realized that they were made by burrowing creatures and that ashlike material was silt from the soil through which Boykin Creek flowed. I followed the trail and the creek to the Neches and the ruin of an old sawmill.

I was alone with the river and my thoughts. I wasn't there to fish or float. I was just there, absorbing the beauty of a morning in the woods along a slow-flowing river. I was reminded of the passage from Norman Maclean's *A River Runs Through It* when the narrator "sat there and forgot and forgot, until what remained was the river that went by and I who watched." And so I sat, and the river went by, and I remembered that Maclean had written to me that this was his favorite passage in the book. He was writing about the Big Blackfoot River in Montana, but his image was as apt here on the banks of the Neches in East Texas.

The Nueces of South Texas

LOCATION: *Edwards Plateau southeast to Gulf Coast at Corpus Christi*
NAME: *Spanish for nut, apparently meaning pecans growing on the banks*
CITIES: *Corpus Christi at its mouth*
IMPOUNDMENTS: *Choke Canyon Lake (on the Frio), Lake Corpus Christi*
TRIBUTARIES: *Frio, Sabinal, Atascosa, Leona*
RECREATION: *Hunting, fishing, power boating*
WATERSHED: *17,000 square miles*
DISCHARGE: *620,000 acre feet*
LENGTH: *416 miles*
PUBLIC LANDS: *Lost Maples State Natural Area, Kickapoo Caverns State Natural Area, Garner State Park, Choke Canyon State Park, Tips State Park, Lake Corpus Christi State Park, Mustang Island State Park, Lipantitlan State Park*
FEATURES: *Nueces Canyon, Frio Canyon, Copano Bay*

ONCE A DISPUTED BOUNDARY of Spanish Texas and later of the Republic of Texas, the Nueces River typifies South Texas, J. Frank Dobie's Brush Country, a dry land of mesquite, cactus, cattle, and oil. From a watershed almost equal to that of the Trinity River's, the Nueces generates roughly a tenth as much water, for it lies in a much drier region largely west and south of San Antonio.

"The Nueces," Mary Austin Holley wrote in her 1836 *Texas,* "forms part of the western boundary of Texas, . . . runs southeast a distance of more than 350 miles and discharges into the Gulf of Mexico, forming a considerable bay at its mouth." This bay is, of course, Corpus Christi Bay, the western reach of it called Nueces Bay, which lies north of the city. Holley further extols the area through which the Nueces flows as "one of the healthiest and most valuable in Texas," affording "pasturage of the finest kind." It was already cattle country, had been for almost a century, when she described its value as range land.

Almost the entire Nueces watershed lies west of the modern highway between San Antonio and Corpus Christi, Interstate 37, which essentially parallels the lower Nueces and its tributary the Atascosa. Many an early expedition into southern and coastal Texas had to cross the Nueces. Alonso de León, who crossed the Nueces in 1689 on his way to establish missions in East Texas, has been credited with naming it (nueces being the plural of *nuez*, meaning "nut" in Spanish). Two years later Teran de los Ríos called it the San Diego, but that name never caught on. Cabeza de Vaca referred to a Río de las Nueces in the region through which he passed, noting that the Indians lived for two or three months every year on the nuts from the river-bottom pecan trees.

The Nueces served as the boundary between the Spanish provinces of Texas and Nuevo Santander, background for the dispute over the Texas-Mexico boundary after Texas won her independence from Mexico in 1836. This dispute was not settled until the Treaty of Guadalupe Hidalgo (1848) that ended the Mexican War (the one Henry David Thoreau protested through his acts of civil disobedience). Thus the Rio Grande became the official boundary between Texas and Mexico; other boundary disputes remained to be settled.

But long before boundaries and border disputes, the Nueces River and its primary tributaries, the Frio, Sabinal, and Atascosa rivers, established boundaries of their own, vegetational boundaries based on the availability of water. All three rivers originate on the western fringe of the Edwards Plateau, an uplift of some two thousand vertical feet that occurred roughly ten million years ago. When the region that ultimately became the Edwards Plateau rose, about the same time as the Llano Estacado, erosion began to cut into the higher ground, exposing the limestone layers beneath the surface and leaving thin layers of soil on broad expanses of bedrock known as Edwards limestone, which had formed beneath ancient seas.

Rivers that originate in this limestone formation usually flow clear because they are spring-fed and have little soil to wash away when it rains. Even though the region averages less than twenty inches of rainfall annually, it produces more runoff than other areas of equal rainfall because the limestone does not absorb the water as readily as do areas of deeper soil. However, surface water does recharge the water table, percolating through cracks and crevices in the limestone to form sinkholes, caves, and springs characteristic of what geologists call Karst topography. Such landscapes earned their name from an area with similar characteristics in Yugoslavia, where they were first described scientifically. Underground water from sinks in the Nueces and Frio rivers

39. Nueces River flows over limestone ledges.

actually flows downhill within the bowels of the earth toward the San Antonio area, where the water emerges at the surface in the form of springs.

Many streams that head in the Edwards Plateau produce a limestone gravel rich in chert, a material from which early Indians often crafted their arrowheads and spear points. The Nueces, Frio, the Frio tributary Sabinal, and the Atascosa rivers all drop out of the Edwards Plateau, flowing southeastward over the Balcones Fault. The lower Nueces flows through the coastal plains, an area composed of relatively recent (Pleistocene) sediments. A fluvial and deltaic sandstone formation known as the Frio formation, which underlies the area northwest of Corpus Christi, contains major oil and gas reservoirs.

Few people traveling through the Brush Country of the lower Nueces pay much attention to the geology of this relatively flat region of mesquite, stunted oak, and pricklypear cactus, but the southern stretch of Interstate 37 between San Antonio and Corpus Christi—after the highway crosses the river at Nueces River Park—follows the river terrace along the drainage divide, offering travelers a good view of the river and its valley. Because of modern "improvements," the Nueces now discharges directly into Corpus Christi Bay, with substantial wetlands north of the river feeding into Nueces Bay.

Early Inhabitants

With an understanding of the lie of the land, the nature of the area and of its aboriginal people becomes clearer. According to W. W. Newcomb, Jr., in prehistoric times bands of Payaya Indians, one of the Coahuiltecan tribes whose focal point was San Pedro Springs (in San Antonio), lived on the headwaters of the Frio, but by the end of the eighteenth century the area had become home to the Lower Lipan Apaches. Bands of another Coahuiltecan tribe, the Pachal, lived in the vicinity of the Frio-Nueces confluence, and a third group, the Orejons, lived along the lower Nueces. Never unified tribes, they are little known today. Living in an area with few large animals, they depended primarily on native vegetation—cacti, mesquite, sotol, agave, and nuts—and on

40. The Frio River, Nueces tributary, flows through Garner State Park.

reptiles, birds, and small rodents for food. Only occasionally did bison migrate this far south. Deer, pronghorn, and javelina supplemented their diet rather then playing a vital role in it.

Some anthropologists believe that these original residents of South Texas, linguistically related to Indians of California, may have been split from their California relatives by the invasion of Athapascan tribes migrating into the southwest from Canada, the Apaches and Navajo. In any case, the Nueces Coahuiltecans were too busy making a living in the harsh semidesert environment to have time for sophisticated cultural evolution. Much of what is known of them comes from a careful study of Cabeza de Vaca's journal, for he knew these people, having spent time with them between 1528 and 1536.

After de Vaca's trek through South Texas, a century passed before the Spanish entered the area again. In 1579 Luis de Carabajal was authorized to establish Nuevo León in what is now northern Mexico and to expand into Texas; by 1583 he had founded his capital city of León, now a small village a few miles south of the Rio Grande, but he failed to expand northward beyond the Rio Grande. In 1655 a Spanish punitive expedition against the natives led by Fernande de Azcue entered South Texas, killing a hundred Indians and taking seventy prisoners. In 1675 an expedition led by Fernando del Bosque crossed the Rio Grande near Eagle Pass and reached the Edwards Plateau, where they found local tribes already decimated by smallpox. Essentially the Coahuiltecans, in the words of historian Leon C. Metz, "vanished as a people, victims of battle, disease, and assimilation" (230).

Although several Spanish expeditions passed through the area and a few settlements were attempted (I use the passive voice here to a purpose—it was a passive conquest), the Spanish never really controlled the region. They converted and conquered few Indians, never recreated a new Spain on the Nueces, and eventually lost it to American influence. When José de Escandón (El Conde, "the count") was ordered, in the 1740s, to colonize Nuevo Santander—northern Mexico and what became the Nueces Strip in Texas— his Spanish settlements generally evolved on the south bank of the Rio Grande since the region north of the Rio Grande remained Indian country.

It was Domingo Teran de los Ríos, the Spanish governor of provincial Texas, who established the Old Spanish Trail, originally known as the San Antonio Road for its first major destination. It eventually ran all the way to Nacogdoches in East Texas, crossing the Rio Grande near Eagle Pass, the Nueces where it drops off the Edwards Plateau, and the Frio on the open plains. However, the

Nueces-Frio area still had few settlers. Even when Texas won its independence from Mexico in 1836, the Nueces remained largely unsettled. It was simply too dry and too dangerous.

Bad Old Days of the Nueces Strip

Texas claimed the Rio Grande as border; Mexico claimed the Nueces. The area between the two rivers became known as the Nueces Strip. Both countries invaded it, but neither controlled it or settled it—it was even more dangerous and just as dry. It became another border no-man's-land. Even though, as noted, the border dispute was officially settled by the 1848 Treaty of Guadalupe Hidalgo ending the Mexican War, it was not until the mid-1870s that the Nueces Strip was tamed by a company of Texas Rangers under Capt. Leander H. McNelly, as chronicled by George Durham in *Taming the Nueces Strip.*

The primary problem was Juan Nepomuceno (Cheno) Cortinas, an intelligent and well-organized Mexican-born outlaw who spent much of his time raiding Texas ranches in the Nueces Strip, stealing nearly a million head of Texas cattle between 1859 and 1875, when the rangers were called in. On orders from Governor Richard Coke, a special force of roughly thirty men (the number varied from time to time) took on the task of bringing law and order to the Strip. Using what today would be considered lawless, brutal tactics, McNelly's rangers got the job done.

The Nueces Strip was an exceptional case requiring special treatment. On more than one occasion the rangers actually invaded Mexican territory. As Walter Prescott Webb observes in the foreword to Durham's book, "They justified everything they did, including the unvarying execution of prisoners *thought* to be from a foreign country" (my emphasis). Most of these foreign prisoners were, of course, Mexican, but some were American. Although many died without any kind of trial, the Nueces Strip became livable for ordinary people.

The taming of the Strip evokes another event in the history of South Texas, the Nueces River, and the Texas Rangers, an episode that occurred a generation later at the turn of the century. Those who have seen the excellent movie *The Ballad of Gregorio Cortez,* starring Edward James Olmos, or read *With His Pistol in His Hand* by Americo Paredes will know the story.

Gregorio Cortez was a simple Mexican vaquero who killed a Karnes County sheriff in a confusing accident precipitated by an interpreter's misunderstanding. Accused of stealing a horse he'd actually bought, Cortez shot the sheriff in self-defense after the sheriff had shot Cortez's brother. Then Cortez led a chase to the border during which he first walked more than a hundred miles, generally away from the border, then rode three different horses for more than four hundred miles, crossing several South Texas rivers including the Nueces near Cotulla.

Cortez's entire family was incarcerated; any Mexican found in the area of the chase was brutalized as a possible member of the "Gregorio Cortez Gang" (which never existed), and Cortez eventually served twelve years in prison. He was pardoned by Governor O. B. Colquitt in 1913, moved to revolutionary Mexico for a time, and died in 1916 at the age of forty-one in Anson. Even before his death, Cortez had became a folk hero along the Mexican border where the *corrido* (folk ballad) about his exploits is still sung.

In the generations since Gregorio Cortez, the Nueces valley from its Edwards Plateau origins to its discharge into Corpus Christi Bay, has changed. While it still grows good crops of mesquite and pricklypear and continues to fatten cattle as well as sheep and goats, some of the flat land has been irrigated for crops. Oil and gas discoveries have decorated the landscape with storage tanks, refineries, and Texas grasshoppers. Two major reservoirs in the watershed—Coke Canyon Lake on the lower Frio and Lake Corpus Christi on the lower Nueces itself—provide new recreational opportunities.

Retired Texas Parks and Wildlife fisheries biologist Ernest G. Simmons in an unpublished document calls the Nueces a "sometimes" river: "Sometimes it has water in it, sometimes it doesn't. Sometimes it is beautiful, sometimes it's rather unattractive. Sometimes it is fresh; sometimes it is salty—this is a highly variable stream." He recalls aborting a canoe trip with a group of Boy Scouts because some of the boys got sick, "possibly from contaminated water." But Simmons also reports "the privilege of fishing some of the deep isolated pools" in a highly variable stream.

Rising in northern Real County not far from its tributary Frio, the Nueces runs clear over a limestone bottom pitted with deeper pools. Spring-fed and lined with cypress trees, the river offers canoeing possibilities, although Nolen and Narramore fail to include it in their book on Texas rivers and rapids, probably because it has few public access points. When it has enough water to canoe, it also has enough rapids to challenge good paddlers. Its west fork, which begins in Edwards County, offers similar scenery and recreational possibilities.

The West Fork joins the main Nueces northwest of Uvalde, then it all but disappears into its bed, apparently to recharge the aquifer. For the next hundred miles, running now with perennial flow through private ranch lands, it has good fishing in deep pools if you can gain legal access. The Sabinal, which enjoys a lively life of its own in the Hill Country, joins the Frio between Uvalde and Pearsall. The Lost Maples of Texas lie along its headwaters in Bandera County.

Water quality on the lower Nueces hasn't always been the best, even before the oil and gas boom and more recent assaults on the natural environment. But its upper reaches and its tributaries flowing out of the Edwards Plateau west of San Antonio produce cool, clear, clean water. I remember hearing about the clarity of the Frio River, a major Nueces tributary, from Myrtle Bell, then my boss at the Austin Recreation Department in the mid-1950s and now an old friend. She said the water in the Frio at Concan was "so clear you can see the hair on your toes in five feet of water." I was impressed and looked forward to seeing it for myself.

I'd missed a great opportunity to see it when my high school senior class spent a week at Garner State Park just after graduation. A summer job starting immediately meant I had to forgo the experience of a lifetime, a week at Garner. It wasn't until I'd been drafted into the army during the Korean War years later and gone through basic training that I finally saw the Frio for myself, driving home from Fort Bliss in El Paso. I'd driven as far as Uvalde on my first day of leave, and when I awoke in a cheap motel and began to study my road map, I realized I was within striking distance of the Frio. I drove the twenty-something miles after breakfast to discover the clear water of the frigid Frio, which became one of my favorite rivers.

Several years after my brief army career, I visited the Frio again, this time on my way back home to Andrews in the Permian Basin, where I served as director of a youth center. I'd just spent Thanksgiving weekend participating in a Texas Folk Dance Camp on another cypress-lined Hill Country river, and I felt the need to visit the Frio again. Besides, it was on my shortest route home. It was as clear as I'd remembered it, and cold in late November, the hardwoods still bright with autumn leaves and the cypress trees shedding their golden needles, as lovely a sight as I've seen in Texas.

The Nueces on the National Stage

In the mid-1970s, this beautiful country surrounding the headwaters of the Frio and Nueces, more sheep and goat country than cattle country, became the setting for one of the more notorious moments of national insight into a negative aspect of the Texas psyche: a minority attitude, widespread in Texas, that certain people are above the law, that they can ignore the law with impunity, that laws are for others, the mental set that says "I'll select the laws that apply to me and ignore the others." The issue was aerial shooting on the Nueces of bald and golden eagles, both protected under federal law.

As a columnist for the *High Country News,* an environmental newspaper now published in Colorado but at that time edited in Wyoming where I was living, I had been researching, both in the library and in the field, predator control practices in the West. The Caine Report, published in 1969 I believe, was the result of a congressionally mandated study of the effectiveness of predator control as practiced by the U.S. Fish and Wildlife Service. As a nation we were spending millions of dollars annually to kill coyotes, cougars, rodents, and numerous other wild creatures. Members of Congress wanted to know if the practice was cost-effective. The Caine Report had found that predator control was not only a waste of money—a kind of subsidy to the sheep, goat, and cattle industries—but also that it was biologically unsound.

Three separate times during the last half-century, Congress has asked for studies of federal predator control programs; each time the report has been the same, and each time it has been ignored. The federal government still subsidizes ranchers by providing predator control on public as well as private lands. Such programs have led to the near extinction of the black-footed ferret and have killed millions of nontarget animals, including numerous domestic pets. The programs still make no sense.

I had come under the influence of Adolph Murie, a wildlife biologist who lived in Jackson Hole and who had written *The Wolves of Mount McKinley* and *The Coyote in Yellowstone,* two ecological studies of predatory species and their relationships to the animals on which they live. We met frequently to discuss many wildlife matters; he served as my mentor as I wrote a series of articles on predator control for *High Country News* that found their way into the *Congressional Record.* Shortly after my articles appeared, a Wyoming sheep rancher had been discovered poisoning eagles, but before he'd been brought to trial, he had died in an automobile accident. There was no test case to support federal laws protecting eagles.

Then a few years later, in 1975, the test case came in Real County, Texas. "Out on the range, where no one can see, the varmint haters have it all their own way" (xv), wrote Donald G. Schueler in *Incident at Eagle Ranch.* Highly regarded ranchers, corrupt elected officials, and go-along bureaucrats were implicated in the illegal killing of bald and golden eagles, which were being shot from aircraft, both fixed-wing airplanes and helicopters. The first observation of this activity was made by a ranch manager near "two shallow crossings of the Nueces River" (3).

While there were arrests and ultimately convictions, the real perpetrators pretty well got off scot-free. But the incident at Eagle Ranch briefly focused the eyes of the nation on Real County and on the illegal practices of a few of its leading citizens. It led to greater protection for the eagle through closer scrutiny of Animal Damage Control within the Fish and Wildlife Service. It seems ironic that the mascot of nearby Leakey High School athletic teams is, yes, the eagle.

In his book Schueler notes—and my own observations in the Texas Hill Country bear him out—that "the phenomenon of investment buying of ranch lands has reached epidemic proportions. . . . The motivation in many cases is tax write-offs on long-term investments; meanwhile, cattle and game ranching pays the taxes" (130), another kind of government subsidy. His point is that "the older order is changing," and the people "used to having their own ways," who "detest government handouts even while they accept their share of them" (131), are giving way grudgingly to what Schueler calls the New People, who are taking over. Like the old gray mare, the old Nueces sheep and goat range ain't what it used to be.

The Lower Nueces

Nueces tributaries provide much of the water for the lower river. The Leona flows into the Frio, as do two Live Oak creeks, one heading west of Hondo, the other heading west of Pearsall. The Atascosa ("boggy"), which begins near Devine southwest of San Antonio, joins the Frio immediately below Choke Canyon Lake, a few miles above the confluence of the Frio with the Nueces. The old cowtown of Three Rivers, obviously named for this juncture, caters to ranchers and recreationists and has joined the petrochemical age with a refinery.

The Atascosa is lined with treasure trees, ancient live oaks that have treasure signs carved into their bark. Mallory Franklin, "the Singing Turtle" who lived for many years near Poteet, told the story of meeting a horseback traveler who asked about a grave with an iron cross near one of the old oaks. Mallory told him where to find the grave, then grew suspicious, and the next day visited the site himself. He found a freshly dug hole in the ground where the grave had been, not as big as a coffin but big enough to reveal the outline of a smaller box, but both the box and the iron cross were gone. There were all kinds of buried treasure stories, many of which J. Frank Dobie recorded (this was his country), and much digging occurred along the banks of the Atascosa, the Frio, and the Nueces.

El Camino Real, the old road between northern Mexico and San Antonio, crossed the Atascosa near Poteet. Parties in the early days often camped by the river, a source of fresh water after a long day of crossing the semiarid region. To keep their family treasures safe, should they be attacked by Indians or bandits, people often buried valuables overnight, digging them up when they continued their journey the next day. If they were attacked but escaped, they could return later to collect their property when it was safer to do so. However, there might be no one left to retrieve the buried goods.

Mallory's daughter Analyn Franklin Gilbreath, wife of my old Hardin-Simmons college buddy Billy Gilbreath, a retired science teacher who lives in Midland, shared with me some stories from her father. Analyn tells me that her father ran away from home at twelve and became an excellent horseman who wandered the West from the Mexican border to Wyoming and Montana, knew Cheyenne and Lakota Indians, joined a wild west show, and trained horses for a circus. His daughter, Sammy Franklin, tells more.

Living outdoors most of his life, Mallory learned to observe the natural world and became something of a weather prophet. He got his nickname from a story a reporter wrote about him. In an extensive interview, the reporter from a San Antonio newspaper kept digging for Mallory's secret, which was no secret at all but simply a matter of having observed weather patterns over a lifetime of living in the open. Finally, in exasperation, Mallory confided to the reporter, "You see, I have this turtle that sings, and it tells me what the weather's going to do." The reporter bought into the story and used it in his feature, but all of the locals understood that it was a tall tale. Ever afterward, Mallory was known as the Singing Turtle. His weather predictions were featured for years on a San Antonio radio station.

So well known was he that during the big drought in the 1950s he'd often receive mail asking his advice about the weather: "I can afford one more planting. Had I better wait 'til next year or plant now?" Mallory felt a great responsibility to the people who put so much trust in him and worried a good deal about the drought. I wonder what he'd have had to say about the El Niño year of 1998.

Analyn told me of growing up along the Atascosa, "a small river, just a creek, really, with willows growing close to the water." She remembers once seeing something strange, a willow covered with a mass of writhing water moccasins that began falling into the water as she and her sister approached. She told me of mussels in the river ("we never thought to eat them or look for pearls") and of eating wild grapes and pecans that grew along the stream. "It was a great place to grow up, and the cow community was so close-knit that we knew everyone in the neighborhood," she said.

The Nueces remains largely cattle country even today, but the livestock industry has been augmented by oil and gas and by tourism at state parks: Choke Canyon Reservoir, Lake Corpus Christi, and Garner. Garner State Park in the Hill Country was developed by the Civilian Conservation Corps during the 1930s. Lake Corpus Christi, created in 1935 after an earlier dam had failed, was also improved by the CCC crews during the Great Depression.

Choke Canyon Reservoir, created in the 1970s by damming the Nueces River at a narrow canyon or "choke" point, covers twenty-six thousand acres. Several park units have been developed in and adjacent to a wildlife management area, where native species of birds and animals may have lost some of their natural habitat but they've also lost some of their native shyness. It's a good place to see wildlife and catch fish and the most westerly site in the state to see alligators. It boasts nearly two hundred species of birds and half a dozen species of catchable fish. A few miles below the reservoir lies the little-known Lipantitlan State Historical Park near the Nueces, built by the Spanish in 1728 near a Lipan Apache village of that name and used by various forces through 1842.

Upstream at Chaparral Wildlife Management Area near Artesia Wells (off IH 35), three species of endangered reptiles live: the Texas tortoise, the Texas horned lizard, and the Texas indigo snake. Two dozen more reptiles, eleven migrating warblers, and six kinds of owls live here too, along with deer, javelina, feral hogs, and other wild creatures typical of South Texas. Daugherty Wildlife Management Area adjacent to Choke Canyon Reservoir has similar wildlife and birds, including the black-bellied tree duck and crested caracara, a noble looking raptor sometimes called the Mexican eagle.

Welder Wildlife Refuge at Sinton northeast of the Nueces, a privately owned reserve, has recorded 380 species of birds, 1,400 plant species, 55 species of mammals, and 55 species of amphibians and reptiles. White-tailed hawks, common south of the border all the way to Argentina, are found in the open country of South Texas, the only place in the United States where they are common. Mustang Island protects Corpus Christi Bay, into which

41. A stretch of the lower Nueces shows some of the pecan trees for which the river was named.

the Nueces River flows. Mustang Island State Park lies in the middle of a typical barrier island, a mix of shore and sand dunes, of freshwater marsh and saltwater lagoon. Copano Bay State Fishing Pier is an old causeway, breached to allow boat traffic to pass through. It has been closed to vehicle traffic and opened as a fishing pier.

From its Hill Country origins and its clean, clear tributaries to its saltwater meeting with the Gulf, the Nueces flows through the core of South Texas, capturing virtually every stream that produces enough water to flow. A few South Texas rivers flow directly to the Gulf and a few flow to the Rio Grande, but this is dry country that counts the Nueces as its major river, an important axis of its history and its future. The riches of the river and its riparian woodland are all the more a source for celebration in a region where the surrounding terrain is so sparse and demanding.

The Mythical Pecos

LOCATION: *West Texas, the Trans-Pecos*
NAME: *Numerous suggestions, none ascertained*
CITIES: *Pecos, Fort Stockton*
IMPOUNDMENTS: *Red Bluff, Amistad (on the Rio Grande)*
TRIBUTARIES: *Toyah Creek*
RECREATION: *Fishing, canoeing, swimming, rock hounding*
WATERSHED: *33,000 square miles*
DISCHARGE: *Largely used for irrigation*
LENGTH: *926 miles, roughly 650 miles in Texas*
PUBLIC LANDS: *Balmorhea State Park, Fort Lancaster State Historical Park, Devil's River State Natural Area, Seminole Canyon State Historical Park, Amistad National Recreation Area*
FEATURES: *Horsehead Crossing, Langtry (Judge Roy Bean's Jersey Lilly Saloon and Law West of the Pecos)*

THE PECOS RIVER, better known in myth than in reality, demarcates an entire region of Texas known as the Trans-Pecos. It includes all of West Texas south and west of the Pecos River, an area of thirty thousand square miles—larger than several eastern states—containing all of Texas' true mountains in semiarid rangeland dominated by the livestock industry, with oil and gas interests and some limited irrigated farming.

Pecos Bill, a legendary cowboy who sometimes rode a mountain lion (once he rode a cyclone *without a saddle*) and used a rattlesnake for a whip, may be known more widely than the fact that he was the literary creation of Edward O'Reilly writing in the *Century* magazine (1923). Supposed to have been weaned on moonshine, he grew up among coyotes (now where did they get any moonshine?) along the Pecos River in Texas and rode a horse named WidowMaker. The popular mind has absorbed the character and has been building on him ever since, driving him west to Hollywood. He even appeared on a U.S. postage stamp in the mid-1990s.

Stories of Judge Roy Bean's "Law West of the Pecos" appear throughout tall-tale and Texas humor literature, but the mythic judge, pudgy and profane, is based on a real character, who became justice of the peace in the tiny town of Langtry on the Rio Grande, near the mouth of the Pecos. Born in Kentucky, Bean (1825–1903) spent the Civil War years in San Antonio, where he married Virginia Chávez, a teenager at the time, who bore four children before divorcing him.

Bean participated in the freighting business during the Civil War, hauling cotton to Mexico. Later he kept a saloon in San Diego, where his brother was mayor. Roy Bean had to leave town after a knife scrape. He opened the Jersey Lilly Saloon near the confluence of the Pecos with the Rio Grande during the railroad-building boom of the early 1880s, and was shortly thereafter appointed justice of the peace. Not always sober, he frequently dispensed frontier justice in his barroom, sometimes protecting his wayward son Sam from the full enforcement of the law. While the Pecos River gave the judge his title, he actually lived nearer the Rio Grande at the town of Langtry above the canyons.

Perhaps his greatest claim to fame arose when he staged the 1896 world-championship boxing match between Australian Bob Fitzsimmons and Irish champion Peter Maher in Mexico, just across the Rio Grande from Langtry. Boxing had been outlawed at the time in most of the United States and parts of Mexico, but the Law West of the Pecos hosted the illegal match on a sandbar on the south side of the river opposite the mouth of Eagle Nest Canyon.

Because its promoters had to keep the location quiet until the last minute for fear of being caught by higher authorities on both sides of the border, only 182 fans paid to see the poorly advertised fight. Other boxing fans watched from surrounding bluffs. Fitzsimmons won in a minute-and-a-half in a fight that brought brief but international notice to Langtry, to Bean, and to his brand of law west of the Pecos. One of my correspondents and sources of information on the Pecos, Charlena Vargas-Prada of Irann, writes in "Remembering the Pecos as It Was," *San Angelo Standard-Times,* Nov. 30, 1998, "my grandfather used to drink (not coffee) with Judge Roy Bean." She remembers the Pecos "when it was cleaner and wider and deeper, swimming its clear pools beneath jagged bluffs."

Long before Judge Bean found his way to the mouth of the Pecos, however, Cabeza de Vaca had crossed it on his westward trek through West Texas in 1535. Half a century later Antonio de Espejo (1583) followed it from near Santa Fe, New Mexico, into the Trans-Pecos area of Texas, calling it Río de las Vacas (river of cows) for the numerous buffalo he found along its banks. Gaspar Castaño de Sosa (1590) called it the Río Salado (salt river). It was also known as the Río Puerco (pig-like or dirty), but by 1599 Pecos had become its acknowledged name. No one knows for certain just why. *Puerco* seems too far removed from *Pecos* to have had anything to do with the naming of this desert river. Who knows?

When Juan de Oñate (1592) settled the region that came to be known as New Mexico, he brought along seven thousand horses, many of which escaped to the wild or were stolen by raiding Apaches. By 1654 Apaches north of the Pecos had horses. During the Pueblo Revolt (1680) when Pueblo peoples drove out the Spanish conquerors and attempted to eradicate everything Spanish, considerable additional numbers of horses and mules were released to the wild.

By 1700 the nomadic Comanches had become horse warriors, changing the southern plains forever. Except for annual autumn raids the Comanches made into Mexico, the Pecos River essentially marked the southwestern boundary of Comanchería, the homeland of these wide-ranging horsemen. They came to be known as the lords of the southern plains, hunting bison as far north as Kansas and raiding into central Mexico. Their territory in Texas ran from the Llano Estacado to the Gulf Coast plains, depending on the season. They often spent most of the winter in Mexico—the original snowbirds.

But it was the Apaches, upper Lipan and Mescalero, who dominated the Pecos River in Texas. Santa Fe anthropologist Curt Schaafsma believes the basic difference between Navajos and Apaches, both Athapascan-speaking tribes, is that the Navajos found a place they liked and stayed put, whereas the Apaches continued to wander, living a nomadic life. In any case, between Indian depredations and the semiarid condition of the country along the Pecos, this region remained largely unsettled and rarely traveled until the latter years of the nineteenth century.

Where the West Begins

Loving County, along the Pecos adjacent to the New Mexico state line, is not only the least populated county in Texas even today; it is the least populated in the whole United States south of Canada. The county was created in 1887 but not organized until 1931, the last county in Texas to form a local government.

Like the Canadian River that flows through the Texas Panhandle, the Pecos begins in the southern Rocky Mountain range of New Mexico known as the Sangre de Cristo. A few miles northeast of the Santa Fe Ski Area, where so many Texans ski, the snowmelt from 13,102-foot Truchas Peak and 12,622-foot Santa Fe Baldy help form the Pecos River, a mountain stream well-known for fine trout fishing and spectacular scenery.

It runs south out of the Pecos Wilderness, then turns southeast for a hundred miles to Fort Sumner, where the Navajo people were held captive for four years (1864–68) and where Billy the Kid was killed (1879). From Fort Sumner the Pecos flows primarily south past Roswell and Artesia to Carlsbad, where it turns southeast again as it moves into Texas through a reservoir. Roughly 70 percent of its total 926-mile length lies in the Lone Star state, where today it flows not into the Rio Grande proper but into Amistad Reservoir, a major impoundment on the Rio Grande.

Through stream piracy and headward erosion, the Pecos River, which embraces the western edge of the Llano Estacado and defines its southern extremity, has separated the Llano from its geological connection to the southern Rockies. This massive formless feature commonly called the Staked Plain was created by sediments eroded from the Rocky Mountains and deposited in an ancient shallow sea. Rain falling on the Llano, which is topped with a layer of caliche largely impervious to water, runs off rather than soaking in, a major reason that the underlying Ogallala Aquifer recharges so slowly.

The Pecos River has supplied drinking water for wildlife, humankind, and livestock—prehistorically, historically, and in modern times. Flowing through the driest part of Texas, its alkaline waters sustained life even though it became infamous for its unpleasant taste, so salty and foul smelling that only the thirstiest could tolerate it. The Pecos became famous too for its dangerous crossings, which presented the combined risks of shifting quicksand, swift and curious currents, steep banks, and Indian ambushes.

The river's reputation as a gateway to the West did not evolve until the California Gold Rush (1849–50) created a demand for a quick route to the west coast. U.S. Army Brevet Capt. John Pope, for whom Pope's Crossing was named, began exploring the Pecos in the early 1850s and drilling wells in an attempt to find water sweet enough to sustain people; that crossing is now inundated by Red Bluff Reservoir on the Texas–New Mexico state line.

So negative was the historical attitude toward the Pecos that the term *pecos swap* meant a theft, and the expression *to pecos* someone meant to kill him and throw his body into the river. Charles Goodnight called the Pecos River country the graveyard of the cowman's hopes. It was Goodnight, along with Oliver

Loving, who, pioneered a major route through this dry region in the mid-nineteenth century. Loving was wounded soon afterward by Indians in New Mexico, and when he died of gangrene from his wounds, Goodnight took Loving's body back to Weatherford for burial, perhaps the source of Larry McMurtry's similar story in *Lonesome Dove.* Cattlemen driving herds to market or to new ranges farther west and north made good use of the Goodnight-Loving Trail.

Crossings

Many military and civilian travelers used the route during the next few decades, but they all dreaded the Pecos crossings and the long dry treks through the desert to reach the Pecos. The trail west ran from the headwaters of the Middle Concho to the Pecos and beyond, an arduous three-day waterless trek through high, dry Castle Gap to Horsehead Crossing. Many travelers failed to survive the long overland haul: they either ran out of water before they reached the Pecos or succumbed to Comanche attack, occasionally at the river crossing itself. Even when they reached the Pecos safely, the alkaline water, especially at low river levels, often caused major gastrointestinal problems and in extreme circumstances even led to death.

Horsehead Crossing became notorious for several reasons. Named for the numerous horse skulls at the crossing, it lies on the Pecos River a few miles north of present-day Girvin. If livestock driven west across this long dry route drank too much too quickly, the animals often died from the salty water. Others were trampled to death in their hell-for-water rush; some even drowned when the river was high or they were crowded into the current by other cattle crazy for water. The river's high banks and the short but dense surrounding vegetation, which hid the river until the cattle were on its brink, added to the complexity of this ford on the Pecos, probably the best known historically if the least visited today, but only one of several famous Pecos River crossings.

Patrick Dearen, a western writer living in Midland, knows the Trans-Pecos as well as Thad Sitton knows the Neches and other East Texas rivers. Dearen has written several good books on the Pecos River country: *Crossing Rio Pecos,* which documents more than a dozen famous crossings (nine major ones, seven minor ones), *A Cowboy on the Pecos, Portraits of the Pecos Frontier,* and *Castle Gap and the Pecos Frontier.*

In the fall of 1997, retired Midland science teacher Billy Gilbreath and I stopped to meet Dearen and to learn how to find Horsehead Crossing. I'd read Dearen's *Crossing Rio Pecos,* and I wanted to talk to the man who knows so much about the river that defines this dry region. "There's no one spot," Dearen told me. "It kept changing. You can see where the trail comes in, but it spreads out at the river." Dearen pointed out that the Pecos was a faster-flowing stream in the early days before irrigation took so much water out of the river.

Gilbreath and I drove south to Crane, then west to Grandfalls (what were the grand falls like?). Following Dearen's directions and State Highway 11 downstream paralleling the Pecos, we saw the faint sign to Horsehead Crossing and followed the road to the river. We also found a large bullsnake in the middle of the gravel road, pretending it was a rattler.

After photographing the snake and the crossing from several points of view, we spent a while looking it over, trying to figure out what had happened here. We could see Castle Gap in the distance, could imagine the long dry treks across that waterless wasteland. The water was cool and clear that November day, but we didn't sample it. Several parties of locals visited the crossing during our stay, having a picnic, skipping rocks on the still surface of the quiet river, exploring the vicinity for signs of the old trail, which we failed to find.

Another famous Pecos passage, Lancaster Crossing, once known as Indian Ford, lay on the military road between San Antonio and El Paso. Named for nearby Fort Lancaster, which had been established in 1855 as part of the military defense against Indians, the ford saw the coming of camels to the Southwest. When Secretary of War Jefferson Davis, who later became president of the Confederacy, ordered the experimental use of the exotic ships of the desert in West Texas, the camel train stopped overnight at Fort Lancaster (July 1857). They crossed the Pecos, watered at the crossing—they also watered at nearby Independence Creek—and continued on their way to explore the Big Bend country. Fort Lancaster little deterred the Apaches, who continued to raid throughout the Pecos River watershed and beyond.

I first saw the Pecos at night in the spring of 1953 on my way to basic training camp at Fort Bliss near El Paso. I saw it from a bridge, with moonlight reflecting off its shimmering waters. As a young draftee on my way by bus to two years in the U.S. Army during the Korean War, I crossed the Pecos by means of the Old High Bridge.

On two subsequent leaves, I headed home to Central Texas and got a better look at the Pecos by daylight, crossing it by that same bridge on U.S. 90 shortly before the flood of 1954 destroyed it. That same flood destroyed

Charlena Vargas-Prada's family home and guest ranch. In a heavy rainstorm similar to the 1998 storm that flooded Del Rio, the Pecos River in its deep canyon rose *ninety-six feet* overnight, blasting the bridge from its foundation. Traffic was detoured for months over the old low-water bridge at Pandale Crossing many miles upstream, the launch site for canoe trips on the lower Pecos and also the take-out for a John Graves canoe trip that started upstream at the Chandler Ranch, according to Charlena Vargas-Prada.

The Gorge and the Dam

That was well before the damming of the Rio Grande backed Amistad Reservoir eighteen miles into the spectacular lower gorge of the Pecos River, drowning numerous paleo-Indian sites. The dam was completed in 1969. When I stopped at the new high bridge over the drowned Pecos in November, 1997, I found hundreds of black and turkey vultures roosting on the bridge girders. They seemed to me a symbolic bow to the dead river, which offers enough fish carcasses and drowned rodents to keep the carrion eaters interested. Before the dam was built, catfish up to eighty-six pounds were caught in the Pecos.

In an insightful recent article in *Audubon* magazine, Marc Reisner, author of *Cadillac Desert,* points out that generally speaking, "dam building has been a potently disruptive ecological force" (60). His article outlines a contemporary trend to tear out environmentally inappropriate dams. "In a time of environmental enlightenment," he continues, "the economics of water and watersheds are beginning to turn upside down—or, if you prefer, right side up" (60).

All natural lakes and artificial impoundments or reservoirs, by their very nature, are dying, as I learned decades ago in a basic geology course. They fill with evaporites, vegetation, silt, and sand; or the barrier that creates them, whether natural or man-made, eventually erodes away; or they ultimately lose their source of water. We're addressing geological process here, time and the river flowing, carrying dissolved, organic, and inorganic materials, and eroding away solid stone. The river dissolves some of it, abrades more of it, frost-heaves a tiny bit during extreme cold augmented by severe temperature variations from frosty night to high-heat midday, and violently hacks away at it during flash floods and sudden storms. Plants and animals participate both in deposition, when they die and defecate, and in erosion, when they dig dens and scramble about the landscape, shifting rock rubble and forming trails.

42. The new high bridge crosses the Pecos River on U.S. Highway 90 east of Langtry (note vultures in flight).

Human activity, of course, has even more impact: building roads, damming rivers, bulldozing landscapes, and destroying natural cover through plowing and overgrazing the range. Nature has a means to prevent overpopulation of wildlife and overgrazing by livestock: predators. But as human beings have decimated predator populations to protect both wildlife and domestic stock, the range has deteriorated. Too few ranchers seem to realize that five jackrabbits eat as much grass as one sheep and that predators enhance the health of the land and the wildlife. We continue to upset nature's balance through thoughtless and self-centered activities like predator control.

Ranchers and ranch managers who live on the land are generally pretty good stewards, but since so many Texas ranches have become tax write-offs, fewer and fewer ranchers actually live on the land and see what goes on day by day. Many make more money today by leasing their lands for hunting or birding than they do from livestock. Ecotourism and nonconsumptive outdoor recreation, however, have begun to change the way some owners view their land. They are learning to leave it alone to revert to its natural qualities and are even beginning to enhance these.

As a species, we too often fail to recognize or respect natural processes and the results of human actions. Thoughtful people today often question the plowing of the Great Plains, an activity that led to the Dust Bowl in the 1930s. Only recently have we begun to understand the patterns in nature that affect our own lives and to pay attention to the impacts of collective human actions. We seemed to believe that technology could solve any problem, that we could forever abuse any natural system with impunity, that we could dominate nature, ignore its most basic patterns. Not until the hole in the ozone layer began to be felt in profound ways did we respond, perhaps too little and too late. Not until there is crisis do we begin to think beyond our own special interests and realize that everything really *is* connected to everything else. After the El Niño year, we pay more attention to discussion of large-scale global warming.

With the attitude that technology will save us from ourselves, we have destroyed the planet's ability to renew itself in certain ways: free-flowing streams can no longer cleanse themselves of the inorganic poisons we have created through our technology. In some areas even our drinking water, one

43. Turkey vultures and black vultures roost on rocks above the drowned Pecos River at the Pecos Arm of Amistad Reservoir.

of the vital ingredients of life, is no longer safe enough to sustain us. Charlena Vargas-Prada writes in "Remembering the Pecos as It Was," *San Angelo Standard-Times,* Nov. 30, 1998, "My river is plagued by pollution, fought over by farmers, ranchers, and environmental groups, choked by salt cedar, littered with aluminum and styrofoam artifacts, visited periodically by algae blooms and fish kills."

Southwest of the little hamlet of Pandale, where El Paso novelist Cormac McCarthy's two runaway boys, John Grady Cole and Lacey Rawlins, cross the Pecos on horseback in *All the Pretty Horses,* the river flows across shallow bedrock limestone shelves. A bend below it enters its canyon course to the Rio Grande. At the point where a new bridge was under construction when I last visited the crossing the winter of 1997–98, the Pecos flows clear and cold from upstream springs after its tortuous path across some of the most desolate lands in Texas. Here it passes through a landscape covered with lechuguilla, agave, mesquite, catclaw acacia, pricklypear, and sotol.

Not that such a landscape doesn't have its own special beauty: the Pecos River waters a subtle riparian habitat where many songbirds thrive along with quail and doves, roadrunners and shrikes, raptors and occasional ducks. The limestone hills squeeze the valley between long rocky fingers that offer ideal javelina and mule deer habitat. During hunting season this relatively barren landscape finds favor with hunters.

At the Pandale Crossing the river's flow is strong with new water from more springs and from Independence Creek. Isolated and off the tourist track on a long, dusty road, this crossing nonetheless had several visitors when I was there, on the last weekend of November, and not all were deer hunters. Many were families out for a Sunday drive. I met Ken Gully, who told me a story from the mid-1950s when, because the Old Pecos High Bridge had washed away, the main highway detoured through Pandale and across this Pecos River ford.

Gully told me that H. J. W. (Henry) Mills owned the Pandale store in those days and maintained a bumper gate, a swinging gate across the road to keep livestock in or out. It would open when a car bumped it lightly, then swing back into place. A detoured easterner came by in a big fancy car and stopped at the gate, puzzled at the apparent barrier. He asked Mills, who had been watching, what to do. Mills said, "Just bump it, and it'll open." The fellow backed up and, with a running start, hit the gate a powerful blow, tearing it loose from its pivot point, and he went roaring down the gravel road dragging the mangled gate.

44. Water ripples over limestone ledges at Pandale Crossing on the Pecos River.

Also known as Bed Rock Ford, the Pandale Crossing is the launch site for river trips running the lower canyon-bound stretch of the Pecos. This multiday river trip, one of the most isolated in the state, is a popular favorite with canoeists from several surrounding states, who often run it in late fall or early winter. The sixty-mile segment offers roughly fifty miles (depending on reservoir levels at Amistad) of rocky rapids and long pools, major archeological sites, and scenic beauty in a remote wilderness. Too shallow for rafts and too narrow in places, it begs for open canoes to run the eighteen rapids, only a few of which are serious enough to suggest scouting.

The river enters the canyon almost immediately below the ford for the sixty-mile paddle to a take-out on Lake Amistad. Nolen and Narramore describe the trip in *Rivers and Rapids* as running through an extremely remote, rough, unforgiving area. Pat Dearen, who has also made the run, counts it as one of his most memorable experiences. Albuquerque canoeist Joe Butler, who grew up in Dallas and for many years lived in Houston and paddled with the canoe clubs there, loves it too, but he recalls massive mats of floating cane blocking the route on the reservoir after major floods had scoured the Pecos shorelines.

In their excellent book, *The Lower Pecos River,* Louis F. Aulbach and Jack

Richardson note that "the area around the confluence of the Pecos and the Rio Grande has more recorded archeological sites per square mile than any other place in Texas" (22). This confluence, now drowned by Amistad Reservoir, marks the center of an ancient paleo-Indian civilization that left numerous pictographs (images painted on the canyon walls in coral snake colors of red, black, and yellow) and petroglyphs (images carved into the stone surfaces).

Seminole Canyon State Historical Park northwest of Del Rio celebrates a major paleo-Indian site that represents what was drowned along the lower Pecos by Amistad Reservoir—similar to the Anasazi sites in Glen Canyon that were lost to Lake Powell in southern Utah. Glen Canyon, known as "the place no one knew" well enough to save it from the dam, had more Anasazi ruins than any comparable site in North America. Indeed, no one really knew it except the ancient people who had lived there, and they no longer communicate with the modern world now that their sacred landscape has been inundated.

Parks, Wildlife, and Tired Towns

Through much of Trans-Pecos Texas the oil boom has come and gone. Here and there it remains in Texas grasshoppers pumping endlessly, but its ruined towns—two-thirds of the businesses boarded up and empty—and the crossroads tin shacks that once were cotton gins, now opened by the wind and rusting, serve as sad testimony to the area's boom-and-bust economy. Drained of its life-giving water to irrigate poor cotton fields and sorghum patches, the Pecos in places runs more like a cane-lined ditch than a real river, until sudden heavy rains bring floods and turn unpaved roads and open fields to gumbo.

An article titled "Pecos River: River of Hard-won Dreams" by Cathy Newman in *National Geographic* (September 1993) features the Girvin Social Club, a tin-shack saloon that matches many of the buildings in the tiny town, which has certainly seen better days. Photographs of some of the paleo-Indian sites near the confluence also appear in the piece, which highlights the area's lack of reliable water. Charlena Vargas-Prada, librarian at Irann High School, grew up on the Pecos. She referred to it in "Remembering the Pecos as It Was," *San Angelo Standard-Times,* Nov. 30, 1998, as "an unlovely stream, in perspective now no more than a wide and mucky irrigation ditch in places, albeit a ditch which has achieved mythological proportions in the area of men's imagination."

My own notes for November 22, 1997, say: "The Pecos River is a sorry sight east of the town of Pecos, full of concrete debris and trash, flowing through a ditch lined with salt cedar, junked car bodies, ugly graffiti on the bridge abutments, a sadly neglected river." I note the town's elevation (2,580) and population (12,069). I note too that the sand from the sometimes dry Pecos River downstream from the town supplies the sand for 3,840-acre Monahans Sandhills State Park forty miles to the northeast.

Near the railroad tracks, Pecos has a fine historical museum, which I visited, a complex of old cowboy saloon and Orient Hotel, with a third building a block away housing an old chuck wagon representative of early ranching days. Pecos bills itself as the site of the world's first rodeo, a test of cowboy skills held on July 4, 1883—the same year that cowboys unionized and went on strike on the Canadian River in the Texas Panhandle.

Historically the Pecos River has seen impressive floods. In 1904 it spread across the plain more than a mile wide at the town of Pecos. Today, dammed and diverted to irrigate melons, cotton, and alfalfa, it trickles through the landscape, invisible from fifty feet away. So flat is the land, so minor the flow, and so dense the tamarisk (salt cedar) that you don't see the river until you are upon its banks. This plant, an exotic ornamental brought in a century ago from the Middle East, now dominates the shoreline, sucking up water.

Despite the harsh reality of its semiarid nature, the Trans-Pecos has several special places. On my first trip to the Big Bend country on the Rio Grande, I stopped at Balmorhea State Park to swim in a perfect pool with natural bottom, fed by the artesian San Solomon Springs. The forty-six-acre park four miles southwest of the town of Balmorhea is home to a unique pupfish. The Davis Mountains State Park and Old Fort Davis National Historic Site lie a few dozen miles to the southwest of Balmorhea.

Monahans Sandhills State Park is several miles northeast of the Pecos River, but as noted, the river provides the sand. Carried downstream from the mountains of New Mexico and from the fringes of the Llano Estacado, the sand settles along the Pecos floodplain in high water; then, blown by the prevailing southwest wind, it helps create the dunes characterizing the park northeast of Monahans.

The Diamond Y Springs Preserve, owned by the Texas Nature Conservancy, is one of the few remaining natural springs in the region, now that Comanche Springs and several others in the area have dried up. The preserve is home to three rare snails, an unusual plant species, and six native fish, two of them endangered species: the Leon Springs pupfish and the Pecos mos-

45. The Pecos River flows smoothly as it winds through salt cedar and tall grass near Girvin.

quito fish. This preserve also harbors numerous songbirds and raptors as well as regional wildflowers, including the rare salt-tolerant puzzle sunflower.

Guadalupe Mountains National Park now protects an area I knew before it became a park. As director of the Andrews Youth Center (1956–57), I led the Andrews Amateur Alpine Association, a group of high-school students, into the Guadalupes on several occasions. On one trip we successfully climbed Guadalupe Peak, the state's highest at 8,749 feet above sea level. On another we explored the possibilities of climbing the sheer El Capitan (8,085 feet) from the saddle between El Cap and Guadalupe Peak, but we were thwarted when one of the boys took a nasty fall that led to a successful rescue effort.

From several points along the road (U.S. 285) that roughly parallels the Pecos River between Red Bluff Lake on the Texas–New Mexico state line and the town of Pecos, you can see the distant outline of the Guadalupes from prominent El Capitan eastward. Usually there is too little water in the river for boating.

Devil's River is not a Pecos tributary, but it flows through the same harsh semiarid terrain at the junction of the Edwards Plateau with the Rio Grande north of Del Rio. Historically it did flow into the Rio Grande, a few miles below the Pecos confluence with the Rio Grande, but today it helps fill Lake Amistad. Although nowhere near as long as the Pecos, Devil's River shares with it many characteristics, and yet remains unique, a special river that until a few years ago had a reputation for hostile landowners unwilling to share its beauty with the general public.

Now, with the acquisition by the State of Texas of twenty thousand acres of riverfront land, the public has access at Devil's River State Natural Area. Visitation is limited, requiring reservations with the Texas Parks and Wildlife Department and a Texas Conservation Passport (a $50 annual ticket to all state parks and several other special places), but the experience is well worth the cost and effort. The endangered Devil's River minnow and the Concho pupfish live in the springs and river. Elf owls and endangered black-capped vireo, Merriam's canyon lizards and Texas earless lizards find the riparian habitat suitable, and wildflowers brighten the landscape many months of the year.

The Nature Conservancy of Texas has also purchased land along Devil's River. A site at Dolan Falls offers spring wildflower displays, seasonal birding with good opportunities to see black-capped vireos, and a monarch butterfly migration in mid-autumn. Along the lower Pecos Chandler Independence Creek Preserve near Sheffield harbors seventeen species of fish, including the proserpine shiner; deer, wild turkey, and predators; and raptors and a wide variety of songbirds, including—you guessed it—the black-capped vireo.

The Pecos River today flows like a shadow of its former self, deprived of its water by dams and diversions. Yet it continues to define the region, and its canyon near the Rio Grande remains imposing, despite its current status as a reservoir. Perhaps the least-known rivers in Texas outside their own neighborhood, the Pecos and Devil's rivers and their subtle wildlife and scenic splendor have been discovered by paddlers, bird-watchers, and a growing cadre of those who love the outdoors. These people have begun to make their presence known, in their use of the great outdoors as well as in the voting booth and the state capitol. Writing half a century ago as an advocate of the delights of the Texas wilds, naturalist Roy Bedichek was a voice in the wilderness, but his voice rings louder every year.

Canadian River of the Texas Panhandle

LOCATION: *Northern Panhandle*
NAME: *Accounts conflict*
CITIES: *Borger, Canadian*
IMPOUNDMENTS: *Lake Meredith*
TRIBUTARIES: *Rita Blanca, Amarillo Creek, Red Deer Creek*
RECREATION: *Fishing, boating, shooting*
WATERSHED: *46,900 square miles in three states*
DISCHARGE: *Minimal for so large a watershed*
LENGTH: *906 miles, 225 miles across Texas*
PUBLIC LANDS: *Alibates Flint Quarries National Monument, Lake Meredith National Recreation Area, Black Kettle National Grasslands, Lake Rita Blanca State Park*
FEATURES: *Adobe Walls, Old Tascosa, XIT Ranch Headquarters*

FOR MOST OF ITS LENGTH, the Canadian River flows through states other than Texas. Much of the year it barely flows at all, and in drought years, it simply doesn't flow. Nevertheless, the Canadian is the setting for a vital part of Texas history.

The first time I saw the Canadian—in midsummer of a wet year—it ran bankfull, like a rich sorrel mare lolling in the desert sun after a rain, nibbling away at its sandy banks: a chocolate-borscht mousse gurgling and gliding, swirling along at a pace faster than I could walk, the color of the rusty car bodies used as riprap in a vain attempt to prevent inevitable erosion.

The Canadian drains 46,900 square miles of New Mexico, Texas, and Oklahoma. It starts in New Mexico; its main branch bisects the Texas Panhandle north of Amarillo and flows into Oklahoma. The north branch dips briefly into Texas, draining the northern Panhandle through streams named

Coldwater, Palo Duro, Kiowa, and Wolf, recalling its former occupants. The dry, narrow valley of the Canadian harbors few towns even today in a sparsely settled region, but events in its watershed have had important historical and cultural significance for the high plains of Texas through which it courses.

Often referred to as "Little Texas," eastern New Mexico was part of Texas until the Compromise of 1850 when the present state line was established. All of New Mexico east of the Rio Grande was once claimed by the independent nation that became the State of Texas. (A trivia question: Which state once included four present-day state capitals? Yes, the answer is Texas, which once took in Cheyenne, Denver, and Santa Fe as well as Austin.)

Eastern New Mexico and Panhandle Texas share a common history, matching climates, and similar cultures. The same Indian tribes lived here before European settlement, the Spanish initiated European invasion, and the similar terrain and climate have dictated comparable local livelihoods. Although oil and gas discoveries during the 1920s and 1930s provided an early boom, today residents of the Canadian River area still depend largely on ranching and irrigated farming, regardless of state affiliation.

Texas and New Mexico also share the major high, flat, formless landscape feature known as the Llano Estacado or Staked Plain. Reasons advanced for the name include the ideas that travelers had to drive stakes into the plain to find their way or to secure their horses; that seen from the east, the edge of the steep-edged, fortresslike high plain looks like a palisade or stockade; and that the abundant yucca stalks punctuating the plain look like stakes.

Whatever the true source of the name, the Canadian River essentially forms the northern boundary of this thirty-thousand-square-mile area of semiarid high plains (averaging between 3,000 and 4,000 feet above sea level). Characterized by fertile soil but meager rainfall and high evaporation, the area grows few crops without irrigation but offers ideal grazing for livestock, especially cattle and horses and, historically, sheep. The earliest European explorers of the Llano Estacado marveled at the native cattle, the bison or buffalo, that thrived here.

Beneath the Llano Estacado lies one of the largest, most productive aquifers in North America, the Ogallala, underlying so much of the high plains of the West: all of Nebraska, most of Kansas, and portions of South Dakota, Colorado, Oklahoma, New Mexico and Texas, including the Panhandle and the Canadian River watershed as well as the headwaters of three other Texas rivers: the Red, the Brazos, and the Colorado. The surface area of the aquifer covers a region of some seven hundred by three hundred miles, and the aquifer's capacity is 3 billion acre feet.

46. The Canadian River runs bankfull after heavy August rains near Old Tascosa.

Ogallala water supports one fifth of the nation's total irrigated cropland and 40 percent of the grain-fed beef sold on American markets. This vital aquifer of fossil water 3 million years old is being withdrawn—mined, so to speak—at 21 million acre feet a year (an acre foot is enough water to cover an acre of land to a depth of one foot). It is recharged, however, at only about 100,000 acre feet per year, because the 220,000-square-mile surface area of the aquifer has low rainfall and much of the land surface is capped with impermeable caliche, which prevents the water from percolating back into the aquifer.

The buffalo that once flourished across this vast area could have been a renewable resource, but the fossil water is a finite one. Water users have been mining this fossil water for decades. Consequently the aquifer has been dropping by as much as ten feet a year, and some areas, especially in the southern reaches of the Ogallala (the Texas Panhandle), have been so seriously depleted that irrigated farming has become less than profitable.

Spring snowmelt or summer thunderstorms may turn a dry streambed into a raging torrent. John J. (Jack) Culley observed in *Cattle, Horses, and Men* that the Canadian can "become mighty treacherous—death traps, indeed—when the red flood comes down." When it runs "normal," it braids through interlacing channels, but much of the time its riverbed in the western Panhandle is bone-dry. In the eastern Panhandle the river flows with reservoir releases from Lake Meredith.

Flowing Red across the Panhandle

The color of the Texas stretch of the Canadian is produced to a large extent by New Mexican sandstone that the river carries with it. Early names for the river derived from this characteristic; it was known as the Río Rojo, meaning "red river," and the Río Colorado. The Kiowa called it *Geoalpay,* meaning "alongside a red hill or bluff." Although the Caddo Indians lived hundreds of miles to the east, their word *Kanohatino,* meaning "red river," may be a source of the modern name, for the Canadian is as red as the Red, Colorado, or Brazos rivers. It flows through the same geological formations that have painted these other Texas rivers red.

Texas cowboy Charles Siringo (1855–1928), who spent time along the Canadian River and wrote about his experiences in *A Texas Cowboy: Fifteen Years on the Hurricane Deck of a Spanish Pony,* avers that the river was named for Canadian fur trappers, a concept also subscribed to by David Lavender, author of more than twenty books on western history and one of the most thorough, yet readable, historians of the century. Indeed, four Canadian trappers, led by Paul and Pierre Mallet, left Santa Fe to explore the river in 1740, following its south bank past the Llano Estacado. When they found that Caprock streams added to the river's flow, they built elm-bark canoes and continued their journey all the way to the Arkansas and ultimately to the Mississippi and New Orleans by boat. Another Frenchman, Pierre Vial, who lived on the Red River, blazed a trail from San Antonio to Santa Fe in the winter of 1786–87, following the headwater streams of the Red, then crossing north to the Canadian, known to the French as Rivière Rouge.

There have also been suggestions that the name Canadian came from the Spanish *cañon,* meaning "canyon," or from *cañada,* meaning "ravine," and another story suggests that early visitors believed the river ran out of Canada. *¿Quien sabe?*

The Canadian River consists of two major branches heading on the southeastern slopes of the highest mountains of northern New Mexico. Here the southern reaches of the Rocky Mountain chain, known as the Sangre de Cristo (Blood of Christ) Range, rise to elevations of more than two miles above sea level. The landscape is largely dry and forbidding, with sparse population and few towns.

The South Canadian, normally referred to simply as the Canadian River, begins in a series of small streams along the New Mexico–Colorado state line from the Sangre de Cristos east to Johnson Mesa. Southeast of Springer, New Mexico, it has carved a fifteen-hundred-foot gorge that rivals Santa Elena Canyon on the Rio Grande but reminds me more of Labyrinth Canyon on Utah's Green River with its subtle colors, convoluted course, and abandoned and entrenched meanders.

Major tributaries of the Canadian in New Mexico include East Fork Creek near Raton Pass, Vermejo River, Cimarron Creek, (which flows through Philmont Boy Scout Ranch), Mora River, Gallinas Creek and River, Conchas River, and, near the Texas border, Ute Creek. When it flows at all with Sangre de Cristo snowmelt or thunderstorm runoff, the Canadian adds its subtle sands to the entire downstream landscape.

The headwaters of Corrumpa Creek, which flows eastward through New Mexico's Kiowa National Grasslands, lie on volcanic Sierra Grande (8,720 feet), the highest peak between the Black Hills and the southern Rockies. Corrumpa Creek becomes the Beaver River as it crosses from New Mexico into Oklahoma's panhandle. Several dozen miles into the Sooner state, it dips briefly south into Texas, which is drained by Beaver River tributaries. Shortly after its return to Oklahoma, it becomes the North Canadian, paralleling the South Canadian for hundreds of miles before joining it in a reservoir, Eufaula Lake, between Muskogee and McAlester in eastern Oklahoma near their mutual confluence with the Arkansas.

While the Canadian may begin along the New Mexico–Colorado state line and flow into the Arkansas River in Oklahoma, it qualifies as a Texas river because it flows completely across Texas from one border to another as it bisects the Panhandle north of Amarillo, cutting across six counties: Oldham, Potter, Moore, Hutchinson, Roberts, and Hemphill.

The Canadian and its tributaries served as homeland for Native American people who lived along this meager flow, perhaps for as long as twelve thousand years: paleo-Indians and Panhandle Pueblos followed by Kiowa, Comanche, Southern Cheyenne, Arapaho, and even Kiowa Apaches, who followed the buffalo to these southern high plains. The river flows through a series of canyons that the Comanches knew well, for the Canadian lay in the heart of the southern Plains Indians' buffalo country. Coronado's expedition, seeking imagined riches on the Great Plains, traveled eastward across the Llano Estacado the spring of 1541, then northward, no doubt crossing the Canadian in the search for the seven cities of gold.

From Buffalo Hunting to Indian Wars

Known as *ciboleros,* early Spanish settlers in New Mexico and Pueblo Indians from the Rio Grande hunted buffalo (*cíbolo*) here. Mexicans who traded with the Comanches were commonly known as Comancheros. These Hispanic traders safely traveled the Canadian watershed, but none of them settled the Staked Plain, for this was Comanchería, traditional home of the Comanches.

Even the Comancheros had to watch their scalps, from time to time, for as buffalo became scarce and the People, as the Comanches called themselves, were pressed more severely by invading Americans, they became less friendly, especially when whites hunted buffalo in areas secured by treaty as Indian lands. Buffalo numbers plunged from an estimated 20 million in 1850 to only five hundred animals in 1890, a trend that Cheyenne warrior Yellow Wolf predicted in 1846.

While the Santa Fe Trail, which came into use in 1821, lies north and west of the Texas Panhandle, one Santa Fe trader, Josiah Gregg, pioneered a route along the Canadian River the spring of 1840. It became part of the trail between river ports in Arkansas and Santa Fe in the southern Rockies and saw extensive use during the California Gold Rush days.

Entering the Texas Panhandle today in an isolated landscape without towns, the Canadian River flows eastward through the old XIT Ranch, the name a shortening for Ten (counties) in Texas. At the U.S. Highway 385 bridge, the river passes near what would be the ghost town of Tascosa had the townsite not been given to Cal Farley in 1939 as the foundation for his now famous Boys Ranch. Farley, a world-class wrestler and successful Amarillo businessman, founded the Boys Ranch when Julian Bivins gave him the historic Tascosa courthouse and 120 acres of land to help Farley help needy boys. In the nearly sixty years since it began, Cal Farley's Boys' Ranch has grown to more than ten thousand acres and from five boys to over five hundred.

Tascosa seems to be a corruption of the Spanish *atascosa,* meaning "boggy." The old town of that name, once known as "the cowboy capital of the plains" and which Culley called "the toughest town in the Southwest," essentially became the ranch that now gives hundreds of "troubled, homeless, confused, delinquent or problem" boys, and recently a few girls, a second chance. In 1945 MGM made a movie titled *Boys Ranch,* filmed on the Canadian River site, about Farley's private helping hand for these youngsters.

This part of the river valley, site of an easy crossing, was settled by New Mexican sheepherders Casimiro Romero and Agapito Sandoval in 1876 shortly after the Comanches finally trailed to their nearby Oklahoma reservation. In fact, several Canadian River communities established in the 1870s and 1880s by New Mexican sheep ranchers were known as "plazas" rather than towns because of central squares built in the Mexican style.

Pauline Durrett Robertson's and R. L. Robertson's extensive historic research on the area is reported in *Tascosa: Historic Site in the Texas Panhandle.* According to the Robertsons, the first settlers described the Canadian as "a beautiful stream (with) no sand bars at all, . . . deep, clear, living water" (8), in which early residents caught channel catfish. Herds of buffalo still roamed the area along with antelope, deer, and wild mustangs, while beaver and muskrats lived in the river, and long-billed curlew, sharp-tailed grouse, and prairie-chickens nested on the shortgrass prairie. Then the cattle "destroyed the bushes. Trappers caught the beaver, their dams deteriorated, turning the water loose, and this altered the nature of the river," reported Jose Romero in later life (8).

The first Anglo settlers were army buddies Henry Kimball and Theodore Briggs, who had seen the Canadian River Valley on a buffalo hunt from Fort Union in 1874. Kimball settled into the Tascosa Valley as a blacksmith in 1876 near "where a big spring gushed from the side of a hill," and Briggs later settled on nearby Rico Creek. A Jewish merchant, John Cone, opened a general store in 1879 on land controlled by Romero. Several other New Mexican families from the Mora area moved into the valley, which had a predominantly Hispanic flavor by 1880, when the population approached three hundred.

A range war was to blow apart the cooperative tranquility of the valley, however. A certain Sostenes l'Archévêque, distinguished by his huge size and French, Mexican, and Indian blood, killed two Anglo sheepmen, the Casner brothers. Local Hispanic leaders brought the murderer to frontier justice, killing him, but the Casners' father and a third brother, seeking revenge, killed several local Hispanics, leading some families to head back to the relative safety of New Mexico.

At about this time, with the Canadian River country cleared of Comanches, the big cattlemen—including George Washington Littlefield and Charles Goodnight—began to move into the Panhandle, buying up the land on which the New Mexican sheepmen had grazed their sheep. Early during the settlement of the area, Goodnight and the sheepmen reached an agreement on a division of the range: the cattlemen would stay south of the Canadian and the sheepmen north of it.

While no real range war occurred, much of the Hispanic population, feeling threatened, began to move back west. All of this happened against the background of the Lincoln County War in New Mexico (1879–81). Billy the Kid hung out in Tascosa during 1877–78, but the only real shootout, known locally as the "Big Fight," occurred the spring of 1886, long after the Kid was dead.

The shootout grew out of the first attempt by cowboys to organize a union and strike for higher wages, better working conditions, and more independence. In the spring of 1883 in the Canadian River country around Tascosa, the big cattle interests began to enforce what the cowboys considered unreasonable restrictions, and Pat Garrett, who had killed Billy the Kid, went to work for the big ranchers as an enforcer. Elmer Kelton, one of Texas' best writers of western fiction, recreates the situation in his novel *The Day the Cowboys Quit.*

Several dozen cowboys were involved in the ineffectual strike, many were fired (eighty by one rancher alone); replacement cowboys were easy to hire. Some of the disgruntled cowboys began resisting the unreasonable rules (cowboys were not allowed to wear guns or keep their own cattle or horses, small cattle operations were not allowed to participate in roundups, certain brands were declared illegal). A few actually resorted to rustling. Four men died in the Big Fight, including one innocent bystander, and two were wounded. The dead men were all buried in Boot Hill Cemetery at Old Tascosa, above the Canadian River just west of town.

East of Tascosa the river jogs northeast through an impoundment known as Lake Meredith, and below the Bureau of Reclamation dam impounding this lake, the Canadian flows eastward again, passing near Black Kettle National Grassland, named for the Cheyenne chief whose small village on the Washita River was wiped out by Gen. George Armstrong Custer and the Seventh Cavalry on November 27, 1868. Black Kettle had survived a vicious attack by Colonel Chivington's volunteers on this same peaceful band of Southern Cheyenne at Sand Creek in 1864. As it flows into Oklahoma, the Canadian loops through the Antelope Hills north of another unit of Black Kettle National Grassland that surrounds the Washita Battle Site in extreme western Oklahoma.

Capt. Joel H. Eliott of Custer's command, following the Canadian River downstream, found Indian pony tracks that led to the Cheyenne village on the Washita, proof enough for Custer that Black Kettle's village harbored "hostiles." Eliott and eighteen men died in the Battle of the Washita when Custer failed to support them or to heed suggestions from Indian scouts that Elliott's command was in trouble. The Washita begins in the Texas Panhandle south of the Canadian and flows into the Canadian south of Oklahoma City.

47. The cemetery at Old Tascosa has been touched up. It contains the remains of several cowboys who pioneered the Texas Panhandle cattle industry, some of whom participated in the first cowboy labor strike.

Through Time and the Valley by Panhandle writer John Erickson gives an account of the Canadian River in its Texas crossing. Erickson documents a 140-mile horseback trek he and a friend made through the Canadian River canyons in the eastern Panhandle. Early in their trip, they stopped at Adobe Walls, the ruin of a William Bent-Ceran St. Vrain trading post built in 1842 that failed because of the Comanches' strong ties to the Comancheros from New Mexico. The ruins of the old trading post served as the site for two major battles of the Indian wars.

In 1864 Kit Carson led a party of 335 New Mexican volunteers against a combined force of Kiowa, Comanche, Cheyenne, Arapaho, and Apache Indians. The soldiers overran a small Kiowa village (176 lodges) on the Canadian River four or five miles upstream from Bent Creek, the location of Adobe Walls. What had started as a surprise attack soon became a more even match. As Carson led his troops downstream beyond the Kiowa village, they ran into several Comanche villages wintering along the Canadian River. The Indian numbers grew to thousands as hundreds of warriors from several downstream villages joined the fight. Carson wisely began "an orderly but difficult" retreat.

Hard pressed, the volunteers might very well have been overrun by the Indians and wiped out like Custer at the Little Bighorn twelve years later, had they not had two small howitzers. They escaped with the loss of only two men killed and twenty-one wounded; the Indians had sixty casualties, killed and wounded. Neither side could claim victory, but the battle discouraged Indian attacks on nearby settlers and ranchers for a brief period.

The second Battle of Adobe Walls (1874) resulted from white buffalo hunters' invading Indian territory: all lands south of the Arkansas River were off limits to whites. Hundreds of warriors, perhaps as many as a thousand, from several tribes, surrounded the small trading post that had sprung up at Adobe Walls to serve the hide hunters. A lucky accident—the breaking of a ridge pole in one of the buildings—awoke the hide hunters at 2:00 A.M. They numbered twenty-six, including Billy Dixon and Bat Masterson and one woman. Still working on repairs at dawn, they were awake when the Indians attacked. The buffalo hunters saw the attack coming and were prepared to resist.

Led by Comanche Quanah Parker—son of captive Cynthia Ann Parker and Comanche chief Peta Nocona (for whom the town of Nocona is named)—and the Kiowa medicine man Ishatai (Coyote Droppings), the consolidated Indians killed fifty-six horses, twenty-eight oxen, three white men, and a Newfoundland dog during the two-day siege. The buffalo hunters' numbers increased almost hourly, for the Indians failed to secure the surround.

Using .45 and .50 caliber Sharps rifles, accurate at a thousand yards, the buffalo hunters simply outgunned the more numerous Comanches. The Indians lost thirteen men, including one shot at 1,538 yards by Billy Dixon (they stepped it off after the battle), with many more wounded. The Panhandle Indians never again organized such a concerted attack, and within a year, the Indian wars had ended on the southern plains.

After the Indian wars and the buffalo-hunting days, Dixon settled along the Canadian for a while (1883–1904), but shortly after he married, he left the Adobe Walls neighborhood. Billy Dixon loved the area; when he established his ranch, he apparently wanted to be near the spot of his moment of celebrated marksmanship.

San Angelo–based western writer Elmer Kelton has recreated the Panhandle hide-hunter days in his novel *Slaughter*. In Lucia St. Clair Robson's *Ride the Wind*, a fictional biography of Cynthia Ann Parker, the reader sees the battles from the Comanches' perspective. Charlie Siringo mentions the battles in his *A Texas Cowboy*, which also gives details of Billy the Kid's presence along the Canadian River in Texas.

Places to Visit

Rita Blanca State Park, southwest of Dalhart and about fifty miles northwest of Lake Meredith, is Texas' northernmost state park. The 1,500-acre area at 4,000-foot elevation offers characteristic high plains vegetation in blue grama and buffalo grass. The impoundment on Rita Blanca Creek attracts wintering ducks and geese. As noted, the Bureau of Reclamation dammed the Canadian between 1962 and 1968 to create Lake Meredith. Three counties share the lake. With a storage capacity of 864,400 acre feet, it supplies water to eleven Panhandle communities, including Amarillo and Lubbock.

The reservoir and its surrounding hills are now known as Lake Meredith National Recreation Area and administered by the National Park Service. Sailing, water-skiing, scuba diving, windsurfing, power boating, jet-skiing, and fishing are all popular activities on the reservoir. Eleven campgrounds accommodate hundreds of Panhandle campers and visitors from nearby states. Incongruous as they may seem in the parched semiarid region, the sky-reflecting blue waters of Lake Meredith offer a pleasant change of scene in the Texas Panhandle.

Named for an early settler, Allie Bates, Alibates Flint Quarries National Monument lies on a promontory near the eastern lakeshore, commemorating an ancient flint chipping site used as early as 10,000 B.C. by prehistoric Indians of the Ice Age Clovis Culture, who hunted mammoths. Between 1050 and 1500 paleo-Indians lived in the site, which was used well into the nineteenth century. Littered with chips, points, drills, and scrapers as well as colorful native flint from the site, the national monument also offers good birding.

In its incision across the Texas Panhandle, the dammed Canadian River creates an important wildlife habitat around Lake Meredith. Waterfowl, wintering bald eagles, songbirds including both mountain and eastern bluebirds, golden eagles, beavers, badgers, bobcats, porcupines, skunks, raccoons, white-tailed and mule deer, pronghorns and wild turkeys all occupy the environment surrounding the dam. The downstream flow created by the impounded waters creates additional wildlife habitat in the naturally dry northern Panhandle.

Lake Marvin east of the town of Canadian is a good place to find wood ducks as well as migratory waterfowl, wild turkeys, Mississippi kites, beaver, white-tailed deer, and the elusive bobcat. Gene Howe Wildlife Management Area, a few miles east of Canadian, offers similar wildlife: spring prairie-chicken booming (the stylistic nuptial behavior of the plains grouse) draws bird-watchers from a wide area. Spectacular fall colors enhance the autumn scene.

People speculate about present Canadian River populations compared to those of the paleo-Indians or Panhandle Pueblos; some believe the ancient population may have been greater than today's. Several ghost towns lie along the Canadian; the only real town on the river itself as it crosses the Texas Panhandle is Canadian, established in 1887. Historical museums exist in Borger and Canadian—and in Canyon, south of Amarillo—to help visitors piece together the past life of the Canadian River valley on the Staked Plain.

Oil and gas discoveries beginning in the 1920s helped the northern Panhandle through the Great Depression, and postwar industry in nearby Amarillo changed the local economy forever. But despite the arrival of the twentieth century along the Canadian River, the old ways die hard. Farmers who can no longer afford to drill into the dwindling Ogallala Aquifer have joined ranchers whose grass has withered during periodic drought. Even the petroleum industry has fallen on hard times in recent decades.

Just as the river itself swings between boom and bust, between flash flood and dry bottom, the Canadian River country in the Texas Panhandle is no longer booming now as it has done from time to time in the past. But if the country is rarefied, the people of the Canadian River's sweep across the Panhandle are also determined, fitting denizens for a landscape marked by its primary river and carved into strong relief by that river as it rolls on through Oklahoma toward the Arkansas.

PART 4

Into the Gulf

San Jacinto River and Buffalo Bayou

LOCATION: *Houston and vicinity, largely north and east of the city*
NAMES: *San Jacinto for its discovery on that saint's day (August 17); Buffalo Bayou named not for bison but for abundant buffalo fish*
CITIES: *Houston, Pasadena, Deer Park, Conroe, Baytown*
IMPOUNDMENTS: *Lake Conroe, Lake Houston, Sheldon Reservoir*
TRIBUTARIES: *White Oak Bayou, Brays Bayou, Buffalo Bayou, Greens Bayou, Clear Creek*
RECREATION: *Power boating, canoeing, fishing*
WATERSHED: *3,976 square miles*
DISCHARGE: *2 million acre feet—high for so small an area*
LENGTH: *85 miles*
PUBLIC LANDS: *Lake Houston State Park, Dwight D. Eisenhower Park, Sheldon Lake State Park and Wildlife Management Area, San Jacinto Monument, San Jacinto Battlefield State Park, Battleship Texas State Historical Park, Armand Bayou Nature Center*
FEATURES: *San Jacinto Monument, Battleship Texas*

HOUSTON, TEXAS' LARGEST CITY, grew up on a network of bayous, most of them now concreted into a storm drainage system that flows into Buffalo Bayou, which serves as the upper Houston Ship Channel. It flows into the area's major river, the San Jacinto, which lies at the eastern edge of the city and accepts the polluted waters of the urban bayous. This entire complex constitutes a small watershed but, with heavy rainfall in the area, produces major discharge into Galveston Bay and the Gulf of Mexico; the Trinity River also discharges into this bay. The heavy runoff helps dilute local pollution.

Urban rivers have traditionally been badly abused, especially in larger cities, where street and highway, roof, driveway, and parking-lot runoff produces massive amounts of nonpoint-source pollution. Given the magnitude of petrochemical and other industrial development in the Greater Houston area, accepting pollution has become a way of life for many dwellers of this city named for General Sam Houston. He was the man who commanded the ragtag Texas army that won independence from Mexico in a brief but decisive battle at the very edge of this great metropolis. A piece of Texas history lies at the confluence of Buffalo Bayou with the San Jacinto River.

The San Jacinto begins with an East Fork in San Jacinto County and a West Fork in Walker County. They merge in a reservoir in northeast Harris County, Lake Houston, created by a dam on the main San Jacinto below their traditional confluence. The West Fork is also dammed northwest of Conroe to form Lake Conroe. Below Lake Houston, the San Jacinto is joined by Buffalo Bayou, which, by the time it reaches the river, has collected water from most of Houston's other major bayous.

Confluence of Texas Independence

The 1836 Battle of San Jacinto that ended Texas' War of Independence was fought at the confluence of these two streams, now commemorated by the San Jacinto Battlefield State Historical Park and the San Jacinto Museum of History. Nearby is moored the modern battleship *Texas,* another state historic site. A 570-foot-high masonry obelisk topped with a gigantic lone star is known as the San Jacinto Monument; it marks the site of the battle that earned Texas her independence from Mexico, its base decorated with names of those who fought here.

That battlefield, one of Texas' most sacred places, is described in Marquis James's Pulitzer Prize–winning biography of Sam Houston, *The Raven,* as "lying at the tip of a point of lowland where Buffalo Bayou flowed into the San Jacinto River" (245). The Texans set up in an oak woods along the bayou near its mouth, within sight of Lynchburg, "a scattering of unpainted houses" across the San Jacinto, their backs to the bayou and overlooking an open prairie.

Throughout the brief war, Houston had an excellent intelligence network: he knew where the enemy was, in what force and in what condition. For example, the 540 men under General Cos who joined Mexico's president and commanding general, Santa Anna, at San Jacinto early on the day of the battle were exhausted after a long forced march. A key scout was Hendrick Arnold, a free Negro who posed as a runaway slave to gather information on Mexican troop movements. Erastus (Deaf) Smith, commander of scouts, seemed to be everywhere at once. He captured a Mexican courier and the Texans learned

Santa Anna's battle plan. The Texans, after weeks of inglorious retreat, were ready to fight at last.

A brief skirmish had occurred April 20, but the main battle came on April 21. Houston had between eight and nine hundred men; Santa Anna, between eleven and thirteen hundred. The Texas infantry lined up across a thousand-foot front flanked by two cannons, the Twin Sisters, and Mirabeau B. Lamar led sixty Texas horsemen in an attack on the Mexican camp enjoying a siesta. The Texans marched into battle, hidden by a swell in the prairie until they were within two hundred yards of the Mexican encampment.

In the bloody one-sided twenty-minute engagement, 630 Mexican soldiers were killed, another 208 wounded, and 730 were captured, according to Texan accounts. Gen. Santa Anna was captured the following day, disguised as a peon. His men, recognizing their commander, gave him away by their startled comment, "El Presidente." The Texans lost six or seven or nine killed (accounts vary) and twenty-four to thirty-four wounded, including General Houston. The date, April 21, 1836, is celebrated annually throughout the Lone Star state. I've always felt an affinity with Sam Houston because we share a birthday, March 2, which is also Texas Independence Day, the other major time to celebrate Texas history.

Buffalo Bayou has been dredged to create the upper Houston Ship Channel. The San Jacinto, serving as the lower ship channel, flows into Galveston Bay from the northwest at Atkinson Island off Morgans Point. To the northeast is Trinity Bay, where the Trinity River flows into Galveston Bay on the eastern side of the Cedar Point promontory drained by Cedar Bayou, which forms the boundary between Harris and Chambers counties and flows into the bay opposite Morgans Point. The lower San Jacinto River constitutes a complex of bayous, tidal marshes, and industrial development between Pasadena and Baytown.

In this part of the country almost every body of slightly moving but sluggish water is called a bayou. (As far away as Central Texas, Pecan Bayou flows into the middle Colorado. A stream heading between Nacogdoches and San Augustine is called Attoyac Bayou, and Big Cypress Bayou flows into and out of Caddo Lake.) Houston has swallowed much of the natural beauty of its bayous, yet some of them retain a natural splendor similar to Louisiana's bayou country, at least in isolated segments. Clear Creek, one of only four natural bayous remaining in the Houston area, is under attack at this writing. (See Wendee Holtcamp's "Turbulence Over Clear Creek," *Texas Parks and Wildlife*, Feb., 1999, pp. 12–19.)

The Brazos flows nearby, a few dozen miles to the west, and the Trinity, a few dozen miles to the east. Since it rains a good deal (an annual average of forty-two inches), the runoff rainwater has found numerous routes to the nearby Gulf of Mexico. The combination of high rainfall and low elevation makes the Houston vicinity prone to flooding, especially when high water in Galveston Bay as a result of southerly winds slows drainage into the bay; there really isn't any place for the bayous to go but up.

Gulf Coast Barrier Islands

Part of the Gulf Coastal Basin, the Houston area, is underlain by Pleistocene sediments, relatively recent, geologically speaking—deriving from the past two million years. The Texas Gulf Coast is a low-lying flat strip of land some three hundred miles long by fifty to a hundred miles wide. As the land is flat inland, so the submerged land beneath the waters of the Gulf is flat and shallow offshore, composed of even younger sediments than those on the adjacent land. I recall as a small boy riding on my father's shoulders as he walked into a moonlit Gulf for miles, or so it seemed to me at the time—it was probably only a few hundred yards. The experience was both thrilling and frightening.

Typically, the Texas coastal plain is characterized by slow, winding rivers carrying silt and sand to the sea. The rivers create oxbow lakes in broad flat floodplains as they meander near the coast. Usually they create bay-head deltas at their mouths where the sluggish rivers enter their respective drowned bays. The result of changes in the elevation of the sea over geologic time, these drowned bays are, for the most part, protected by barrier islands resulting from the great quantities of silt and sand carried to the coast by the turbid rivers. These sediments, continually redistributed by wave and tidal action and hurricanes—which visit the coast with great frequency, on average one big one every other year—protect the tidal marshes and estuaries from the full brunt of storms.

Long, narrow salt-water lagoons are impounded landward of the barrier islands. Tidal deltas form at the passes cut through the islands and peninsulas in a constantly changing pattern. Water flowing through these passes deposits sand and silt, which form bars, shoal areas that create turbulence as the waves break over these shallows. Many Texas river mouths were well guarded by bars that were difficult for ships to cross until channels were dredged through them to facilitate shipping. These artificial channels have to be maintained continually because Gulf currents constantly try to close them in the natural process of current deposition.

Barrier islands are fascinating creatures; they almost seem alive, and they do move, changing in a never-ending pattern. Padre Island, which stretches for 113 miles along the Texas coast from Corpus Christi at the mouth of the Nueces River to Boca Chica at the mouth of the Rio Grande, is the longest barrier island in the United States.

Galveston Island is a barrier island too. These islands are interesting places to visit, though I wouldn't want to live on one. Yet thousands of people do and are forced to rebuild whenever natural forces strike them, just as those who live in river floodplains sometimes have to do. They often rebuild in the same locations with financial aid from the federal government. Should taxpayers have to foot the bill for people's poor decisions?

Galveston Bay, into which both the San Jacinto River and the nearby Trinity flow, is protected by Galveston Island and the Bolivar Peninsula as well as by Smith Point on the east side of the bay itself. A series of small islands known as Red Fish Bar trails westward off Smith Point, further protecting the inner bay. Artificial barriers such as the Texas City Dike also add protection, but when hurricane season comes around, there is little humankind can do in the face of such devastating natural forces.

A tremendous hurricane in 1900 virtually destroyed Galveston and helped Houston evolve into the major seaport it is today. Galveston's location places it at the hub of the coastal petrochemical complex, but it has also become a financial and educational center and a favorite tourist attraction. It remains a ship-building and commercial fishing center as well.

Development of Houston

In 1836 on the site of a Karankawa Indian village, New York land speculators Augustus C. and John K. Allen, brothers who had lived in Texas for only four years at the time of the Texas War of Independence, set up a trading post on Buffalo Bayou. They named it Houston for the general who had commanded the Texas troops at the Battle of San Jacinto. A tiny frontier town grew up on the banks of the bayou, and in 1837 it briefly became the state capital, before Texas had reached its first birthday as a nation.

Mary Austin Holley noted in the 1830s that "San Jacinto, Buffalo Bayou, and a number of small streams discharge their waters into Galveston Bay, after plentifully irrigating the surrounding country. The San Jacinto forms a very beautiful bay at its mouth, and is navigable for any vessel that can pass Red Fish bar, as far as the mouth of Buffalo Bayou. The Buffalo Bayou is also navigable to its forks above Harrisburg, within forty miles of San Felipe de Austin, which interval is a level prairie. It resembles a wide canal, with high and heavily timbered banks. The tide flows up as far as the forks" (34).

Few government officials, except Sam Houston, liked the hot lowland location. It took the steamboat *Laura* three days to get up the log-obstructed Buffalo Bayou in 1837. After a log-clearing operation in 1838 removed most of the snags, four or five steamers engaged in full-time trade between Houston and Galveston, but when a tenth of Houston's population died of a yellow fever epidemic in 1839, the capital moved to Austin. It was simply too hot and humid, too mosquito-infested for most people.

Frederick Law Olmstead, who visited Texas and toured much of the state in 1854, reported that approaching the town from the west, five miles from it he entered a pine forest that continued to the town itself. In his *Journey through Texas* published in 1857, he says that for the year ending September 1, 1856, the town of Houston had shipped 45,557 bales of cotton, or about half the total shipped out of Galveston. Houston was growing in importance as a shipping center, and a great deal of cotton was grown in the area.

The town continued to grow, despite another epidemic of yellow fever (1867), the hot, humid climate, occasional flooding, and periodic hurricanes. Transportation on the nearby Brazos River to the west was hampered by logjams in the lower river and a hazardous bar at its mouth. Cotton shipping helped Houston grow, especially after 1840 with the construction of Houston's first dock and development of a ship channel. In 1869, shortly after the Civil War, the ship channel was deepened and widened. With nearly a dozen railroads heading into or passing through Houston, the city continued expanding. When the Great Storm of 1900 crippled Galveston, then the principal port on the Texas coast, Houston became a significant player in world trade.

Among Houston's growing pains, the sacrifice of its bayous, creeks, and river loomed large, though in the face of booming progress, few people noticed the increasing pollution, loss of wetlands, and stream degradation. As the petrochemical industry evolved in Greater Houston, population soared, and the automobile became a way of life; air quality degradation augmented water pollution problems until quality of life became a major issue. Had it not been for the environmental movement of the late 1960s and 1970s and resultant federal air and water quality legislation, the Houston area might be almost unlivable today. Buffalo Bayou wasn't cleaned up until the 1990s.

Thanks to environmental regulations, public awareness, and the frequent and heavy rainfall that clears the air and washes away much of the pollution, the area's surface waters once again offer pleasant views, recreational opportunities, and abundant wildlife that people once took for granted. It has taken hard work and substantial cost to salvage a natural world from this massive concentration of population. A changing attitude toward nature has made the difference, along with legislation that many business interests continue to try to erode. Coastal streams have begun to recover, positive results of an environmental movement that got much bad press in the Houston area and all over the State of Texas in the decades of its evolution, but that has played a vital role in helping Houston recover.

Paddling the Creeks and Bayous

Several protected areas within Greater Houston suggest the importance to the general public of natural areas and the plants and animals that come with them. One of the most popular such areas lies south of the city center near the NASA Lyndon B. Johnson Space Center, the Armand Bayou Nature Center on Armand Bayou. *An Analysis of Texas Waterways,* published in accordance with the Sixty-Second session of the Texas Legislature, has long been a bible for river recreationists. (Republication of the book has been suppressed by lobbying landowners who don't want boaters on *their* rivers.) It describes Armand Bayou as "an excellent example of a scenic natural bayou in East Texas" representing "an unspoiled area of vegetation (including palmettos, oaks, Spanish moss, cattails, and flowering water plants) close to the Houston Metropolitan area" (70).

Armand Bayou remains a favorite among canoeists, the first that came to mind when I asked Lorraine Bonney, widow of Orrin H. Bonney who did so much to preserve the nearby Big Thicket, for a good piece of paddling water in Greater Houston. In the twenty-five-hundred-acre Armand Bayou Nature Center, operated by a private nonprofit organization but owned by Harris County, you can see white-tailed deer, armadillos, raccoons, snakes, gulls, terns, ducks, raptors, a variety of songbirds, a number of wading birds, alligators, and colorful red-eared sliders (turtles). Clear Creek, which joins Armand Bayou in Clear Lake and forms the southern boundary of Harris County, offers paddling possibilities through a heavily wooded scenic waterway, but power boats have taken it over in recent years. Lorraine Bonney also mentioned "rubber-ducky races" (small inflatable crafts) on Buffalo Bayou in

48. These paddlers on the San Jacinto River had spent several hours in near-wilderness before I shot this scene almost under the Interstate 45 freeway a few miles south of Conroe.

the heart of Houston, and verified Buffalo Bayou is used by many paddlers.

A few miles northwest across the bay, Cedar Bayou, which enters at Shell Point, flows through a series of wooded loops, tidal marshes, and lagoons southeast of Baytown. Wintering bald eagles have been seen here. Just off Morgans Point—and immediately west of Shell Point—lies Atkinson Island, which can be reached only by boat. Here you may find a variety of ducks and other waterfowl, shorebirds, wading birds, marine birds and migrating songbirds as well as ruby-throated hummingbirds sampling honeysuckle and trumpet creeper. Since the use of DDT has been outlawed in the United States (1972), brown pelicans have returned to the area and nest on some of the islands. Ospreys too, recovering their numbers since their decimation by DDT, also nest here, and white ibis and roseate spoonbills appear frequently.

Inland a few miles up the San Jacinto River lies the forty-nine-hundred-acre Lake Houston State Park, where old logging roads winding through stands of loblolly pine, oak, and magnolia have become hiking, biking, and equestrian trails. Many songbirds nest in the dense woods, and while lake access remains limited, streams in the park offer short paddling possibilities. The best canoeing, however, lies upstream on the West Fork of the San Jacinto River below Lake Conroe. I haven't paddled the West Fork myself, but just as I was about to take a picture of the river from beneath the Interstate Highway 45 bridge south of Conroe, a canoe came into my viewfinder. The canoeists had launched at State Highway 105 early that morning and had paddled almost a dozen miles by the time I met them. They planned to leave the river at the north edge of Humble, more than twenty miles downstream, another eight hours of paddling for a long day on the river.

Houston paddler Louis Aulbach tells me a new bridge has recently been built across the West Fork on Needham Road, a farm-to-market road south of Conroe, offering an alternate take-out and a shorter run. Aulbach, who has written excellent river guides to Devil's River, the Pecos, and the Lower Canyons of the Rio Grande, paddles the streams and bayous of the Houston area regularly. He enjoys the San Jacinto's West Fork for its white sands, relatively natural banks, and wilderness feeling, despite occasional gravel pits along the way.

He tells me that on Buffalo Bayou, even in the heart of residential Houston, "the streamside vegetation hides the city," and he refers to Memorial Park, through which the bayou flows, as "still pretty wild." He tells of two- to three-hour trips through northwest Houston, of paddling upstream against the slow current, then returning downstream to obviate the need for a shuttle, and of proposals by the county to develop miniparks along Buffalo Bayou, a concept he loudly applauds. He's seen wintering bald eagles on a few streams not far from downtown Houston, despite relatively poor water quality.

My old army buddy Earle Oldham, who serves on the Tomball City Council, confirms wisdom about the new bridge on Needham Road and tells me of seeing canoes on Spring Creek, a small tributary of the West Fork, during high water. I visited Earle in the spring of 1998 during field research; though not a paddler himself, he knows a lot of East Texas rivers, having grown up in Pittsburg near Big Cypress Bayou and gone to college in Marshall near the upper Sabine.

New Mexico paddler Joe Butler, who grew up in Dallas but lived in Houston for many years, has canoed most of the rivers in Texas, including Spring Creek, which he enjoys for its white sandy beaches and big pines, and Buffalo Bayou, which he says is "neat in the spring" and better in wet weather than in dry. He's done a two-day trip on upper Buffalo Bayou from S.H. 6 well west of the city to downtown Houston, a popular run. Joe also recommends Dickinson Bayou east of Alvin; it flows into Dickinson Bay off April Fool Point, just outside Red Fish Bar.

Farther from the city, near Cleveland lies, the San Jacinto River Canoe Trail, "a scenic and challenging canoe trip with wildlife viewing possibilities around each bend" (78), according to Gary L. Graham in the *Texas Wildlife Viewing Guide,* a multiagency project developed in cooperation with a major national conservation organization, Defenders of Wildlife. The first printing of this popular guide quickly sold out and one hopes it will be kept in print. I bought the last copy on my visit to Landa Park in New Braunfels. Dog-eared and dirty, it shows evidence of heavy use. The book has been such a useful guide for me that I recently bought a second copy at a used book store in Albuquerque.

The canoe trail follows the East Fork of the San Jacinto for about ten miles through the southeast corner of Sam Houston National Forest. Although many canoeists consider the East Fork too lean to paddle, spring and fall offer the best possibilities. While fallen trees may be a problem and the going may be slow, seeing and hearing such resident songbirds as hooded and prothonotary warblers can make the trip worthwhile. The opportunity to see a river otter adds to its mystique. The U.S. Forest Service can provide current river-flow information.

Just a few miles southwest of Lake Houston lies Sheldon Lake State Park and the adjacent Sheldon Wildlife Management Area. Only thirteen miles from downtown Houston, this twenty-five-hundred-acre double unit of the Texas state park system provides winter food for ducks and geese in the form of cultivated grain crops. Heron and egret rookeries exist on small islands in the lake, and fishing is allowed. Florida bass, crappie, sunfish, and catfish have been stocked. The shallow lake is closed to boating from November through February, the best months to see wintering bald eagles here. Motors during the remainder of the year are limited to ten horsepower. Just north of Sheldon Lake immediately downstream from Lake Houston lies Dwight D. Eisenhower Park, bordered on the east by the San Jacinto River. It includes a slough known as Big Eddy where you can find a wilderness world of water only by boat.

To know the rivers in the Houston area, and any coastal estuary, it pays to consult a cruising guide, for cruising has become a major recreational activity on the salty waterways of the Texas coast: the bays and inlets and the Gulf Intracoastal Waterway. Chambers of commerce may offer localized detail, and I have found the second edition of the *Texas/Louisiana Coastal Cruising Guide* quite useful. This guide to coastal waters in both Louisiana and Texas points out that practically all of the world's domestic and major international energy companies have a presence in the Port of Houston. Although the city lies many miles inland, it has been a major seaport for generations. Recreational boaters need to be aware of shipping activities in the port as well as of recreational opportunities in the bay.

Thus the San Jacinto and its tributaries and the other streams that flow into Galveston Bay form a vast network of waterways that receive heavy use recreationally and commercially in a major industrial city that includes large petrochemical complexes. Yet the whole watershed retains vestiges of natural Texas in its small headwater streams and coastal bayous. Waterfowl and shorebirds, migrating and nesting songbirds, wintering ducks and geese, even osprey and bald eagles use these waterways, which, though by no means without pollution, still offer marvelous opportunities for people to enjoy the natural world.

The San Jacinto may be dammed and considerably less than pristine, and the Greater Houston area may be crowded with too many people, but in a canoe you can get away from the modern world to visit a more natural Texas, screened from the harsh realities of today. It's a temporary escape when we need an escape. I like to think of paddling experiences as a return to myself and a visit to a more peaceful world that lies all around us as well as within us.

San Antonio

LOCATION: *San Antonio southeast to Gulf Coast south of Victoria*
NAME: *San Antonio de Valero (1691)*
CITIES: *San Antonio, Bandera, Castroville, Floresville, Karnes City, Goliad*
IMPOUNDMENTS: *Medina Lake, Braunig Lake, Calaveras Lake on tributaries*
TRIBUTARIES: *Medina River, Medio Creek, Leon Creek, Salado Creek, Cibolo Creek, Calaveras Creek, Woman Hollering Creek, Martinez Creek, Santa Clara Creek*
RECREATION: *Boating, swimming, fishing, hiking, biking, bird watching, polo*
WATERSHED: *4,180 square miles*
DISCHARGE: *350,000 acre feet annually*
LENGTH: *180 miles*
PUBLIC LANDS: *State historical parks at Landmark Inn, Casa Navarro, Rancho de las Cabras, Goliad, and Fannin Battlefield; Government Canyon State Park, San Antonio Missions National Historic Park, Aransas National Wildlife Refuge*
FEATURES: *The Alamo, Espada Aqueduct*

THE UPPER SAN ANTONIO RIVER may be the best-known urban stream in America for its famous River Walk and the spectacular San Jacinto Day float parades through the heart of the city. My mother, who lived in San Antonio for the last thirty years of her life, was more impressed with that spectacle than with anything she'd experienced at the Texas Centennial celebration of 1936. She took everyone who visited her—family, friends, business associates—to see the river as it sweeps through the downtown area near Texas' most sacred shrine and historical site, the Alamo.

Having grown up only a hundred miles from the Alamo, I came to know it well, just around the corner from Joshke's, where we usually did our Christmas shopping—they always had a wonderful display for the holidays. As excited as I always was during our Christmas-shopping visit to San Antonio in early December, I was equally drawn to the Alamo. I memorized every detail of the battle as presented in the displays, knew the name of every defender, where each had fallen. I got a lump in my throat and tears in my eyes every time I heard or read the story. The Alamo has always been special to me. So was the San Antonio River, which flows nearby.

Less than two hundred miles long and relatively unattractive for most of its course to the Gulf, the San Antonio shines in the city of its origin. When Queen Elizabeth of England visited San Antonio, she appeared on the news beaming her way down the river listening to a mariachi band, obviously enjoying herself thoroughly. Spring-fed and clear, it provides a steady year-round source of water, one of the most dependable rivers in the state. More like the Nueces than the Guadalupe in its course to the Gulf, the San Antonio River flows turbid and silty through a tree-lined ditch, but in the city where it has become a showplace of urban river development, it has charm and clarity, a European scene set into the Texas landscape.

Only eleven years after the establishment of the first mission on the river, its life-giving waters began to be siphoned off to serve human populations, an early irrigation project. The upper watershed lies in a region of relatively low rainfall and thin limestone soils that grow better pricklypear cactus and mesquite than potatoes and corn, an area that has more underground water than surface water.

That surface water was put to good use by the five early missions in San Antonio. The river's water, diverted into an acequia system, was used for drinking, cooking, washing, and irrigation. The Espada Aqueduct, dating to the middle of the eighteenth century, is still in use today. Protected from wandering livestock by a live-cactus fence, the water ran through a series of ditches mortared with a mixture of fine baked limestone powder and goats' milk, the animal fat in the milk sealing the ditch against water loss. The purity of the water was protected as well as its quantity by local laws passed as early as 1830.

The abundant clear springs and the limestone topography reflect the geology of the region, which lies at the edge of the Edwards Plateau, raised some two thousand feet above the surrounding landscape by an ancient uplift. Long before this great rising occurred, ten to twenty million years ago during Miocene times, massive layers of marine shale, sandstone, and limestone had formed beneath an ancestral sea. The uplift raised these marine sediments high above the surrounding landscape, and surface erosion began to carve the present vista. As the whole region rose, underground drainage caused by the uplift began to create caves and sinkholes as the water drained away, leaving the characteristics of Karst topography throughout the area.

As the Gulf of Mexico began to form, fractures occurred along the Balcones fault zone that, during Cretaceous times, allowed molten magma beneath the earth to blast through sediments and water to the surface, causing steam-driven explosions that formed craters on the ocean floor and depositing ash and pyroclastics (volcanic debris). A line of volcanoes lies between Austin and Uvalde just north of San Antonio along the Medina River headwaters. Texas' major volcanic activity, however, occurred later and farther west.

The Balcones Escarpment marks the southeastern edge of the Edwards Plateau and provides the San Antonio River with its potential for producing power from falling water. A number of early Texas towns grew up along the fault line because of the power potential. The Balcones fault zone was named Los Balcones (the balconies) by Spanish explorer Bernardo de Miranda in 1756. Balcones describes well the geological stair-step or balcony-like nature of the escarpment's edge, which runs through San Antonio and impacts the course and flow of the river. Several rivers that head on the Edwards Plateau are similarly influenced by this major fault zone, which stretches in a great curve from Del Rio on the Rio Grande to Waco on the Brazos.

The San Antonio River has a moderate slope near its Hill Country origin, a steeper slope as it runs over the Balcones Escarpment, then a gentler and gentler gradient as it flows through rolling hills to the coastal prairies. Near the Gulf it meanders perceptibly before flowing into the Guadalupe River only a few miles from the Gulf. It is best known and most admired in its Hill Country headwaters, where lush springs and cypress-lined clear-water streams characterize its birthplace.

In Mary Austin Holley's account of the San Antonio River in *Texas,* she reports that "its crystal waters flow off with a rapid current over a bed of limestone" (34) and predicts that because of the river's many mill-seats (possible sites for mills) in San Antonio, the city "will probably become the great manufacturing district of Texas" (34). It hasn't turned out that way, but the city has become one of Texas' largest, a major governmental and military center, with several air bases and an army base (Fort Sam Houston, where I was inducted into the army), a retirement community for many military personnel, and a thriving tourist center.

Spanish Settlement and Missions

The river begins at San Pedro Springs within the limits of San Antonio, one of the oldest cities in Texas. The Mission San Antonio de Valero—part of which eventually became the Alamo (built in 1724)—and the presidio San Antonio de Béxar were established at the springs in 1718 as a halfway point along the road connecting the presidios in northern Mexico and missions in East Texas. It became one of the most successful Spanish settlements in Texas and for the first time gave the Spanish a real economic base north of the Rio Grande, one that grew because of the abundant spring water.

Several more missions were established in the vicinity to serve different Indian tribes: San José de Aguayo (1720) and a trio farther east, reestablishing missions that had failed and had been abandoned: La Purisima Concepción de Acuña, San Juan Capistrano, and San Francisco de la Espada, all in the same decade. Collectively they turned the upper San Antonio River Valley into the first permanent major Spanish settlement in Texas. Settlers in Texas soon came to be known as Tejanos.

Mission Espíritu Santo, originally located on Matagorda Bay (1722) and later moved to the Guadalupe River near Victoria (1726), was eventually relocated on a bend of the San Antonio River southwest of Victoria (1749) and became the impetus for the settlement at Goliad. Taking advantage of the lush grass then growing along the river, the mission developed the first major cattle-raising operation in Texas, expanding the cattle range to the Gulf Coast. Two roads, one on the east side of the river (used in dry weather) and one on the west (wet weather), linked the San Antonio missions to the one on the lower river. The only link between the two roads was Conquista Pitaias Crossing (near present-day Falls City in Karnes County), established in 1739 even before the lower mission was moved and named for the Spanish conquest of the local Pitaias Indians. This crossing was still used well into the twentieth century until FM-791 between Falls City and Campbellton was built and the river was bridged.

At one time the mission at Goliad held jurisdiction over all the land between the Guadalupe and San Antonio rivers below Gonzales. The mission's cattle, said to number more than forty thousand, helped to establish the cattle industry in Texas. Secularized in 1831, the mission fell into a state of ruin, but the Goliad City Council rebuilt the basic structures in 1848 to use as a school. In 1849 the Presidio La Bahía moved to the area to guard the mission.

San Antonio became the provincial capital of Spanish Texas in 1772, with

49. La Bahía Mission on the San Antonio River in Goliad exemplifies early Spanish settlements.

the Alamo at its center. Its name is thought to come from the cottonwood trees (*álamos*) growing along the nearby San Antonio River, but according to Paul Horgan in *Great River* (New York: Rinehart, 1954), 2:529, "It took its popular name from the fact that a company of soldiers from El Alamo, a garrison post in Coahuila, had once been stationed there." It was part of the original mission, but after secularization, it became a military depot (like the Parthenon in Athens at one time) and later a symbol for solidarity among Texans during the War of Texas Independence. Anglo-Americans, European immigrants, and Mexicans fought side by side against the Mexican central government's forces. This was more a war against the dictator Santa Anna, who had revoked the Mexican Constitution of 1824, than against Mexico itself, and many Mexicans living in Texas fought alongside the Anglo Tejanos.

War for Independence

During this war for Texas independence, the early battle lines were drawn along the San Antonio River. Initially the Texans held both San Antonio and

Goliad, and they had won minor skirmishes against Mexican authority at Anahuac, Nacogdoches, and Gonzales as well as in San Antonio and Goliad the fall of 1835.

However, as thousands of Mexican troops massed under General Santa Anna and his brother-in-law General Martín Perfecto de Cos, the Texans took defensive positions at the Alamo and in Goliad. Everyone knows the story of the defense of the Alamo, how 180 Texans under William B. Travis and James Bowie withstood the Mexican attack for thirteen days, how the Alamo fell with all its defenders killed.

The Texans at the Alamo could not have known about the Declaration of Texas Independence, for that was signed on March 2, only a few days before the Alamo fell on March 6. No one from outside the Alamo could have brought them word of the historic act of defiance. The defenders of the Alamo were fighting superior Mexican forces for the Mexican Constitution of 1824, which the dictator Santa Anna had ignored after he grabbed the reins of power. The Texans had flown a Mexican flag emblazoned with the date "1824" above the Alamo, an act said to have enraged Santa Anna, a true tyrant.

The Mexican general could easily have bypassed the Alamo, but he wanted to teach the upstart Texans a lesson: that he was in complete control and that the Constitution of 1824 was history. In doing so, he allowed the main Texas army under Gen. Sam Houston to escape eastward, where they could not only muster and train more soldiers but also choose their own terrain for the decisive battle of the war.

At Goliad an indecisive West Point graduate, Col. J. W. Fannin, led an army of some four hundred Texans. Fannin couldn't seem to make up his mind which way to go or when to leave, but when he finally did set out (March 20, two weeks after the Alamo fell), his troops were caught in the open near Coleto Creek and surrendered to superior Mexican forces after a brief battle. Gen. José de Urrea's recommendation of clemency for the captive Texans infuriated Santa Anna, who ordered them all executed. On Palm Sunday, March 27, Fannin and most of his men were shot down by firing squads. Only twenty-eight escaped. Elmer Kelton used the event as the basis for his 1965 novel, *Massacre at Goliad.*

The Battle of the Alamo, along with the Battle of Goliad, became the Texas cause for revenge in the Battle of San Jacinto a few weeks later. In an arrogant military stupidity, Santa Anna, who as noted was both president of Mexico and commanding general of Mexican forces in Texas, had every defender of the Alamo and every prisoner at Goliad, except the few who escaped, killed to make a point. The point has been forgotten, but the Alamo and Goliad have been remembered.

After Texas had become a nation, the area along the San Antonio River seemed to have fallen from grace. Most of the activity of organizing the new nation occurred in the eastern part of the country—or at least well east of San Antonio, which was too near the border, too subject to attack, perhaps too Mexican. It was, in fact, attacked a number of times by a series of Mexican armies.

There was to be another war (1846–48) with Mexico soon after Texas had become part of the United States (1845). It started as a border dispute over whether the Rio Grande or the Nueces was the legal boundary between the two countries; once Santa Anna had returned safely to Mexico after the Texas War of Independence, he seemed to have forgotten his signed promise. Yet many in the United States saw that war as a land grab. However, as Pat Kelley writes in *River of Lost Dreams* (about the Rio Grande), looking at the period and the man in historic perspective, "Santa Anna's actions [in the Texas War of Independence and in the Mexican War] turned an attempt to restore constitutional rule into a rebellion that eventually cost Mexico her northern provinces from Texas to California" (26).

During the turbulent years of Texas history from the early 1830s, when Anglo-American settlers began grasping for democracy, through the late 1870s, when Reconstruction had ended and the Indians had been removed to reservations north of the Red River, San Antonio continued to expand in population and importance. Its ready water supply from the many springs at the head of the San Antonio River helped it thrive. Downriver communities were thriving as well, using the river's water for irrigation and domestic consumption.

During the Civil War with cattle reproducing and running wild, the range along the San Antonio erupted with an abundance of marketable meat on the hoof. When the men returned from the war, they began looking for markets, found them at the railheads in Kansas, and began collecting cattle all over South Texas for the long drives north, and later for stocking ranges in the Rockies of Colorado, Wyoming, and Montana.

Samuel A. Maverick's name lives on in the term *maverick* for unbranded cattle. Practice on the open range was to brand any calf with its mother's brand, but unbranded calves old enough to be on their own were fair game for anyone to brand with his own mark. Sam Maverick never bothered to brand his cattle, and after four years of war, during which few cattle had been rounded up for marking or for market, the range was crowded with mavericks. Ambitious cowboys who were good with a rope and a branding iron became cattlemen after the Civil War, many of them along the San Antonio River.

Bandera and the Medina River

A principal tributary of the San Antonio, the Medina, reaches northwestward for more than a hundred miles, a longer arm than the main San Antonio from its source to its confluence with the Medina. The Medina flows along the edge of the Edwards Plateau to extend the tentacles of the San Antonio River's watershed into the southern portions of Kerr County near the Guadalupe River headwaters. Essentially the Medina drains Bandera County. Less well-known than the adjacent Guadalupe, which rises just north of the Medina headwaters (they share a ridge), the upper Medina is as lovely as any stream in the Hill Country, with clear water flowing over a limestone bed and rocky outcrops towering above the river-fringing bald cypress trees.

North of Bandera, which lies at a sharp S bend of the Medina River and bills itself as the "Cowboy Capital of the World," the Battle of Bandera Pass occurred in 1840. Only 500 yards long and 125 feet wide, the pass between the Medina and Guadalupe rivers has been a major travel route since paleo-Indian times. The Spanish, under a General Bandera, defeated a band of Apaches here in the middle of the eighteenth century. In the spring of 1840 a troop of forty Texas Rangers under the command of Capt. John (Jack) Coffee Hays fought a battle against Comanche Indians at the pass, which lies fifty miles west of San Antonio, about twelve miles north of Bandera.

One of the better-known rangers, Hays had become a captain at the age of twenty-three. He raised a company of rangers to protect Texas' southwest border against Mexicans, Indians, and a lawless element of Anglos. Headquartered in San Antonio, Hays's company had beaten the Comanches at the Battle of Nueces Canyon (Hays himself had killed a dozen Comanche raiders in Uvalde Canyon). After camping at the site of the present town of Bandera, the rangers had headed north through Bandera Canyon, where the Comanches were waiting for them. Ambushed in the pass by the Indians and totally surrounded, the rangers fought their way out, decisively defeating the Indians, who lost sixty warriors killed or wounded while the entrapped troop of Texans suffered five killed and six wounded.

Hays eventually moved to California, where he was the first sheriff of San Francisco, became federal surveyor general, and founded the city of Oakland. Another ranger, "Big Foot" Wallace, who had joined the Hays command,

50. The Medina River flows through an avenue of cypress trees near Bandera.

liked the surrounding country so well that he eventually settled on the Medina River and made a personal treaty with the local Lipans. When the Indians soon broke it, Wallace made life so hot for them that "the Lipans concluded to emigrate from that part of the country to the headwaters of the Guadalupe River," according to John C. Duval in *The Adventures of Big Foot Wallace* (112).

The site of the battle, which occurred only a year after the Battle of Plum Creek (see chapter on the Guadalupe), has become an important part of local history. Bandera began as a cypress-shingle camp in 1853, then became a Mormon colony, followed by a large contingent of Poles, who built St. Stanislaus Catholic Church in 1876. Restored in modern times to its original condition, it still functions as a church, one of the oldest Polish parishes in the country. Since World War II Bandera has become a major tourist area with ten dude ranches and a dozen bed-and-breakfast facilities. The Frontier Times Museum in Bandera helps interpret local history.

A few dozen miles northwest of San Antonio, roughly halfway between the Medina's headwaters and its confluence with the San Antonio southeast of the city, lies Medina Lake, its only major impoundment. A Catholic priest in Schulenburg once took a trio of us high school boys, one a Catholic, one a Baptist, and one a pagan, on a day's bass-fishing trip on the impoundment for an early lesson in religious tolerance and reservoir fishing. I'll not forget the clear dark waters of the artificial lake lying between steep cliffs, dropping deeper into the lake than the cliffs rose above the lake's surface.

Fifteen miles south of the lake lies Castroville. According to historian Rupert Norval Richardson, who taught at Hardin-Simmons University during my graduate-school days there, Green De Witt was "next to Austin the most important proprietor" or head of a colony in early Texas. However, according to a Castroville Chamber of Commerce brochure, Henri Castro "was second only to Stephen F. Austin in the number of settlers he brought to Texas." Whatever the case, Castro, "a gentleman of French birth, Portuguese ancestry, Jewish faith, and American citizenship," did bring numerous settlers from the Rhine Valley, many of them from the French province of Alsace, to a bend of the Medina River in 1844 to create Castroville twenty miles west of San Antonio.

Parks

Since San Antonio is the city I knew best during my childhood, the San Antonio River played a significant role in determining what I thought a river should be. I dearly loved Brackenridge Park, through which the upper river flows. The park's open space and varied attractions all thrilled me as a child: the Sunken Gardens, the Polo Field, and especially the zoo, known as the San Antonio Zoological Gardens and Aquarium, which exhibits more than thirty-four hundred creatures of more than seven hundred species.

In those days we used to picnic in the park nearly every time we visited my Aunt Rose and Uncle Gus Richter, who lived on Meerscheidt Street, a reflection of their Germanic background. While San Antonio is much more a Hispanic than a German city and its population is largely Latino (49.7 percent in 1998), it nonetheless has a substantial Germanic population. The San Antonio City Council in 1894 included a number of Germans—Albert F. and Joe Beckmann, William Hoefling, Henry Limburger, and Erich Menger—as well as the Scotsmen F. W. McAllister and Nelson Mackey, a Smith, a Newton, and a Hice; not a Spanish name among them.

So well-known had San Antonio become for its abundant water and its irrigation system that a group of Belgian vegetable farmers moved en mass to Texas in the 1880s and settled along the San Pedro Acequia. The entire watershed was heavily settled by immigrants from every corner of Europe. In the traditional vaquero country, European and Anglo-Americans become dominant over the majority Hispanics, a point well illustrated by the story of Gregorio Cortez (in the Nueces chapter). Historically Hispanic communities found themselves shut out by the growing Anglo and European society, to some extent as a result of oil and gas discoveries. When the Great Depression came, the Anglo-European community was the harder hit along the San Antonio River, but out of the New Deal some positive changes occurred.

In 1931, a century after it was secularized, the mission at Goliad became part of the 178-acre Goliad State Historical Park, less than a mile south of Goliad. Fannin Battleground State Historical Park lies a few miles east of Goliad. In 1936, the Texas centennial year, the Civilian Conservation Corps began work restoring the old mission. The park includes the birthplace of Ignacio Zaragoza, hero of the Battle of Puebla in Mexico on May 5, 1862, for which the holiday Cinco de Mayo is celebrated. A nature trail runs through the park, which is located at the junction of three major natural regions—coastal prairie, oak woods and prairies, and the South Texas brush country—and includes elements of four different biotic provinces.

When I hiked the Aranama Trail along the San Antonio River in the spring of 1996, I used the park's nature trail guide to help me identify plants I'd known as a boy growing up less than a hundred miles away—plants I hadn't seen for years because I'd been living outside Texas. I saw Texas persimmon, small but with bark like the madroña; lime pricklyash and spiny hackberry, honey mesquite, sweet acacia, live oak, Texas mountain laurel, and blackbrush acacia. There were pricklypear cactus (here commonly known as nopal) yucca, mustang grape, and poison ivy, an old friend and an old foe. The Goliad State

Historical Park bird checklist includes more than three hundred species. Camping facilities are available in the park.

San Antonio features several parks and historic sites: the Alamo, of course, lies in the heart of downtown San Antonio; Jose Antonio Navarro (also known as Casa Navarro) State Historical Park, home of an important Tejano leader who was one of two native-born Texans to sign the Texas Declaration of Independence; San Antonio Missions National Historic Park, which includes four Spanish colonial missions plus the Espada dam and aqueduct, part of the early irrigation system; and the recently acquired Government Canyon State Park at the northwest edge of the city.

And here we are more than a hundred and fifty years after the Republic of Texas became the Lone Star state: Texas is the nation's second largest and the second most populous state; San Antonio is the state's second most populous city (barely ahead of Dallas in the 1996 census). The San Antonio River still runs through its heart and flows to the Gulf. Except for the city itself, the major economy is still agriculture, augmented by oil and tourism, the latter two, twentieth-century inventions. The San Antonio River and its Hill Country tributaries remain largely free-flowing and offer many natural advantages to the people of the watershed.

Lavaca and Navidad

LOCATION: *Principal watershed between the Colorado and Guadalupe*
NAME: *Lavaca is Spanish for cow, named for the many bison found; Navidad is Spanish for birth (meaning the birth of Christ or Christmas)*
CITIES: *Schulenburg, Hallettsville, Yoakum, Edna*
IMPOUNDMENTS: *Lake Texana*
TRIBUTARIES: *Big Rocky Creek, Yellowbank Creek (Lavaca), Sandy Creek, Mustang Creek (Navidad)*
RECREATION: *Bank fishing, swimming, and boating on lower reaches*
WATERSHED: *Small*
DISCHARGE: *600,000 acre feet*
LENGTH: *Lavaca—94 miles; Navidad—82*
PUBLIC LANDS: *Lake Texana State Park, Port Lavaca State Fishing Pier*
FEATURES: *La Salle colony*

THE LAVACA RIVER, the largest stream flowing into the Gulf of Mexico between the Colorado and Guadalupe rivers, marked the southwestern extent of the Stephen F. Austin colony, as Mary Austin Holley, a cousin of Austin's, observed in her book *Texas.* Calling it the La Baca, she wrote, "From its source to its entrance into Matagorda Bay [it] serves to form the western boundary of Austin's colony, separating it from DeWitt's and St. Leon's grants" (35). The Navidad, the Lavaca's major tributary, lay entirely within the Austin colony. While several of the Old Three Hundred took up land in the watershed of the twin rivers, much of it was not settled until Bohemian/Czechoslovakian and German immigrants came to the area in the 1840s and 1850s. Another wave of Czechs, Germans, and Poles came after the Civil War.

Listen to the names of the towns and villages in the combined watershed of the Navidad and Lavaca rivers: Breslau, Dubina, Freyburg, Kinkler, Komensky, Mikeska, New Bielau, Obeigoner, Praha, Shimek, St. Wenceslaus, Weimar. In Schulenburg, I went to school with children who entered first grade knowing only German or Czech. My next-door neighbors to the south were German-Czech: he German, she Czech. She made wonderful poppyseed kolaches on special occasions, and I remember her admonitions, "Ah lay yeah dah-netch-key." At least that's the way my ear caught it. It means something in the neighborhood of "Oh, my goodness."

The only Hispanics in town were the Molanos. He served as school janitor, and his wife's tamales were so popular that you had to order them a week before; she sold them from their home every Saturday. One of their daughters, Juanita, was a classmate of mine. Another classmate, Raymond Soso, moved to town in third grade but moved away before the end of the school year.

African American children in Schulenburg went to a different school. I knew black people primarily from working in the summer at the cotton compress only a block from home. Several became good friends, and Albert Stevens of the Lone Star Gospel Singers, at my invitation, once brought his group to a Youth Fellowship meeting at my church. I was called on the carpet for daring to bring African Americans into the church! What had been Indian country a century before had become, by the end of the nineteenth century, an enclave of central Europeans and West Africans. When I talk about my hometown in south-central Texas, I often say that the population was a third German, a third Czech, and a third African American.

The strong European influence in the upper Navidad watershed is reflected in its painted churches. At least four Catholic churches have become tourist attractions for their colorful artistic interiors: the Gothic Revival–style St. Mary's Catholic Church in High Hill (1868), two miles northwest of Schulenburg; the Czech-Moravian Blessed Virgin Mary Church in Praha (1895), two miles east of Flatonia; the Czech St. Cyril and Methadius Catholic Church in Dubina (1877, repaired in 1912), four miles northwest of Weimar; and St. John the Baptist Catholic Church in Ammannsville (1917), two or three miles west of U.S. Highway 77 between Schulenburg and La Grange.

French, Spanish, and Indian Occupants

When the first Europeans arrived, the Karankawan tribes dominated the lower Lavaca and Navidad rivers, for they ranged along Matagorda Bay, into which these rivers discharge, and along the Matagorda Peninsula. When Robert Cavelier, Sieur de La Salle, who had navigated the Mississippi on an earlier expedition, missed the mouth of the Mississippi where he had hoped to settle a French colony, he landed instead at Matagorda Bay. He settled the colony on Garcitas Creek a few miles north of what is today Port Lavaca. Garcitas Creek flows into the northwest corner of Lavaca Bay; the Lavaca River flows into its northeast corner. La Salle's settlement lay within a few miles of the mouth of the Lavaca, and the Navidad joined the Lavaca nearby.

This first European settlement in Texas failed. Karankawa Indians and dissent among the leaders—La Salle was killed by his men somewhere east of the Brazos—put an end to it before the Spanish governor of Coahuila, Alonso de León, was able to do so. De León's 1689–90 expedition to remove the French settlement near Lavaca Bay found tribes related to the Tonkawas farther upriver in what became Victoria and Lavaca counties. W. W. Newcomb suggests that they were probably members of the smaller, more obscure groups of Tonkawan people known as the Emets and Lavas or Cavas.

Governor Domingo Teran de los Ríos's 1691–92 expedition into the region involved Ríos sending a Captain Martínez—with twenty soldiers, more than fifty mules, and nearly three hundred horses—from a camp near present-day La Grange on the Colorado south to the coast at Garcitas Creek to meet a resupply party. According to William Foster, they traveled "over open grasslands to camp on an upper tributary of the Navidad River" (61), which he called Arroyo San Laureano, then covered twenty-eight miles the next day following the Navidad. Martínez "was able to secure by force the services of an unidentified local Indian guide." A quarter-century later Governor Martín de Alarcón, who camped on both the Lavaca and the Navidad during his 1718 expedition, described the area through which he traveled as "an extensive fertile plain" (136).

Obviously the Spanish had begun to meet the local inhabitants and launch their cruel conquest; equally obviously, the Spanish had brought a great many horses and mules into Texas. In 1693 Governor Gregorio de Salinas Varona's resupply expedition crossed the Lavaca traveling east in late May and, returning westward in late June, crossed both the upper Navidad and the Lavaca. On the Navidad he found local Sana Indians and Tohanas trading with Simaoma and Mescal Indians from south of the Rio Grande, suggesting how widely indigenous people traveled and traded.

On an inspection tour in 1767, the French Marquis de Rubi reported seeing "innumerable herds of deer and flocks of wild turkey" on the headwaters of the Lavaca in the fall (October 26–27). The following year Fray Gaspar José de Solio camped at Breviario (April 19 and again July 14), then a popular campsite on Rocky Creek between modern-day Flatonia and Shiner. The headwater areas of the Navidad and Lavaca were known terrain according to William C. Foster, writing in *Spanish Expedition into Texas, 1689–1768.*

However, the whole watershed passed to the Comanches once they acquired the horse and became the lords of the plains, for they raided all the way to the Gulf Coast. Linnville, where a well-known Comanche attack occurred on August 8, 1840, lay on Lavaca Bay at the mouth of the Lavaca River. Thirty-five Comanche leaders had been killed in the infamous Council House Fight in San Antonio five months before on March 19. The Comanche chiefs, who sought peace with the Texans, had come into the city to parley, but when they were all in the building, the Texans indicated that the chiefs would be held captive until they returned a number of white captives. In the ensuing fight, all of the chiefs were killed; fewer than a dozen Texans lost their lives. It was treachery similar to the Bascomb affair with Cochise in Arizona that started a twenty-year war with the Apaches.

Seeking revenge, the Comanches bided their time, waiting for their horses to fatten on the summer grass, taking time to scout the situation and develop the best plan for retaliation. As many as a thousand warriors made a massive sweep to the Gulf, hitting several Texas towns on their way south, including Victoria. They burned Linnville, but most of the residents escaped by retreating into the bay by boat. The Comanches killed or captured about twenty-five Texans and rounded up between two and three thousand horses and mules.

As the Comanches headed back to their high plains homeland, a group of more than two hundred Texas volunteers, including Texas Rangers Ed Burleson, Matthew (Old Paint) Caldwell, Jack Hays, and Ben McCullough, surprised the Comanches near the Plum Creek crossing of the San Antonio Road, killing about eighty Indians, recapturing most of the stock, and freeing the white prisoners. Such was the situation in much of Texas in the 1840s. Indian raids continued for another third of a century, and the Comanches were not forced onto a reservation in Oklahoma until 1874.

Linnville occupied part of the de León land grant, which Mary Austin Holley had mentioned along with the De Witt grant in describing the Lavaca. These two grants lay nearer the coast than the Austin colony in an area of coastal prairies and heavily wooded valleys that enjoyed a more-than-nine-month growing season (290 days), an annual average rainfall of thirty-nine inches, and abundant coastal livestock grazing. Another early observer remarked that the Navidad's banks were lined with large trees draped with mustang grapevines and flanked by natural fields separated by thick hedgerows. A modern analysis of Texas waterways terms the Lavaca a typical coastal plains river, heavily vegetated with coastal hardwoods and depending entirely upon runoff for its flow.

In *The Indians of Texas,* Newcomb suggests, in a chapter entitled "Extermination and Oblivion," that colonists' relations with local Indians had been rough from the beginning, that forces set in motion by earlier European contacts, including those with the French pirate Lafitte, had precipitated bad feeling and mistrust among at least some of the native people. Newcomb writes: "Once hostilities had begun, enduring peace was impossible. . . . The enmity between Austin's colonists and the Karankawas was extended to the colonies of Green C. DeWitt and Martin de Leon. By 1825 Austin was forced to undertake a campaign against the Karankawas." Such action went against Austin's grain, but to save the colony, he took it, and by 1827 a treaty ending hostilities removed a major barrier to settlement. It is not coincidental that the lower Lavaca-Navidad watershed was settled primarily after 1827.

That same year, Noah Smithwick appeared in De Witt's colony, an ordinary man who performed extraordinary deeds and wrote about his frontier experiences in his delightful *The Evolution of a State, or Recollections of Old Texas Days.* Smithwick arrived in Texas by "coasting schooner" at the mouth of the Lavaca River after the ship threaded the Paso Caballo into Matagorda Bay. "The weather was lovely as a dream of Venice," he recorded.

Smithwick had his prejudices; he dismissed the local Karankawa Indians as "a fierce tribe whose hand was against every man. They lived mostly on fish and alligators, with a man for fete days when they could catch one" (3). But he was a keen observer who lived through interesting times. Although his insightful views of the evolving Texas include perspectives on many different rivers— he spent most of his later years on the Brazos and Colorado—I introduce him here because he arrived at the mouth of the Lavaca and spent his first night on Texas soil on the lower Lavaca, where his first meal was "dried venison sopped in honey." The next day he walked to De Witt's colony ten miles up the Lavaca River. He commented on "herds of fine, fat deer . . . vast canebrakes along the . . . sluggish river, which crept along between low banks thickly set with tall trees," from which hung "long streamers of Spanish moss." He also noted abundant alligators and ubiquitous mosquitoes.

Smithwick, a blacksmith at times, left Texas four years later, then returned just as the War of Independence began to take form. He missed the major battles but got caught up in the Runaway Scrape, which he describes in some detail. As a frequent scout who fought many brief battles on the Indian frontier, Noah Smithwick was one Texan who had attempted to negotiate with the Comanches, but anti-Indian sentiment prevailed to prevent any real peace.

Smithwick spent thirty years in Texas, leaving for the last time when the Lone Star state left the Union to enter the Civil War, an action he opposed.

Farming Towns Grow Up

By the time Smithwick left Texas, my hometown had been settled. The fourth edition of his *Texas Handbook,* Joe Cummings reports the year of Schulenburg's founding as 1831, but the town's official history marks it as 1873, when it was incorporated and got its first post office. Kesiah Crier (Cryer) settled on a league of land (4,428 acres) along the West Branch of the Navidad under a Mexican land grant on April 25, 1831. I've seen a copy of the surveyor's report sent to me by the current owner, my high school English teachers I. E. and Lila Clark; Thomas H. Borden of evaporated milk fame was the surveyor. The grant included the townsites of both Lyons, the first town in the area, and Schulenburg, which evolved after the Civil War.

The first grave in the Schulenburg cemetery, not far from my mother's grave, is marked with a tombstone dated 1837, indicating that James Lyons had been "killed by Indians." The thirty Comanches also kidnapped his thirteen-year-old son Warren, who lived with the Indians until he was found near Fredericksburg ten years later. In the 1840s and 1850s the surrounding area began filling in with immigrants from Germany and Bohemia—even as Comanches continued to raid.

A few miles to the south, the town of Hallettsville on the Lavaca—named for the Hallett family, whose descendants still live in the area—was established by Germans and Poles. Local legend includes the story of a lost lead mine, the German owner of which supplied early settlers with lead for their rifles. He is supposed to have been killed for not revealing the location of his mine, which came to be known as the "Lost Dutchman's Lead Mine." Of course, most of the settlers were farmers; relatively few people lived in town.

Nearer the Gulf Coast where cattle ranged across the coastal plains, Ganada was founded in 1883, named for the cattle so plentiful in the area. Most settlers hunted, fished, and trapped to augment their meager food supply. Some hunted professionally. In *Tales of Old-Time Texas,* J. Frank Dobie writes of Pal Ballard, sheriff of Lavaca County, who "had sixty long-eared hounds to run deer out of the Devil's Pocket on the Navidad River" (115). Dobie reports that "deer ran like antelope on Goldenrod Prairie, between the Navidad and Lavaca rivers" until they became wary and took to the thickets, from which

Ballard's dogs routed them. The Lavaca watershed knew something of the Sutton-Taylor feud (see Guadalupe chapter), for several of the killings took place in Lavaca County near Hallettsville.

Abel Head "Shanghai" Pierce, one of the early Texas cattle kings, whose ranch lay between the lower Navidad and Colorado rivers and whose cattle ranged for miles, brought the first Brahma cattle from India to the Texas coastal prairies. His packing plants on Matagorda Bay took the cattle industry a step closer to markets and modern industry. Pierce claimed thousands of acres in central Jackson County, where Lake Texana now lies. He is buried on Tres Palacios Creek.

Edna grew with oil development to become the largest town in the lower watershed. Today Edna remains the major community in Jackson County and the gateway to Lake Texana on the lower Navidad. Ganada serves the Mustang Creek arm of the reservoir and in State Highway 172 enjoys a more direct route to the coast than does Edna.

Twin Sisters on the Gulf Coast

Growing up in Schulenburg between the East and West forks of the Navidad, principal tributary of the Lavaca, I watched the West Navidad nearly wash away the newly completed bridge on U.S. Highway 90 west of town, witnessed the same stream flooding across U.S. 77 south of town, and saw the flood damage to the Lavaca County Courthouse in Hallettsville, all in the 1930s. I was born in the Runge Hospital in Hallettsville, where the Lavaca River is a mere weedy ditch most of the time. That courthouse sits on a rise, but floodwaters reached three feet high in the building. Hallettsville survived major floods in 1936, 1940, and again in 1980.

Although these are my home rivers, I haven't canoed either of them; they're normally either too low for paddling or too high to canoe safely when they come up after heavy rains. I've seen each river more than a mile wide, evoking Wendell Berry's "The Rise," from his book *The Long-Legged House,* about a flood on his home river in Kentucky—he paddles a canoe through the treetops.

Neither the Navidad nor the Lavaca is spring-fed; they both depend on rainfall and extremely rare snowmelt (I first saw snow when I was in the third grade, and we experienced another snowfall during my junior year in high school). Roughly halfway between San Antonio and Houston and less than a hundred miles from the Gulf Coast, Schulenburg has an elevation of 345 feet

51. The West Navidad near my hometown flows shallow and narrow beneath a canopy of tall trees festooned with grapevines.

above sea level. While the immediate vicinity is characterized by low rolling hills—you can see buildings in Weimar eight miles away—the land to the south flattens quickly.

The Lavaca heads near the small town of Moulton, between Flatonia on Interstate 10 and Shiner, which is notable for brewing beer. Moulton once had excellent high school basketball teams—I don't think we ever beat them. Rocky Creek, which heads near Shiner and goes by the brewery, is one of the Lavaca's significant tributaries, though that's not saying much except when there are heavy rains.

Geologically, the Lavaca and Navidad rivers occupy an area of fairly recent sedimentary deposits. The area was a shallow sea into which the Rocky Mountains and other highlands began to erode, the sediments settling on the sea floor. Because various animals in the sea had shells composed of calcium, limestone formed along with sandstone and other sedimentary rocks, depending on the nature, texture, and timing of the deposits. Consequently almost the entire watershed of the Lavaca and Navidad rivers lies in an area known as the Gulf Coast Basin, the coastal plain that runs along the Gulf. The ecological regions these rivers cross are the blackland prairies, the post oak belt, and the Gulf prairies and marshes.

The whole watershed is primarily farming country with some light manufacturing. One of three major milk-producing areas in Texas, it had so many dairy cattle in the 1920s that the Carnation Evaporated Milk Company established a major plant in Schulenburg to encourage the dairy industry. My father worked for many years as a fieldman for Carnation, teaching farmers better milk-handling practices and helping them increase their milk production. He directed construction of Fayette County's first silo, which was dug and blasted out of yellowish bedrock, in the mid-1930s near the Navidad's West Fork.

Cotton has been a major farm product too; as a boy I used to pick cotton to earn a little spending money in the summer, but it was hard, hot work. At one time Schulenburg had the only cotton compress between Houston and El Paso, owned and operated by F. O. Brown, mayor of Schulenburg and father of one of my best friends; as mentioned, I lived with the Browns for a few months during World War II to finish a school year, when my parents moved to Orange.

In Schulenburg we lived only a block from Gus Baumgarten's Cotton Seed Oil Mill, which we could smell whenever it operated and the breeze was right—the most wonderful aroma. Baumgarten was an inventive soul who had developed a fine flour, deep yellow in color and delicious to the taste, from cotton seeds. Just as sugar beet pulp is used for cattle fodder in many parts of the world, cottonseed hulls are used in much of the South, especially in Texas.

But Baumgarten went a step further, developing not only protein-rich cottonseed meal cakes for cattle but highly refined cottonseed flour for human consumption. It was used to treat pellagra, a deficiency of nicotinic acid (a vitamin B complex) in the diet. He named it Allison Flour after his daughter. My mother used to bake the most wonderful cakes using Allison cottonseed flour. One of my favorites was the Allison lazy daisy upside-down cake, covered with pecans in a molasses glaze.

During my boyhood there was also a molasses mill near the East Navidad a few miles south of Dubina just off U.S. 90. A mule walking around a center-stone crusher provided the power, and oak fires burning beneath big vats of sugarcane juice rendered the sweet liquids into delicious dark molasses. My mouth waters at the memory. The summer I worked cutting cane, part of my pay was buckets of molasses.

Beef production is likewise an important industry, and many of the field crops help feed dairy and beef cattle, especially now that silage has become acceptable cattle fodder. Another favorite crop, watermelons, grew fat and sweet along the Navidad. The family of one of my classmates, the Zimmermans, had a farm along the river and grew melons in the sandy loam along the bench above the bottomlands, which nurtured huge pecan trees. Some years the melons were so numerous that we'd take a mule-drawn wagon out to the field, load up with ripe melons, and bring them back to the barn to feed to the hogs, cutting out the melon hearts to feed ourselves until we were as ripe as the melons.

My high school English teachers, I. E. and Lila Clark, live on the West Navidad on a place he inherited from his family, Bermuda Valley Farm, which is featured on a Texas historical marker. It was once a famous horse farm with a race track (1894–1920), and the Clarks had raised fine racing horses. One summer I helped harvest loose hay on one of their pastures adjacent to the Navidad. Two of us high school boys would fork the hay onto a tractor-drawn wagon, and I. E. would stack it for the trip to the barn. I remember forking up a writhing copperhead that I only noticed as it dangled over my head just out of reach—I'd run a tine through its body as it rested in the shade beneath a clump of hay. All four of Texas' venomous snakes—copperhead, water moccasin, rattler, and coral snake—live in the Navidad bottom.

Enjoying the Rivers and Pools

It was along the West Navidad and Navidad that, as described earlier, my father and older brother gathered sand for my sandbox, I cut yaupon for vaulting poles and cane for crossbars, and we fished the deep pools and hunted raccoon and opossum in the river bottoms.

Once Dad took me deer hunting at Thanksgiving on the middle Navidad near Sublime, a fiasco all the way. We packed everything for the trip, except the hamburger meat and hot dogs, before I went to school. Dad was to check the refrigerator before he left home to pick me up. It began to rain as we headed southeast for the hunt. Shortly after we left the main highway in Weimar, we got stuck in the thick black gumbo of a country road. In the heavy rain, we worked for what seemed hours to get unstuck. It was well after dark before we reached the deer lease.

The ground was wet, but the skies had cleared as we began to prepare dinner—only to discover that we had no meat; Dad had forgotten it. Over a meal of buns and mustard, we decided to sleep in the car because the ground was too sodden for our quilts. After a cold, uncomfortable night, I did not want to rise in the dark to go trekking through the damp woods, but I was afraid to stay in the car alone.

However, once I got moving, I came alive to the early morning—mist rising, cardinals singing in the brush, and sunlight glistening on wet limbs. We saw plenty of tracks but no deer, watched an armadillo hunting for its breakfast, walked the cold out of our damp feet, and had a fine time on a bend of the Navidad. By noon we'd given up the planned hunt and headed home for Thanksgiving dinner.

About once a year my dad would take me out to the Klesels' farm, near where that first silo had been dug, for a night of hunting and fishing on the West Navidad: after setting out trotlines in the deep pools, he'd sit with all the older Klesel brothers, sharing a bottle, while the younger Klesel brothers—the next generation—took me hunting.

Foerster's Creek, a tributary of the West Navidad, held a population of secret bass that my next-door neighbor, Clarence Jochen, discovered. His older brother James had come home a casualty of the North African campaign during World War II, with his shattered leg in a cast. I had just learned to drive and would take the Jochen brothers to Rocky Creek, a Lavaca tributary south of town, where James could sit by the hour and fish for sunfish, perch, and catfish while his leg slowly healed. Thus did Clarence learn to fish. Later he found Foerster's Creek northwest of town on the road to High Hill. He became an expert, and would rarely return from a fishing foray without a bass for his next meal.

My experiences with the East Navidad were less frequent and less intimate. It flows south between Schulenburg and Weimar, the nearest town to the east. Weimar had a swimming pool, and at that time Schulenburg didn't. Friends and I would ride our bicycles the eight or ten miles, depending on whether we used the new highway (U.S. 90) or the old one, to go swimming at the Weimar pool. Our parents told us to use the old highway, which we usually did on the way to Weimar, but anxious to get home, we'd often take the shorter route back.

A roadside rest stop on the hill immediately east of the bridge crossing the East Navidad became our rendezvous: here we'd gather to check out the highway traffic on this main route between Houston and San Antonio. When the coast was clear, we'd launch our assault on the bridge, hoping to cross it before a big truck came roaring by, catching us on the bridge. We'd pedal hard down the hill and across the bridge, then ease off as we hit the west side, for we'd cleared the major hurdle on the trip home.

One of our favorite swimming holes, Demel's Pool (on private property but we had permission), lay on a tributary of the East Navidad called Middle Creek; it might as well have been called the Middle Fork of the Navidad, because that's what it is. The creek trickled over a limestone ledge into a clear pool where lilypads grew, shadowing the deep water near the west bank. The east side was deep too, clear and cold, but had no aquatic vegetation. We could dive off the upper bank—if we got a running start to clear the edge. The pool narrowed and shallowed after about a hundred feet to a series of limestone ledges along one bank and a sloping bottom of coarse sand on the other. Below the pool, the creek continued as a shallow trickle where we'd sometimes lie on idyllic afternoons and let the minnows nibble our toes.

Another favored spot, Blue Hole, also on private property, I first heard about from my older brother Paul, an attorney and retired judge who still lives in Schulenburg. Blue Hole is a huge pool in another Navidad tributary, scary in its dark depth. Scoured out by a flood decades ago when the stream was blocked by a huge fallen oak tree, the pool must have been two hundred feet long by a hundred wide and twenty to thirty feet deep, overgrown with dense vegetation. But Paul didn't take me there. I found it the summer of 1950 when I spent a lot of time hanging out with members of the University of Texas baseball team, who were playing semipro baseball for the Herder

52. Remains of a shipwreck or waterfront building at Port Lavaca mark the end of the Navidad and Lavaca Rivers.

Truckers in Weimar. Left-handed pitcher Jimmy Hand had a yellow convertible that we ran around in all summer, and we explored the hinterlands looking for the famous Blue Hole. When we found it, we were too intimidated to try it, but we did try another stretch upstream where a large live oak grew near the water and the stream flowed through a wide deep pool. A rope tied to one of the oak limbs enabled us to swing out over the water and drop in.

Best known among the public recreational sites within the watershed of the Navidad and Lavaca is Lake Texana in the lower basin of the two rivers, an eleven-thousand-acre impoundment formed by the Palmetto Bend Dam, which reaches more than a mile across the Navidad four miles above its confluence with the Lavaca and has nearly seven miles of dikes to augment the impoundment. Built between 1976 and 1980, the rolled earthfill structure with soil cement on its lake side inundates eighteen miles of Navidad bottomlands as well as the lower reaches of Mustang and Sandy creeks. The sixty-nine-million-dollar structure impounds 170,300 acre feet of water and serves as a saltwater barrier, since its base lies fourteen feet below sea level. At high tide, it prevents saltwater intrusion into the former river.

Although federal funds were used to build the dam, the Lavaca-Navidad River Authority operates the Palmetto Bend Project and the recreational facilities on Lake Texana, named for the nearby town of Texana. Established in 1832 as Santa Anna to honor the Mexican president, the town changed its name to Texana when Santa Anna ignored the Mexican Constitution of 1824 and turned on Texas. The first town in Jackson County, it was bypassed by the New York, Texas, and Mexican Railroad in 1883, and died a natural death by 1885.

Another feature on the lower Lavaca, Port Lavaca State Fishing Pier, offers Texans more fishing possibilities. Part of an old causeway, the pier on the west side of Lavaca Bay gives fishermen access to redfish, sheepshead, speckled trout, drum, and flounder. Like most Texas bays, Lavaca Bay formed when sea level rose and drowned part of the valley of the Lavaca River and Garcitas Creek.

The Navidad-Lavaca watershed may be small, but it harbors important early Texas history and the earthly remains of both my parents, plus all the memories of growing up in a quieter and more peaceful time, in a more natural rural Texas. The lower watershed includes the sites of such early Texas towns as La Salle's Fort St. Louis (La Salle) and Indianola, which was second only to Galveston as a port city during Republic of Texas days. Still largely agricultural, the area retains much of its bucolic character even at the dawn of the twenty-first century, despite oil and gas discoveries and growing industrialization. It has changed in the fifty years since I grew up there, but despite my long absence, it still feels like home to me.

Guadalupe

LOCATION: *Northwest, then north of San Antonio, southeast to the Gulf Coast*
NAME: *From Nuestra Señora de Guadalupe (Our Lady of Guadalupe), a Spanish saint, named by Alonso de León*
CITIES: *Kerrville, New Braunfels, Seguin, Gonzales, Cuero, Victoria*
IMPOUNDMENTS: *Canyon Lake, Lake McQueeney*
TRIBUTARIES: *Blanco–San Marcos River, San Antonio River near coast*
RECREATION: *Most famous river in Texas for canoeing, tubing, and rafting; also swimming, fishing (trout, bass, catfish), power boating*
WATERSHED: 6,000 *square miles*
DISCHARGE: *With the San Antonio River, more than 1 million acre feet*
LENGTH: 250 *miles*
PUBLIC LANDS: *Kerr Wildlife Management Area, Kerrville-Schreiner State Park, Blanco State Park, John J. Stokes San Marcos River State Park, Guadalupe River State Park, Honey Creek State Natural Area, Canyon Lake, Sebastopol House (Seguin), Palmetto State Park, Guadalupe Delta Wildlife Management Area, Matagorda Island State Park, Matagorda Island Wildlife Conservation Area, Aransas National Wildlife Refuge*
FEATURES: *Comal River and Landa Park (New Braunfels), Old Indianola Trail, Coleto Creek Park (between Victoria and Goliad)*

A SPRING-FED STREAM that flows out of the Karst topography of the Edwards Plateau, the Guadalupe River is Texas' best known, one of relatively few major rivers that flow from headwaters to Gulf entirely within the boundaries of the Lone Star state. With its clear waters and cypress-lined banks, the Guadalupe draws visitors from all over the state and well beyond. Whitewater enthusiasts nationwide come to the Guadalupe to canoe, kayak, and raft. Anglers seek the Guadalupe bass in its crystalline waters, and many people swim in it. Locals often enjoy it by floating certain segments in inner tubes, the original inflatable craft.

Tubing is as popular on the Guadalupe as on any river anywhere. Even so sophisticated a magazine as *Texas Monthly* has featured tubing, in an article by Joe Nick Patoski. Fishing may come in second to self-powered boating as the most popular recreational activity on the Guadalupe, especially if "tubing" is considered boating, but this is one of the few Texas rivers to offer trout fishing in addition to the normal bass, catfish, and crappie.

The north and south forks of the Guadalupe join at Hunt in Kerr County. It flows through Kerrville, Comfort, and Spring Branch, making an arc around San Antonio, then through New Braunfels and Seguin, still arcing. At Seguin it turns barely south of east to Gonzales, where the San Marcos joins it, then flows almost due south through Yoakum, Cuero, and Victoria to the coast. At Cuero it widens as it enters the coastal plain, the main reason Cuero was hit so hard by the October, 1998, floods. Below Victoria, the river becomes wild and primitive, joined first by Coleto Creek not far south of Victoria, then by the San Antonio River only a few miles from its emergence first into Guadalupe Bay, then into San Antonio Bay, and ultimately into the Gulf of Mexico.

In October of 1998, heavy rain up to twenty-four inches in some areas spawned by a hurricane in the Gulf of Mexico caused the Guadalupe to flood massively, spreading to six miles wide in places and driving thousands of people from their homes. At Victoria it crested at thirty-five feet, fourteen feet above flood stage, breaking by four vertical feet high-water records set in 1936. People living in low-lying areas miles from the river suffered home damage. One friend reported having to shovel three feet of mud out of her living room. The Goyneses, owners of my favorite camp ground in Texas, Pecan Park on the bank of the San Marcos, reported that the area was still inundated two weeks after the rain. The whole lower watershed felt the impact of the enormous flood.

The popular Texas Water Safari, characterized as "the world's toughest boat race," follows the San Marcos and Guadalupe for 265 miles to the Gulf, making it one of the world's longest as well. Beginning at Aquarina Springs in San Marcos, the race is open to seven categories of human-powered watercraft and takes place during the second weekend of June. In the spring of 1997, the flooding San Marcos River aided paddlers in getting downstream to record the shortest times in the history of the race. A six-man team composed of four Texas paddlers—Fred and Brian Mynar, Jerry Cochran, and

53. Cypress trees seem to hold hands above the clear water of the Guadalupe River in the Texas Hill Country.

John Dunn—plus Steve Landick from Michigan and Solomon Carrier from Canada completed the course in twenty-nine hours and forty-five minutes.

The Guadalupe and its tributaries—primarily the San Marcos, its tributary the Blanco, the San Antonio, and its tributary the Medina—typify rivers that head in the Hill Country. Flanked by cypresses along their upper reaches, they run cold with spring-fed clarity over a bed of limestone; then they cross the Edwards Aquifer Recharge Zone as they cascade over the Balcones Escarpment into the flat coastal plain. Here the main river loses much of its force and clarity as it picks up sediments and becomes turbid in its approach to the Gulf.

In 1689 Alonso de León wrote of the Guadalupe, on the day he named it, that "the river has a good ford; its banks are covered with timber," suggesting its practical qualities. Mary Austin Holley, writing in *Texas* (1836), suggested its recreational potential: "Its waters are very transparent and navigable by canoes. It is a beautiful river, passing through a well-timbered country, and affords valuable alluvial bottoms. Its width is in some places as much as sixty yards" (34). Frederick Law Olmsted, referred to the upper Guadalupe as "quick and perfectly transparent" when he saw it in 1854. In her somewhat disorganized but nonetheless delightful *Legends of Texas Rivers* (1937), Fannie May Barbee Hughes mentions an "extensive water power development plan, with six hydroelectric plants" along the Guadalupe, a plan fortunately never completed.

Crown Jewel of Texas Rivers

The Guadalupe's whole headwater region abounds in tourist-oriented facilities and recreational activities. It has become a popular Texas playground featuring camps, dude ranches, hunting leases, exotic game farms, and commercial river running. Bird-watching has also become a major activity along with horseback riding, cave exploring, and photography. Celebrating the Germanic heritage of the area, its food and antiques, its music and folk arts, has become big business, as has exploiting wildlife species from other continents.

Tourism has become a major economic factor during recent decades with recognition of the scenic beauty of the valley and as its rivers have come to be valued as the natural recreational resources they are. Tourism is listed in the 1998–99 *Texas Almanac* as the leading industry for Blanco, Kendall, and Kerr counties, and as second in both Hays and Comal counties. A few wineries have popped up along headwater streams, and certainly real estate plays

54. Lilypads, clear water, and reflections characterize the Guadalupe River.

an important role in the local economy. Let's hope that real estate development doesn't destroy the scenic beauty of the area, as it threatens to do in some parts of the watershed. A proposed withdrawal of water from the river by the Blanco-Guadalupe River Authority for municipal uses presently threatens the viability of fishing and boating activities on the Guadalupe below its major dam.

The counties through which the Guadalupe flows—Kerr, Kendall, Comal, Guadalupe, Gonzales, DeWitt—constitute an area in which tourism has replaced agriculture at extremities of the drainage: its headwaters and its Gulf Coast reaches. In between, the region is focused largely on livestock and poultry raising and dairying, with some oil and gas development and grain and cotton farms. Farmers and ranchers in the area also raise exotics: emus, ostriches, Asian and African game animals, and wildlife species for exhibition.

As a boy of twelve, I went deer hunting with my dad on a lease on the upper Guadalupe one fall. We saw a few does and heard a few turkeys but didn't shoot at anything; however, the outing introduced me to the natural beauty of the Texas Hill Country. We went back the following spring, driving a loop through the Hill Country to see the wildflowers, and I saw my first armadillo—I don't think they were as common in those days as they are now, nor as widespread.

The chances are that Cabeza de Vaca saw no armadillos when he crossed virtually every Texas river that flows into the Gulf of Mexico in the 1530s. One of the first rivers discovered when later Europeans crossed the Rio Grande, the Guadalupe was named for the saint Nuestra Señora de Guadalupe (Our Lady of Guadalupe) by Alonso de León on April 14, 1689. As governor of Coahuila, he had been ordered into Texas to confront and root out the French, and he had brought her image along to protect his expedition.

René Robert Cavelier de La Salle, who had explored the Mississippi River to the Gulf of Mexico, returned to the Gulf Coast to establish a colony, but when he overshot the Mississippi, he settled his people only a few miles from the mouth of the Guadalupe on Garcitas Creek. Here he established Fort Saint Louis near Lavaca Bay. The French had been pretty well wiped out by Karankawa Indians and starvation by the time de León reached the ruins of their settlement, but he followed their trail eastward, looking for survivors and exploring East Texas, where the Spanish crown soon established missions to convert local Indians.

Spanish and German Settlement

The Guadalupe offered only a minor obstacle to travelers on the Old Spanish Trail, also known as El Camino Real (the royal road) and the San Antonio Road, between San Antonio and Nacogdoches, which became the center of the East Texas missions that began to be established in 1690. They failed, were reestablished starting around 1716, and failed again. In 1718, however, when the Mission San Antonio de Valero, which became the Alamo, took hold at San Pedro Springs and succeeded, other missions were established along the San Antonio River. The neighborhood soon became the center of a thriving cattle industry in South Texas that extended down the San Antonio and east to the Guadalupe and beyond. These settlements were among the earliest to succeed in the region north of the Rio Grande.

The first Spanish settlement in the Guadalupe Valley itself was the Nuestra Señora del Espíritu Santo de Zuñiga Mission, involving Franciscan friars who moved in 1749 from Matagorda Bay to a bluff overlooking the river a few miles above present-day Victoria. Near this site the first effort to irrigate lowlands along the river by damming the Guadalupe occurred; it was abandoned in 1736, a century before Texas won independence from Mexico. Other missions begun at Comal Springs (now New Braunfels) and at San Marcos Springs failed, primarily due to Indian raids and poor conversion rates among native people, but floods contributed as well.

What became Guadalupe County, originally used by Karankawas and later by Comanches, experienced the first influx of Mexican settlers in 1806 on a Spanish land grant issued to José de la Baume. An attempt at Spanish settlements near present-day Gonzales (1808) failed because of floods and Indian depredation. In wasn't until Martín de León received a grant in 1824 to settle forty-one Mexican families between the lower Lavaca and Guadalupe rivers that any more permanent community succeeded. When empresario Green De Witt obtained an adjacent grant (between the Lavaca and the divide between the Guadalupe and San Antonio) in 1825, his people established Gonzales on the Guadalupe. Indian raids almost immediately discouraged members of this colony, and they moved onto the de León grant to establish a town on the Lavaca. In 1827 the De Witt settlers were ordered back to Gonzales on the Guadalupe, where a few years later one of the first battles of the Texas War of Independence was fought.

To defend their town against Indians, the people of Gonzales had borrowed a cannon from Mexican authorities. When relationships between Anglo settlers and the Mexican government began to deteriorate, Mexican military forces demanded the return of the cannon, but the Texians, as they now called themselves, refused in the famous response: "Come and Take It," and attacked the Mexican forces sent to recover it. One Mexican soldier was killed in the battle known as the first of the war (October 2, 1835); the remainder of the Mexican army retreated to San Antonio.

During the Texas War of Independence, which followed hard upon that initial skirmish, the Guadalupe River and its tributary San Antonio River were centers of activity. A Texas army organized in Gonzales captured San Antonio, giving Texas forces control of the Alamo. Citizens of Gonzales made the only positive response to an appeal by William B. Travis, commander at the Alamo, for help, sending thirty-two men to augment the Texas forces there. Later floods on the Guadalupe near Gonzales delayed the Mexican army under Santa Anna for at least three days as they tried to catch Sam Houston and the Texas army retreating eastward across Texas.

In the first decade after the war two new towns were established on the Guadalupe: Seguin, named for the Tejano leader Juan N. Seguín in (1838), and New Braunfels, named for the German Prince Carl of Solms-Braunfels (1845). As many as two thirds of the early German immigrants, poorly informed and poorly prepared for the rigors of the frontier, died at the coast from starvation and lack of shelter, but Prince Carl brought organization to the new German colony, which even established positive relations with some local Indian tribes. The upper Guadalupe in what became Kerr County attracted settlers in the late 1840s, including a good many Germans. Indians still claimed much of the Edwards Plateau, and while numerous raids discouraged settlement, the Germans hung on, banded together for protection in their stone houses, and aided by Texas Rangers, fought off the raiders enough times to survive and prosper.

Only a year after the Battle of Plum Creek (see the Lavaca-Navidad chapter), forty Texas Rangers under Capt. John (Jack) Coffee Hays were ambushed and surrounded by a large band of Comanches at Bandera Pass the spring of 1840 (see San Antonio River chapter). Located about fifteen miles south of Kerrville near Camp Verde, the pass lies in a deep gorge a third of a mile long and 125 feet wide some fifty miles west of San Antonio. The pass separates the valleys of the Guadalupe and Medina, a tributary of the San Antonio River.

Texas Rangers became involved a few decades later in a major disagreement among Anglo settlers in De Witt County on the lower Guadalupe, a dispute that bled (literally) over into adjacent Lavaca County, the infamous Sutton-Taylor Feud. Capt. Leander H. McNelly, the ranger whose special troop would later clean up the Nueces Strip, led his command into the fray, which had begun in 1869 and had cost dozens of lives. It has been said that even after all the Suttons and Taylors were dead, the feud went on because everyone in the neighborhood had chosen sides. McNelly and his rangers were sent there to assure that local courts could function without interference from armed gangs from either side. The feud was similar in several ways to the infamous Lincoln County War along the upper Pecos River in New Mexico a few years later and to the similar situation in Tombstone, Arizona Territory.

McNelly sent Sergeant Middleton with three rangers to escort safely an important witness from Yorktown to court in Indianola at the mouth of the Lavaca. The rangers were attacked by a party of fifteen heavily armed men intent upon killing the witness. In the gun battle between the rangers and the Taylor faction, one ranger took a shoulder wound, and the witness escaped unharmed. McNelly found him the next day and delivered him safely to court. The witness's testimony had the potential of convicting William Taylor, who had killed in cold blood one of the Suttons and a man named Slaughter on the steamer *Clinton* a few months earlier.

According to Walter Prescott Webb, in his classic *The Texas Rangers,* NcNelly pointed out in his report on the rangers' involvement that "the method of destroying unfavorable testimony in DeWitt County, one long in vogue, was to murder the witnesses" (235). Taylor had been arrested in Cuero on the Guadalupe, had been delivered to Indianola, and had then been sent to a Galveston jail for safekeeping—on the same steamer on which he'd done the deed. The feud festered for another decade.

From Agriculture to Tourism and Real Estate

Before long the neighborhood was getting crowded. In the early years, the major economic bases were cattle and cotton. Pecan trees along the river bottoms supplied a source of food and commerce. While there was never enough timber in the valley of the Guadalupe to support a real lumber industry, so many native walnut trees were cut to supply eastern furniture companies that much of the valley no longer has any native walnut trees, even in Seguin, which was originally called Walnut Springs. Despite the discovery of oil in the 1920s near Luling on the tributary San Marcos River, the Guadalupe Valley has always been largely agricultural.

Some geographers consider the Edwards Plateau, which spawns the Guadalupe and several other Hill Country streams, to be an extension of the Great Plains, but geologically speaking, it is a separate entity related only in a general way to the Staked Plain of the Panhandle. It represents a major vertical uplift of between 750 and 2,700 feet, averaging about 2,000 feet. Composed primarily of limestone laid down at the bottom of an ancient sea, the plateau offers little topsoil. It grows juniper (commonly called "cedar" in most of Texas), a variety of scrub oak, mesquite, cactus, and several varieties of agave. Grass is less than luxuriant, though the region does produce wonderful and abundant wildflowers in the spring. Sheep, goats, and cattle thrive on the sparse vegetation, making livestock production a prime focus, but the economy is changing.

People from the cities have been buying up Hill Country property for decades as tourism has slowly encroached upon agriculture as an economic factor. A curious thing has happened as more and more city folks have moved into the rural watershed of the upper Guadalupe and its tributaries: people have begun to compete with one another for the most impressive gates, the costliest entrances. At first these entryways were made of native limestone dug from the local hills, but before long exotic stone edifices and elaborate steel structures began to appear, then stone-faced concrete wings and massive piles of imported multicolored rock. A few have turned to natural wood—but wood that doesn't grow within hundreds of miles of the Hill Country. I chuckle at these extravagances, at the apparent need to display wealth in these roadside facades, at people's lack of taste, and at their ridiculous competitiveness, but I'm sure this game of one-up-manship creates jobs and helps the local economy.

Another sign of the times shows itself in fences. "By their fences, ye shall know the stock therein," I wrote in my journal as I drove through mile after mile of layered limestone, loose rock, and neat native stone houses, of pricklypear, cedar, scrub oak, and native wildflowers. High fences indicated either exotic species within or attempts to keep native deer out. Low fences suggested sheep or goats. In one well-fenced pasture I saw wild turkeys feeding with emus; in another, a herd of Angora goats. When I stopped to photograph the goats, they came nearer and nearer until only the low fence stood between them and me. Behind woven-wire fences I saw East African antelope, spotted deer with fawns, and ostriches.

For all the small reservoirs on the Guadalupe's headwater tributaries, only two significant impoundments presently lie in the watershed: the 8,240-acre Canyon Lake on the main river in Comal County and Coleto Creek Reservoir on Coleto Creek, shared by Goliad and Victoria counties. Other major impoundments in the planning stage include a massive Cuero Reservoir that would cover much of De Witt and Gonzales counties and at least two more in the Hill Country north of San Antonio.

Canyon Lake, with a storage capacity of 385,600 acre feet of water, began impounding water in 1966 upon the completion of the Army Corps of Engineers dam north of New Braunfels. The reservoir has become a major flat-water recreation area, but for all the natural beauty of the Canyon Lake area, the rampant real-estate development has spoiled it for me. When I visited the area, a real-estate sign towering high above the Hill Country vegetation so caught my attention that I stopped at the company's nearest office to complain about the visual desecration of the landscape. The agent gave me nothing but a flippant response. Why do developers so often ignore the natural beauty of the areas from which they earn their living?

Enjoying the San Marcos and Guadalupe Rivers

My acquaintance with the rivers of the watershed began during my high school days when class trips introduced me to the Guadalupe at New Braunfels and

55. A marina on Canyon Lake, an impoundment of the Guadalupe River northwest of New Braunfels, suggests the type of use the reservoir receives.

to the San Marcos River, the major Guadalupe tributary, in nearby San Marcos. My sophomore class spent a day at Landa Park in New Braunfels, where we saw Comal Springs, swam in the off-river pool, and tubed the river. In San Marcos we discovered the in-river commercial swimming area that became one of my favorite haunts during college days at the University of Texas in Austin only thirty miles away.

The Blanco River, which flows into the San Marcos just downstream from the Interstate 35 crossing in San Marcos, is more of a series of small lakes than a river in much of its lower course, a common practice in Central Texas. Small dams, four or five to ten or twelve feet high, impound the river every few hundred yards to create a necklace of lakes, so that every property owner along the river has a pond for swimming and fishing. The public is shut out to a large extent, but the state is purchasing more and more land for public waterfront access. The upper reaches of the river as it flows through Blanco and Wimberley offer delightful recreational opportunities and scenic views as well as some paddling possibilities—if you can find access.

A huge pool full of fish surrounded by tropical vegetation, not all of it indigenous to the area, characterizes Aquarena Spring in San Marcos, the origin of the river. At the spring archeologists have found significant evidence of thousands of years of local human habitation. In past years a major commercial enterprise produced an underwater floor show that drew people from around the world, but the spring has become part of Southwest Texas State University's local holdings and is now used primarily for scientific research.

Popular Texas nature writer Stephen Harrigan has written a fine essay about the San Marcos River, entitled "The Perfect River." Harrigan was drawn to the river "for the way the water sounded and the way it held light" (75). I have paddled the San Marcos, the stretch from Pecan Park at Martindale past the old mill to the next low-water crossing downstream, and I can relate to Harrigan's feelings as expressed in the essay. He writes of the archeological discoveries in Spring Lake, where the San Marcos begins, and of the river's unique fauna.

I must say a word about Pecan Park, a small privately owned campground that lies on a bend of the San Marcos River below its confluence with the Blanco, south of San Marcos at the edge of Martindale. Owned and operated by Tom Goynes and his wife, Pecan Park is one of the loveliest places in Texas

56. Sheep graze in a Hill Country pasture near the headwaters of the Blanco River, tributary to the San Marcos.

57. An old mill above a rapid on the San Marcos River has had better days. It lies near the Balcones Escarpment.

to spend a night. Huge, well-spaced pecan trees grow on a river bench that floods at extremely high water (it did in October, 1998), judging by its fine sandy soil. Huge cypress trees line the river. Blue jays and cardinals call in the early morning; small, tasty pecans litter the ground, attracting squirrels; and numerous colorful wildflowers bloom in spring. Goynes is one of Texas' most active paddlers and river advocates. The October, 1998, flood took out some of the big old giant pecan trees, but where the grass grew, little damage occurred. However, the graveled areas washed out as the river dug four- to five-foot trenches. Water was almost a foot deep in the Goynes's home. They've had to rebuild the camping area, essentially start from scratch. At this writing, Pecan Park is open only for church groups and youth groups, but Tom vows it will return. The October flood of 1998 has gone downstream, taking with it much sand and silt, but Pecan Park is back in use again.

The aforementioned private swimming area on the San Marcos River just below the railroad bridge gave me a great deal of joy during my college days. This cool, clear swimming hole in the river offered a high tower with a cable to a midstream island, a trio of trapezes overhanging the river, and a huge anchored top in the shallower water. From the tower we could ride a cable car running on rollers and drop off into the river; from the various trapezes we could do flips and gainers into the deep pool—it was a blast.

The Guadalupe watershed today has a series of public lands to visit. Beginning at Kerr Wildlife Management Area near Hunt, let's have a look at it all the way to the coast. At Kerr you can find the endangered golden-cheeked warbler and the black-capped vireo of the Hill Country in the summer, along with deer, javelina, fox, raccoon, and skunk, and in the winter, wild turkey. At Kerrville-Schreiner State Park at the southeast edge of Kerrville the river offers swimming, fishing, and canoeing; a larger section of the park across State Highway 173 has a good hiking trail through wooded terrain where you can find most of the wildlife.

Guadalupe River State Park and adjacent Honey Creek State Natural Area lie a few dozen miles directly north of San Antonio. Here, in January 1997, I did a short solo canoe trip, poling upstream for a few miles, then drifting back down to enjoy the current. Then in the spring of 1998 I canoed with Henry Holman of Hollywood Park from Golden Crossing on Edge Falls Road to the park. The trips were different because of the season and the company; each was special in its own way. The park itself is special too, with its

58. The San Marcos flows through early-morning fog at Pecan Park, my favorite Texas campground.

59. Huge pecan trees dominate a bench above the San Marcos River at Pecan Park near Martindale.

huge cypress trees and limestone cliffs. The lovely and endangered golden-cheeked warblers nest here in the Ashe juniper and live oak woods, and the rare Honey Creek Cave salamander lives here, in the longest known cave in the state. Many other species of fish, birds, and mammals native to the Hill Country can be seen along the river.

Blanco State Park, on the Blanco River in the town of Blanco, was developed by the Civilian Conservation Corps during the 1930s. Small (105 acres) and urban, in the sense that it lies in town, the park enjoys a mile of riverfront, natural springs, a typical Hill Country limestone riverbed, and two low-water dams that encourage swimming and fishing (rainbow trout are stocked). In tiny (5.6 acres) John J. Stokes San Marcos River State Park, which lies near Interstate 35 not far from the Aquarena Spring headwaters, you can swim, fish, and canoe. The low dam on the river has a canoe slot to obviate portaging the dam. Lying on the Balcones fault zone, the river was used historically to mill grain and to gin and bale cotton.

Sebastopol State Historical Park in Seguin commemorates the 1854 concrete home of Col. Joshua W. Young. The unusual structure was known as Sebastopol, perhaps because of the Battle of Sebastopol fought in the same year during the Crimean War—the battle that prompted Tennyson's famous poem, "The Charge of the Light Brigade." Traveling through Texas in 1854, Frederick Law Olmsted, the architect for Central Park in New York City, stopped in Seguin and marveled at the use of concrete—cheap, neat in appearance, durable—in so small a town on such an isolated frontier. He thought Seguin "the prettiest town in Texas" (136).

As already noted, the town was named for Juan Seguín, one of the Tejanos who played a heroic role in Texas' War of Independence. Colonel Seguín led the only detachment of Texas-born Mexicans in the Battle of San Jacinto, fighting for the Texas cause. The town of Seguin is also the setting for a wonderful historical novel, *True Women* by Janice W. Windle, which covers several generations of delightful background along the Guadalupe River.

Palmetto State Park near Luling I'd never seen, even though it lies less than fifty miles from my hometown, until I began doing field research for this book. It was acquired in 1933, two years after I was born, but I'd never even heard of it. I'm glad I did. Composed of a part of Ottin Swamp and rolling hills covered with post oak woodland, it lies on a terrace of the San Marcos River. The approach road hugs a high hill that offers a fine view of the river valley, but to enjoy the park, you need to walk its three nature trails. The understory of dwarf palmettos and pricklypear cactus highlights an open forest

60. Typical vegetation at Palmetto State Park near Luling on the San Marcos River belies the riparian habitat.

of ash, oak, and sycamore that form a thick canopy. The park boasts 240 species of birds, more than five hundred plant species, and considerable other wildlife.

The Guadalupe Delta Wildlife Management Area lies near the mouth of the river along with Matagorda Island Wildlife Conservation Area, Matagorda Island State Park, and nearby Aransas National Wildlife Refuge, winter home of the rare whooping cranes. I visited the area in January, 1998, and saw a trio of whooping cranes fishing in the bay and herds of deer feeding in the dunes. I camped at nearby Goose Island State Park. The whole river-mouth region of wetlands, estuaries, bays protected by barrier islands, and the barrier islands and peninsulas themselves creates a vital wildlife habitat; it is a recreational resource that needs to be used with care.

Headquartered in San Antonio, one paddle-boating outfitter, Bill Minor, who calls himself the Tide Guide, offers sea-kayak trips to the offshore islands. Clients paddle their own craft through the bays and passes, fighting wind and current to reach isolated campsites, where small individual tents set up within a larger tent protect campers from the weather and insects. These trips, especially popular in late winter or early spring, provide paddlers with excellent opportunities to see many of the nineteen endangered or threatened species and the three hundred species of birds that live here.

From Hill Country headwaters to coastal estuary, the Guadalupe River provides a variety of recreational opportunities as well as a substantial economy based on tourism and agriculture. The major flood in October of 1998 disrupted the neighborhood and rearranged the furniture, but the Guadalupe River and its tributaries quickly began to recover through natural processes and the will of the people living in the watershed.

Without doubt, the Guadalupe is the most popular recreational river in Texas, near enough to major population centers to attract crowds of swimmers, tubers, canoeists, and rafters as well as fishermen and casual picnickers. It's clear pale-green waters offer refreshingly cool magic on a hot summer's day and plenty of sunburn to the careless. Originating in a hot, somewhat dry landscape, the Guadalupe appeals through its contrasts. It's a friendly, accessible river that everyone can enjoy, and many people do. It draws them back time and again, a mecca for recreating multitudes.

Epilogue

We have only recently begun to learn from modern science what Native American people have been trying to tell us for generations: that the whole earth and everything in it and on it are connected, that if we destroy one element, we impact all the others, that if we disrupt its patterns, we lose the whole.

When Europeans came to Texas, they brought horses and cattle, sheep and goats. Their livestock began to strip the land of its natural vegetation, especially after fences blocked their free range and access to water. Then with the plow the settlers opened the land to forces of erosion that had been acting upon the land throughout time but had never had so clear a shot at the fragile soil. It began to wash away with rainfall and snowmelt, to blow away with the wind. Rivers began to choke on the sediments and to cut more deeply into the soil. The water table began to drop as wells sucked water from beneath the land to replace the surface water that was disappearing.

As we have changed the land in the name of progress, we have damaged the social and cultural heritage of the people, destroyed the land's ability to sustain us, and ruined the capacity of our rivers to flow freely. We have built our houses and businesses in floodplains and seen them flooded, yet we fail to learn the simple fact that rivers, designed by nature to drain water from the land, need free range as much as the bison did. When we dam the rivers, dike them, and dewater them, we alter their nature.

We can't turn back time, nor should we try, but we can learn from our mistakes and alter our attitude toward rivers and the land that bears them; we can change our abusive actions and behaviors, shift our philosophy from that of conqueror toward the role of cooperating colleague, from the need to rule nature to a willingness to live with nature and within natural laws. If we don't, we're in serious trouble. As Aldo Leopold so wisely wrote in the introduction to *A Sand County Almanac,* "We abuse the land because we regard it as a commodity belonging to us. When we see land as a community to which we belong, we may begin to use it with love and respect" (viii). We also, unfortunately, see water as a commodity and have been abusing it for decades. I hope it isn't too late to change our ways.

For all the damage done by rivers when they flood, and for all the abuses inflicted on them by civilized society, given half a chance, rivers have an amazing capacity to renew themselves, recover, rejuvenate, and return to their immutable purposes: to drain the land and form its contours, to assist in natural erosion and fertilization of the floodplain, to water the land and return excess water to the oceans to begin anew the wondrous, unique hydrological cycle that makes life on earth possible—we live on the only planet that has one.

Bibliography

Abernethy, Francis Edward, ed. *The Bounty of Texas.* Texas Folklore Society Publication. Denton: University of North Texas Press, 1990.
Alonzo, Armando C. *Tejano Legacy: Rancheros and Settlers in South Texas, 1734–1900.* Albuquerque: University of New Mexico Press, 1998.
Atherton, Lewis. *The Cattle Kings.* Lincoln: University of Nebraska Press, 1972.
Aulbach, Louis F., and Jack Richardson. *The Lower Pecos River.* Houston: Wilderness Area Map Service, 1996.
Barrington, Carol. "A River for All Reasons." *Texas Highways,* Sept. 1995, 4–11.
Bedichek, Roy. *Adventures with a Texas Naturalist.* 1947. Reprint with introduction by Rick Bass, Austin: University of Texas Press, 1994.
———. *Karankaway Country.* Austin: University of Texas Press, 1974.
Bones, Jim. *Texas West of the Pecos.* College Station: Texas A&M University Press, 1981.
Bonney, Orrin H. "Big Thicket: Biological Crossroads of North America." *Living Wilderness* 33, no. 106 (summer 1969): 19–21.
Clayton, Lawrence. *Historic Ranches of Texas.* With paintings by J. U. Salvant. Austin: University of Texas Press, 1993.
Clifford, Craig, and Tom Pilkington. *Range Wars: Heated Debates, Sober Reflections, and Other Assessments of Texas Writing.* Dallas: Southern Methodist University Press, 1989.
Clissold, Stephen. *The Seven Cities of Cibola.* New York: Clarkson N. Potter, 1962.
Cotham, Edward T., Jr. *Battle on the Bay: The Civil War Struggle for Galveston.* Austin: University of Texas Press, 1998.
Couch, Ernie, and Jill Couch. *Texas Trivia.* Nashville: Rutledge Hill Press, 1987.
Cox, Paul W., and Patty Leslie. *Texas Trees: A Friendly Guide.* San Antonio: Corona Publishing Company, 1997.
Crow, Melinda. *The Rockhound's Guide to Texas.* Helena, Mont.: Falcon Press, 1994.
Culley, John J. (Jack). *Cattle, Horses, and Men.* Tucson: University of Arizona Press, 1984.
Cummings, Joe. *Texas Handbook.* 4th ed. Chico, Calif.: Moon Travel Handbooks, 1998.
Dearen, Patrick. *Castle Gap and the Pecos Frontier.* Fort Worth: Texas Christian University Press, 1988.
———. *A Cowboy of the Pecos.* Plano: Republic of Texas Press, 1997.
———. *Crossing Rio Pecos.* Fort Worth: Texas Christian University Press, 1996.
———. *Portraits of the Pecos Frontier.* Lubbock: Texas Tech University Press, 1993.
Dobie, J. Frank. *The Ben Lilly Legend.* Austin: University of Texas Press, 1990.
———. *The Longhorns.* New York: Grosset & Dunlap, 1941.
———. *Out of Old Rock.* Austin: University of Texas Press, 1988.
———. *Rattlesnakes.* 1965. Austin: University of Texas Press, 1984.
———. *Tales of Old-Time Texas.* 1928. Austin: University of Texas Press, 1988.

———. *Voice of the Coyote.* Lincoln: University of Nebraska Press, 1961.

Durham, George, as told to Clyde Wantland. *Taming the Nueces Strip: The Story of McNelly's Rangers.* Austin: University of Texas Press, 1962.

Duval, John C. *The Adventures of Big Foot Wallace.* Edited by Mabel Major and Rebecca W. Smith. Lincoln: University of Nebraska Press, 1966.

Erickson, John R. *Through Time and the Valley.* Austin: Shoal Creek Publishers, 1978.

Fehrenbach, T. R. *Comanches: The Destruction of a People.* New York: Alfred A. Knopf, 1974; New York: Da Capo Press, 1994.

Flores, Dan L. *Jefferson and Southwestern Exploration.* Norman: University of Oklahoma Press, 1984.

Foster, William C. *Spanish Expeditions into Texas, 1689–1768.* Austin: University of Texas, 1955.

Frantz, Joe B. *Texas: A Bicentennial History.* New York: W. W. Norton, 1976.

———. *Aspects of the American West.* College Station: Texas A&M University Press, 1976.

Fritz, Edward C. *Realms of Beauty: A Guide to the Wilderness Areas of East Texas.* Austin: University Of Texas Press, 1993.

Garreau, Joel. *The Nine Nations of North America.* New York: Avon Books, 1981.

Gehlbach, Frederick R. *Mountain Islands and Desert Seas: A Natural History of the U.S. Mexican Borderlands.* College Station: Texas A&M University Press, 1993.

Gentry, Howard Scott. *Agaves of Continental North America.* Tucson: University of Arizona Press, 1998.

Graham, Gary L. *Texas Wildlife Viewing Guide.* Helena, Mont.: Falcon Press, 1992.

Graves, John. *Goodbye to a River.* Austin: Texas Monthly Press, 1960.

———. *Hard Scrabble.* Austin: Texas Monthly Press, 1974.

———. *From a Limestone Ledge.* Houston: Gulf Publishing Co., 1980.

———. *A John Graves Reader.* Austin: University of Texas Press, 1996.

Grider, Sylvia Ann, and Lou Halsell Rodenberger. *Texas Women Writers.* College Station: Texas A&M University Press, 1997.

Gunter, Pete A. Y. *The Big Thicket: An Ecological Reevaluation.* Denton: University of North Texas Press, 1993.

Haley, J. Evetts. *Life on the Texas Range.* Photographs by Erwin E. Smith. Austin: University of Texas Press, 1994.

———. *Charles Goodnight: Cowman and Plainsman.* 1936. Norman: University of Oklahoma Press, 1987.

Harrigan, Stephen. *Comanche Midnight.* Austin: University of Texas Press, 1995.

———. *A Natural State: Essays on Texas.* Austin: University of Texas Press, 1994.

Hendricks, Louie. *"No Rules or Guidelines": Cal Farley's Boys Ranch.* Amarillo: Cal Farley's Boys Ranch, 1996.

Hoagland, Edward. *Red Wolves and Black Bears.* New York: Lyons & Burford, 1995.

Hodge, Larry D. "Rio Grande, Bond of Life," part 1. *Texas Highways,* Feb. 1992, 26–37.

Hogan, William Ransom. *The Texas Republic: A Social and Economic History.* Austin: University of Texas Press, 1969.

Holley, Mary Austin. *Texas.* 1836. Lexington, Ky.: n.p., 1990.

Hughes, Fannie May Barbee. *Legends of Texas Rivers.* Dallas: Mathis, Van Nort & Co., 1937.

James, Marquis. *The Raven: A Biography of Sam Houston.* 1929. Austin: University of Texas Press, 1989.

Kelton, Elmer. "Steamboats on Texas Rivers" in *Water Trails West.* New York: Doubleday, 1978.

Knapik, Jane. *Schulenburg: 100 Years on the Road, 1873–1973.* N.p.: Nortex Offset Publications, 1973.

Langewiesche, William. *Cutting for Sign: The Border.* New York: Pantheon Books, 1993.

Laughmiller, Campbell, and Lynn Laughmiller. *Texas Wildflowers: A Field Guide.* Austin: University of Texas Press, 1992.

Lavender, David. *Bent's Fork.* Lincoln: University of Nebraska Press, 1972.

Leopold, Aldo. *A Sand County Almanac.* New York: Oxford University Press, 1949.

Maclean, Norman. *A River Runs through It.* Chicago: University of Chicago Press, 1976.

Marcy, Capt. Randolph B. *Adventures on Red River: Report on the Exploration of the Headwaters of the Red River.* Report to Secretary of War Jefferson Davis. Philadelphia: n.p., 1854.

McAllister, J. G. "Kiowa-Apache Social Organization." In *Social Anthropology of North American Tribes,* ed. Fred Eggan, 99–169. Chicago: n.p., 1935.

McKinney, Larry. "Troubled Waters." Parts 1 and 2. *Texas Parks and Wildlife,* Jan. and Feb., 1997, 18–27 and 34–41.

McLeRoy, Sherrie S. *Red River Women.* Plano: Republic of Texas Press, 1996.

Metz, Leon C. *Roadside History of Texas.* Missoula, Mont.: Mountain Press Publishing Company, 1994.

Morris, John Miller. *El Llano Estacado: Exploration and Imagination on the High Plains of Texas and New Mexico, 1536–1860.* Austin: Texas State Historical Association, 1997.

Mungall, Elizabeth Carey, and William J. Sheffield. *Exotics on the Range: The Texas Example.* College Station: Texas A&M University Press, 1994.

Newcomb, W. W., Jr. *The Indians of Texas.* Austin: University of Texas Press, 1961.

Nolen, Ben M., and Bob Narramore. *Rivers and Rapids.* Garland, Tex.: n.p., 1992.

Nolen, Ben M. and Val Taylor. *Toobing Texas.* Bandera: Ocean-graphics, 1992.

Olmsted, Frederick Law. *Journey through Texas: A Saddle Trip on the Western Frontier.* 1857. Austin: Von Boeckmann-Jones Press, 1962.

Paredes, Americo. *"With His Pistol in His Hand": A Border Ballad and Its Hero.* Austin: University of Texas Press, 1958.

Parent, Laurence. *Official Guide to Texas State Parks.* Austin: University of Texas Press, 1997.

Parkman, Francis. *La Salle and the Discovery of the Great West.* 1869. New York: Signet Classic edition, New American Library, 1963.

Patoski, Joe Nick. "Take Me to the River." *Texas Monthly,* May 1995.

Peacock, Howard. "Plying the Piney Woods." *Texas Highways,* Sept. 1995, 50–59.

Peeters, Tracy, and Richard Bedard. "At Play on Roy Roberts Lake." *Texas Highways,* July 1997, 42–50.

Perttula, Timothy K. *The Caddo Nation: Archaeological and Ethnohistoric Perspectives.* Austin: University of Texas Press, 1992.

Phelan, Richard, and Jim Bones (photographer). *Texas Wild: The Land, the Plants and Animals of the Lone Star State.* New York: E. P. Dutton, 1976.

Powers, William K. *Indians of the Southern Plains.* New York: Capricorn Books, 1972.

Reisner, Marc. "Coming Undammed." *Audubon* 100, no. 5 (Sept.–Oct. 1998): 58–65.

Richardson, Rupert Norval. *Texas: The Lone Star State.* Englewood, N.J.: Prentice Hall, Inc., 1943.

Rister, Carl Coke. *Fort Griffin on the Texas Frontier.* Norman: University of Oklahoma Press, 1956.

Robertson, Pauline Durrett, and R. L. Robertson. *Tascosa: Historic Site in the Texas Panhandle.* Amarillo: Paramount Publishing Co., 1995.

Robson, Lucia St. Clair. *Ride the Wind.* New York: Ballantine Books, 1982.

———. *Walk in My Soul.* New York: Ballantine Books, 1985.

Schueler, Donald G. *Incident at Eagle Ranch: Predators as Prey in the American West.* Tucson: University of Arizona Press, 1991.

Skiles, Jack. *Judge Roy Bean Country.* Lubbock: Texas Tech University Press, 1996.

Siringo, Charles A. *A Texas Cowboy: Fifteen Years on the Hurricane Deck of a Spanish Pony.* 1885. Lincoln: University of Nebraska Press, 1979.

Sitton, Thad. *Backwoodsmen: Stockmen and Hunters along a Big Thicket River Valley.* Norman: University of Oklahoma Press, 1995.

———. "The Enduring Neches." *Texas Parks and Wildlife,* Mar. 1995.

Smith, Griffin, Jr. *Forgotten Texas: A Wilderness Portfolio.* Photographs by Reagan Bradshaw. Austin: Texas Monthly Press, 1990.

Smithwick, Noah. *The Evolution of a State, or Recollections of Old Texas Days.* 1900. Austin: University of Texas Press, 1983.

Sonnichsen, C. L. *Roy Bean: Law West of the Pecos.* Lincoln: University of Nebraska Press, 1991.

Spearing, Darwin. *Roadside Geology of Texas.* Missoula, Mont: Mountain Press Publishing Company, 1996.

Strickland, Ron. *Texans: Oral Histories from the Lone Star State.* New York: Paragon House, 1991.

Tarpley, Fred. *1001 Texas Place Names.* Austin: University of Texas Press, 1980.

Tjarks, Alicia Vidaurreta. *Southwestern Historical Quarterly* 77 (1974): 291–338.

Telfair, Ray C. "Conservation of the Catfish Creek Ecosystem: A National Natural Landmark in Eastern Texas." *Texas Journal of Science* 40, no. 1 (Feb. 1988).

Texas: A Guide to the Lone Star State. WPA Project. New York: Hastings House, 1940.

Texas Almanac, 1998–1999. Dallas: Dallas Morning News, 1997.

Truett, Joe C., and Daniel W. Lay. *Land of Bears and Honey: A Natural History of East Texas.* Austin: University of Texas Press, 1994.

Vines, Robert A. *Trees of East Texas.* Austin: University of Texas Press, 1990.

Water Trails West. (Western Writers of America.) Garden City, N.Y.: Doubleday, 1978.

Webb, Walter Prescott. *The Texas Rangers: A Century of Frontier Defense.* Austin: University of Texas Press, 1965.

———. *The Great Plains.* New York: Grosset & Dunlap, 1931.

Weber, David J., ed. *New Spain's Far Northern Frontier: Essays on Spain in the American West, 1540–1821.* Dallas: Southern Methodist University Press, 1979.

Williams, John Hoyt. *Sam Houston: A Biography of the Father of Texas.* New York: Simon & Schuster, 1993.

Windle, Janice W. *True Women.* New York: Ivy Books, 1995.

Worcester, Don. *The Texas Longhorns: Relics of the Past, Asset for the Future.* College Station: Texas A&M University Press, 1987.

Index